Defecting
in
Place

Defecting in Place

Women Claiming Responsibility for Their Own Spiritual Lives

MIRIAM THERESE WINTER
ADAIR LUMMIS
ALLISON STOKES

CROSSROAD · NEW YORK

1995

The Crossroad Publishing Company
370 Lexington Avenue, New York, NY 10017

Printed in the United States of America

Library of Congress Cataloging-in-Publication Data

Winter, Miriam Therese.
    Defecting in place : women claiming responsibility for their own
spiritual lives / Miriam Therese Winter, Adair Lummis, Allison
Stokes.
      p. cm.
    Includes bibliographical references.
    ISBN 0-8245-1417-3; 0-8245-1533-1 (pbk.)
    1. Women—Religious life. 2. Feminist theology. I. Lummis,
Adair T. II. Stokes, Allison, 1942– . III. Title.
BV4527. W56 1994
248.8'43—dc20
                                                      94-15875
                                                        CIP

Contents

Acknowledgments

We owe a debt of gratitude to so many women, and a number of men, who encouraged us to undertake this study, who supported its development, contributed to its implementation, and helped us bring it to conclusion.

We especially thank Jeanne Knoerle, S.P., program director at the Lilly Endowment, Inc., who guided our proposal and facilitated the process that led to our receiving a major grant. To all at Lilly Endowment who were part of that process: thank you for funding our study. We hope that this gift you have given to feminist women will bring blessings to you in return.

Thank you to our consultants and advisors who helped shape, evaluate, and affirm our work; our broad-based network of informal advisors for their opinions and support; administrative, secretarial, and coding staff, especially Florence Leduc, Sarah Summers, Mary Jane Ross, and Sheryl Wiggins; administrative assistant Mary Elizabeth Johnson for her many contributions during the project's final phase; and Hartford Seminary for recognizing the importance of this study and for incorporating it into its program. Special thanks to Crossroad publisher Michael Leach and editor John Eagleson, two feminists who worked in partnership with us to give our project visibility and a forum for wider exchange.

We are especially grateful to the many women who are at the heart of our study, whose voices tell how it really is for a multitude of traditionally Christian women in the United States of America, and whose stories fill the pages of this book. We thank you for your words of encouragement and trust, for memos in the margins of surveys, for clippings and poems and pamphlets, and for the promise of your prayers. We would have answered each of you personally if we could have, to tell you that we have heard your concerns, that we have been moved by your wisdom and inspired by who you are. May you find a bit of your spirit here and a glimmer of hope for the future. All that we have learned from this study we owe directly to you.

ADAIR LUMMIS
ALLISON STOKES
MIRIAM THERESE WINTER

December 1993

Project Team

Principal Investigators

Adair Lummis has a Ph.D. in sociology from Columbia University. As adjunct faculty at Hartford Seminary and as an independent research consultant, she has come in contact with a broad range of feminist issues and constituencies within the institutional church. Co-author of *Women of the Cloth* (1983), an assessment of the role and status of clergywomen in the United States made possible by a grant from the Ford Foundation, she is currently working on a follow-up study funded by the Lilly Endowment. Adair is an Episcopal laywoman. She has completed many research projects for the Episcopal Church, several of which have dealt explicitly with the denomination's representation of women in leadership and liturgy. She has also facilitated research with African American, Hispanic, and Korean seminarian and clergy groups, as well as with Muslim communities in the United States.

Allison Stokes, who has her Ph.D. in American studies from Yale University, is an ordained clergywoman in the United Church of Christ and pastor of the Congregational Church of West Stockbridge in Massachusetts. She is a historian of the pastoral care and counseling movement and author of *Ministry after Freud.* Allison has served as college chaplain at both Vassar and Yale and as acting dean, senior research associate, and adjunct faculty at Hartford Seminary. She recently spent a sabbatical semester as a Merrill Fellow at Harvard Divinity School. She is founding director of the Clergywomen's Interfaith Institute in the Berkshires, a nonprofit organization that encourages the ministry of women of all faith communities.

Miriam Therese Winter, a Medical Mission Sister who has her Ph.D. in liturgical studies from Princeton Theological Seminary, is Professor of Liturgy, Worship, Spirituality, and Feminist Studies at Hartford Seminary. Her thirteen albums of biblical/liturgical song include two feminist music collections, *WomanSong* and *EarthSong.* Among her books are *WomanPrayer, WomanSong;* a three-volume feminist lectionary and psalter encompassing all the women in the Bible entitled

WomanWisdom; WomanWitness; WomanWord; and *The Gospel according to Mary.* Miriam Therese has worked with women in Europe and in Asia, throughout Africa and Australia, and across the U.S. and Canada. Her multiple cross-cultural justice ministries include supportive services for a gospel choir in Connecticut's state prison for women and international emergency relief work in Third World settings.

Consultants

Elizabeth Bettenhausen, with a Ph.D. in Christian ethics and literary criticism, has taught and lectured in feminist theology and theory at a number of universities and seminaries and now coordinates the Study/Action Program at the Women's Theological Center in Boston.

Katie Geneva Cannon, author of *Black Womanist Ethics,* has her Ph.D. in Christian ethics from Union Theological Seminary and is Associate Professor of Religion at Temple University in Philadelphia.

Toinette Eugene, who wrote her dissertation on "Black Catholic Belonging" at the Graduate Theological Union in Berkeley for a Ph.D. in religion and society, is Professor of Christian Social Ethics at Garrett-Evangelical Theological Seminary.

Elisabeth Schüssler Fiorenza, who has her doctorate in New Testament studies, is known internationally for her work on biblical interpretation and her pioneering research in feminist theology and hermeneutics. She is the Krister Stendahl Professor of Divinity at Harvard Divinity School. Among her many books are the groundbreaking *In Memory of Her: A Feminist Theological Reconstruction of Christian Origins; Bread Not Stone; Vision of a Just World; But She Said;* and *Discipleship of Equals.*

Beverly Wildung Harrison, author of *Making the Connections: Essays in Feminist Social Ethics,* has her Ph.D. from Union Theological Seminary and is the Carolyn Williams Beaird Professor of Christian Ethics there.

Ada Maria Isasi-Diaz has her Ph.D. in social ethics from Union Theological Seminary and is Associate Professor of Theology and Ethics at the Theological School of Drew University. She is co-author of *Hispanic Women: Prophetic Voice in the Church* and author of *En la lucha/In the Struggle: Elaborating a Mujerista Theology.*

Marie Augusta Neal, S.N.D., has her Ph.D. in sociology from Harvard University and is Professor of Sociology at Emmanuel College.

She is the author of *A Socio-Theology of Letting God, From Nuns to Sisters,* and numerous articles.

Diann Neu has master's degrees in divinity and in sacred theology from the Jesuit School of Theology at Berkeley, is co-founder and co-director of WATER (Women's Alliance for Theology, Ethics and Ritual) in Silver Spring, Maryland, and has published widely on the women-church movement and its rituals.

Rosemary Radford Ruether, with a Ph.D. in classics and patristics from Claremont Graduate School, is the Georgia Harkness Professor of Theology at Garrett-Evangelical Theological Seminary and a prolific author. Among her many works are *The New Woman/New Earth: Sexist Ideologies and Human Liberation; Sexism and God-Talk: Toward a Feminist Theology; WomenChurch: Theology and Practice of Feminist Liturgical Communities;* and *Gaia and God: An Eco-Feminist Theology of Earth Healing.*

Letty M. Russell has a doctorate in mission theology and ecumenics from Union Theological Seminary, is Professor of Theology at Yale Divinity School, and is author and editor of a number of works that include *The Liberating Word: A Guide to Non-Sexist Interpretation of the Bible; Feminist Interpretation of the Bible; Household of Freedom: Authority in Feminist Theology;* and *Church in the Round: Feminist Interpretation of the Church.*

Advisors

Angela Aidala, Ph.D., Associate Research Scientist, Columbia University.

Linda Clark, S.M.D., Assistant Professor of Sacred Music, Boston University, School of Theology.

Marie Cornwall, Ph.D., Associate Professor, Department of Sociology, Brigham Young University.

Lynn Davidman, Ph.D., Associate Professor of Sociology, Brown University.

Estelle Demers, M.A., Sector North America Coordinator, Medical Mission Sisters.

Helen Ebaugh, Ph.D., Associate Professor, Department of Sociology, University of Houston.

Reta Halteman Finger, Ph.D. candidate in New Testament studies; Editor, *Daughters of Sarah.*

The Rev. Cheryl Townsend Gilkes, Ph.D., Associate Professor of Sociology and African American Studies, Colby College.

The Rev. Young Kim, M.Div., founder of Women-Church in Seoul, Korea.

Penny Long Marler, Ph.D., Assistant Professor of Religion, Samford University.

Mary Jo Neitz, Ph.D., Associate Professor of Sociology, University of Missouri.

Marian Ronan, M.Div., M.S., Ph.D. candidate, Temple University.

Ruth Wallace, Ph.D., Professor of Sociology, George Washington University.

Mary-Paula Walsh, Ph.D. in Sociology, adjunct professor at several institutions.

Barbara Brown Zikmund, Ph.D. in American Religious History; President, Hartford Seminary.

Introduction

Individual women have challenged the church in the United States of America from pioneer times to the present, usually with disastrous consequences for themselves and little or no impact on the church as institution. In the Massachusetts Bay Colony Anne Hutchinson, now honored as America's first female theologian but known historically as an "American Jezebel," was excommunicated from her congregation in Boston in 1638 and banished from the colony because she held weekly meetings in her home to discuss the Sunday sermon and to express her theological opinions.[1] In Virginia, Quakers Mary Thompkins and Alice Ambrose were pilloried and whipped because of their preaching. In 1660 Quaker Mary Dyer, a preacher and an outspoken supporter of Anne Hutchinson, was hanged on the Boston Common. In Salem the articulate Mary Oliver was publicly punished and then banished for challenging church authority, and in 1692 Bridget Bishop was hanged. These are only a few of the many women whose defiant critique of organized religion was openly expressed. History, or more accurately herstory, documents what happened to women who chose to preach, teach, or dissent from doctrine. Women who acted independently were accused of heresy or witchcraft and suffered persecution, even execution, for speaking out in the church.[2]

Women's spiritual support groups also have a lengthy history. Anne Hutchinson was surrounded by a circle of females who gathered to read the Bible and talk about the things of God. There were similar groups elsewhere in New England during colonial times. Anne Heaton, a "heretic" in New Haven, Connecticut, was supported by a circle of females who shared her spirit of independence. She was excommunicated for denouncing infant baptism and for walking out of church services before the Lord's Supper because, by her own interpretation, she felt she had not been baptized.[3] Three other women of her company were also brought to trial. One of them, a Mrs. Brewster, was alleged to have said she was "sermon sick" with regard to her pastor's preaching. Her daughter, Mrs. Leach, had considered joining the church but then decided against it "because she found so many untruths" in what she had experienced. She was accused of saying that people would not be turned toward God "until the veil

1

before the eyes of the minister and the people in this place be taken away," a statement she admitted making.[4] During the Great Awakening, Jonathan Edwards advised women to join one of the many women's groups formed for Bible study, discussion, and prayer that were popular throughout New England. Sarah Osborn convened such a group in 1741 in Newport, Rhode Island, which met weekly until her death.[5]

There are similarities between past and present. Women dissenting, women gathering for sharing and support: these are not new initiatives. What then, if anything, is different between women's previous experience and what is happening today? Is the current rebellion of feminists in the church a continuation of isolated cases, albeit on a wider scale, or are we witnessing in our own times a movement in the making?

Janet Chafetz and Anthony Dworkin distinguish between those "forms of female revolt" that "have occurred in many times and places" and the more visible "women's movements":

> In earlier historical epochs, female revolts did not become full-fledged women's movements since a sufficiently large number of women had not yet come to the recognition of the commonality of their plight....Despite the worldwide historical prevalence of female disadvantage, only occasionally have women openly and collectively revolted against their deprivation. In fact, it is safe to assume that many females in any given society have not even been cognizant of the fact that, on the basis of their sex alone, they are systematically disadvantaged.[6]

In their cross-cultural study, Chafetz and Dworkin examine the distinction between "revolt" and "movement" and explain "the circumstances under which large numbers of women have become aware of their collective deprivation, defined it as illegitimate, and organized in an effort to change the structure of society."[7] They differentiate between "movement" in general and a distinctly feminist one:

> The focus of activity in women's movements is consciously oriented to some disadvantages that are unique to the female sex. The first and essentially only priority is to rectify female disadvantage. Women's movements involve the coordinated activities of groups, utilizing networks of communication, and engaging in sustained activities over a number of years. Such movements vary in terms of the scope of their ideology. Some challenge the full range of institutions and definitions. We shall call them feminist.[8]

By their description, which many historians share, there have been two women's movements, or, perhaps more accurately, two waves of a single women's movement in the United States.[9] The first wave of this movement began with the Seneca Falls Convention and its "Declaration of Principles" in 1848 and ended in 1920 with the Nineteenth Amendment, giving women the right to vote.[10] Before Lucretia Mott and Elizabeth Cady Stanton launched this organized movement for women's rights, the rise of feminist consciousness with regard to economics, education, women's suffrage, and the abolition of slavery was already widespread. The second wave of the women's movement, which marks the beginning of the so-called feminist movement, dates from the formation of the National Organization for Women (NOW) in 1966 and subsequently other feminist organizations and caucuses, both professional and political. At the same time local, less visible groups dedicated to "women's liberation" and far more "radical" were springing up everywhere. These quickly coalesced into a single movement. By the early 1970s there was a recognizable feminist movement encompassing diverse entities committed to common goals.[11]

Coming to consciousness of gender oppression is a lengthy and complex process in women's struggle for liberation, as Gerda Lerner explains:

> Feminist consciousness consists of (1) the awareness of women that they belong to a subordinate group and that, as members of such a group, they have suffered wrongs; (2) the recognition that their condition of subordination is not natural, but societally determined; (3) the development of a sense of sisterhood; (4) the autonomous definition by women of their goals and strategies for changing their condition; and (5) the development of an alternate vision of the future.[12]

As in other liberation movements among those who are oppressed, conscientization is key to personal liberation and to systemic change. It begins with seeing one's situation in life as it really is and then moves to a consideration of what it might become. Women's enlightened understanding of God, faith, themselves, and their spiritual life is changing the way some women think about religion and, as this study demonstrates, it is influencing the way they act. Much of this shaping of women's consciousness is due to the creative, courageous, painstaking scholarship of feminist "pioneers."

In her revolutionizing biblical work *In Memory of Her*, Elisabeth Schüssler Fiorenza gave women a feminist theological reconstruction of Christian origins and a liberating "hermeneutic of suspicion."[13] She continues to make the female collective, or women-church, the interpretive center of feminist hermeneutics where women can

> deconstruct the dominant paradigms of biblical interpretation and reconstruct them in terms of a critical rhetoric that understands biblical

texts and traditions as a living and changing heritage, one which does not legitimate patriarchal oppression but can foster emancipatory practices of faith-communities.[14]

Fiorenza offers us a rhetorical model as a feminist interpretive process for transformation, inviting us to move beyond a historical-critical reading and reconstruction of biblical texts to the "cultural-theological practice of resistance and transformation" fostered through storytelling, drama, imaginative ritual, and dance.[15] Biblical scholars and practitioners, theologians and liturgists, have all been influenced by her work.

Rosemary Radford Ruether gave feminists a liberating metaphor and some theological language in a memorable address to the first national gathering of women-church in 1983.[16] She defined feminist women as an exodus community coming out of exile, seeking liberation from patriarchy. She continues to call for an end to the "famine of the words of life" and asks women to

> begin to bake the new bread of life now. We must do more than protest against the old. We must begin to live the new humanity now. We must begin to incarnate the community of faith in the liberation of humanity from patriarchy in words and deed, in new words, new prayers, new symbols, and new praxis. This means that we need to form gathered communities to support us as we set out on our exodus from patriarchy.[17]

As "church," feminists need intentional communities centered in faith-sharing and a meaningful worship that provide strength for the journey, an oasis in the wilderness, and encouragement for continuing on. Ruether identifies two models of church, church as spirit-filled community and church as historical institution, and roots them both in the tradition, as does Fiorenza. Leonard Boff speaks of the Spirit-led base communities of Latin America "reinventing the church." There are some parallels linking the "ecclesiogenesis"[18] of various oppressed peoples building a living church, but many more differences clearly mark the feminist liberation agenda.

Feminists who have struggled to be "church" within the church or wrestled with issues of authority have been helped by the ecclesiology of Letty Russell. Her "partnership" in the "household of freedom" evolves ever so naturally to a "church in the round." There at the welcome table, in a "spirituality of connection" that sees marginality as blessing, "sister outsider" joins "sister circle" for a fully inclusive interpretation and experience of "church."[19] Integral to this understanding of church, which is energetically promoted by Fiorenza and Ruether, is the presence of a pluriformity of races and cultures in the shaping of both substance and structure. The writings of Asian feminist, womanist, and *mujerista* women and face-to-face cross-cultural interaction are revealing how deeply white women in North America have internalized the oppressive attitudes and behaviors of the dominant patriarchal culture. An awareness of the inherent racism in even well-intentioned white North American women has been very slow in coming and still has a long way to go. Once again the oppressed are calling the question, this time, within the sisterhood.[20]

Many women have come to feminist consciousness aided by a biblical and theological framework that begins with women's experience.[21] But almost without exception, women begin with their own experience. Sharing with other women their feelings of pain, frustration, and rage, women discover they are not alone. They learn to identify patriarchy and what it has done to women in society and in the church. Nelle Morton in her classic *The Journey Is Home* describes the women's groups she encountered in her long feminist journey and rejoices in the gift of women to women in hearing one another into speech:

> A new kind of seeing and hearing was beginning to be experienced by one group of women after the other. Once they recognized in themselves a common oppression, they could hear from one another that which many, more astute and intellectual than they, could not hear. Experiencing grace in this manner has become one of the most powerful liberating forces in the lives of women. It is important that the data that these women shared was out of their living, historical experience. Yet, the new words and the new way old words came to expression, while in the context of history, were not evoked by history. Neither oppression nor suffering shaped their speech. Women came to new speech simply because they were being heard. Hearing became an act of receiving the women as well as the words.[22]

Morton goes on to say what other women's experience confirms, that the women in the group heard the speaker speaking not only for herself, but for them, heard her giving voice to their own self-doubt and their struggle with discrimination.

> Tasting a liberation they had never known before, they found it good. They began to appropriate a new kind of courage to explore the future with no known history to inform and a new ability to articulate that which has never before come to speech. They began to know themselves as persons of worth who would pick up their own lives and be responsible for them. They covenanted together that never again would they allow themselves to become isolated from one another.[23]

Feminists often will refer to a similar experience as a turning point in their lives, recounting how a female group was in fact the womb of awareness where they first came to consciousness and were heard into life. As women began to move "beyond God the Father" and a tacit acceptance of their status experienced as "the church and the second sex," they became aware of a "women's reality," of "the original sin of being born female," of "an emerging female system in a white male society," and they began to speak "in a different voice" of "women's ways of knowing." Energized and supported by "womanspirit rising," many made a conscious decision to "kiss Sleeping Beauty goodbye."[24] In telling their story women found their voice and the power to speak with authority. Today feminists no longer accept all that the church is saying simply because it has said it. They are evaluating institutional theology and praxis in light of their own experience and they are finding the institution wanting.[25]

The Study

Why do feminist women remain in congregations? Just how alienated are they from the institutional church? How does their involvement in feminist spirituality groups made up of like-minded women affect their relationship to their denomination and to their congregation? These questions are central to this study. They were asked of a number of feminist women who are or once were within the Christian tradition and who are or once were part of a women's spirituality group.

We three researchers began our formal investigation knowing firsthand the value of such feminist spirituality groups. From our own participation in feminist gatherings and our involvement in the women-church movement, through our teaching, ministry, and travels across this nation and abroad, we have met many women who were part of feminist groups of support and inspiration. It seemed to us that women affiliated with such groups were much more aware of the issues. They were usually open to experiencing new forms of prayer, delighted in feminist ritual, seldom resisted what was radically different, and could clearly articulate the source of their discomfort as feminists in the church. This seemed the ideal place, therefore, to focus an investigation designed to examine the relationship of feminist women to the church, both now and in the future.

This report on our findings is essentially descriptive and proceeds in a feminist way. It features the women surveyed, presenting page after page of testimony documenting women's experiences now. Hundreds of women speak directly to the issues, express their frustration, share their hope, and in their stories, in their struggles, we hear echoes of our own. Their experiences are the essential data, revealing not only present facts but an insight into what may be unfolding.

Chapter 1 begins with an outpouring of the heart from a cross-section of survey respondents, moves to a description of the study, its design and implementation, and concludes with a descriptive analysis of the women in the sample.

Chapters 2 and 3 present feminist women in relationship to the church — the feminist challenge to the institution, the struggle to survive within the system, and the personal cost of a woman's decision either to leave the church or to remain. Chapter 2 focuses on Protestant women, chapter 3 on women in the Catholic Church.

Chapter 4 provides an introduction to feminist spirituality groups and some of their symbols, rituals, and alternative liturgies.

Chapter 5 introduces us to feminist spirituality and its relationship to social justice and concludes with a reflection on the just church, indicating how we feminist women envision that which we seek.

Our report concludes that a growing number of women today are taking responsibility for their own spiritual lives. Many of these women are still affiliated with the church. Many belong to a parish or congregation. Many are active participants in their local church. Many hold significant leadership roles as clergy, lay ministers, educators, administrators. With regard to institutional religion, these women are "defecting in place."

Following our report are the prophetic voices of the project's ten consultants, pioneer feminists who continue to challenge the church for the benefit of us all.

The feminist inclinations of the research team have influenced all aspects of this study, including the shaping of this report. As feminists we set out to identify that feminist element within the church that is actively seeking change, to describe how it is evolving, to locate the source of its strength, to assess the extent of its presence, and to note its potential for impact on congregational life. The study has accomplished its objectives and this additional goal: to give the feminist visibility, to provide her with a forum for voicing her concerns, and to let her know that in her struggle for justice she is not alone.

Chapter 1

The Women in This Study

Listen to the voices of the women in this study as they share with us how they feel about their religion and their spirituality.

~ ~ ~

"While the Catholic Church declares sexism is a sin, it continually perpetuates that sin by excluding women from authority, leadership, and decision-making. Male is normative and female is excluded. Women have been repressed and will no longer tolerate it."[1]

~

"I am constantly saddened by the exclusivity and patriarchal hierarchy of Christian denominations. So many wonderful women are not able to live out their spiritual gifts in this arena. Searching for another place or group in which to live out these gifts is beginning to change how women receive spiritual nourishment and the structures that deliver such services. Telling our stories removes the veil of seclusion and strengthens our connectedness."[2]

~

"I find my current ideas about God at best paradoxical, at worst, contradictory and full of tension. Brought up in a firmly patriarchal tradition, my habits of prayer, meditation, and study are all shadowed by patriarchal imagery, deeply ingrained. But my experiences as a female person and my studies of gender idealogies and images are continually transforming not only my sense of who or what I am but my sense of the nature and identity of God. I often experience a profound longing for an immanent, nurturing, 'maternal' force in my life, but have difficulty catching more than glimpses of a parental rather than paternal God. I have spent most of the last twenty years of my life either studying at or working in conservative evangelical colleges. My gifts are often respected, admired, yet I am seen all too often as an 'exception,' unlike other women—by virtue of my intellect and diligence, 'one of the boys.' At the same time, I can't seem to grasp the 'old boy network' ways of exercising leadership and feel, more often than I should, 'silenced,' not because I am not free to speak, but because I am not fully heard."[3]

~

"I am a Christian feminist. Although I am not alone, I have no personal contact with other Christian feminists. People in my church community don't understand me, and I do not understand them. Still, I firmly believe that God calls us to seek unity within our diversity. Christian feminists are prophets and must remain hopeful while recognizing that we will not be immediately understood. Christ was a feminist. Christ was little understood. I am confident there is a place for me/us in God's holy realm."[4]

~

"Women would have the place in the church they want when we can silence that voice in us that says, 'You are not worthy.'"[5]

~

"I hope that we women would bond and become the body which includes all its members. We must become more outspoken politically, within both the church and our world."[6]

~

"I am in a process of working out a major problem I have with the whole organized aspect of religion. I find that in general the men decide what they want to do and then bulldoze until they achieve what they want. I have felt patronized and bullied and I have given up with the organized side of it all. They can do what they want. I now give where I want and get what I can. I'm working on healing and forgiveness."[7]

~

"I am an angry woman, but I am not angry at men. Women and men benefit from the structure that exists. Women *and* men are oppressed by it. The children suffer. Those who continue to bear the burdens of the old order are increasingly overwhelmed, myself included. No society is free which oppresses its women or children."[8]

~

"As an African American woman participating in a predominantly white church, my first concern is addressing issues of exclusion and discrimination based on race both in the whole church and even the racism among professed liberal women involved in women's groups."[9]

~

"I feel I'm a lonely Catholic voice for women's issues in the state of _____ . I remain with the Catholic Church — when it would be much easier to move over to the Episcopal Church — to keep 'bothering' the males who run things."[10]

~

"As I become a uniquely new woman, a more whole person, I am seeking ways to experience being a woman and finding a greater interest in women's experience in community. I pray the work being done in this direction will continue."[11]

~

"I feel women are oppressed, but I have come to understand that to be set free, the greatest act we can do is to encourage and enable women to set themselves free. The 'system' within the church is oppressive because the skills of self-actualization are not taught and valued as the reason Jesus came, to set us free in the first place. The priests are as oppressed as women are. They have the power, but if one doesn't have the skill to exercise the power, it is like salt that is insipid."[12]

~

"It seems that most of the women I know or have known are not even aware of the extent of their oppression. They just accept the church doctrine that men should be in the positions of leadership and decision-making. I probably would be considered a 'real' heretic since recently coming to the conclusion that my whole belief system is subject to and continually under revision. You know that a real fundie never questions certain doctrinal teachings!"[13]

~

"A university course introduced me to the feminist cause. 'My pain has been named,' I wrote in an early essay. That was twenty years ago, and it wasn't long before I realized that I was too old to benefit from the movement and too young to die. Even so, such an awakening demanded further study, and along with that, expression. Rural areas are not receptive to such 'radicalism,' so my efforts were necessarily confined to private conversation/confrontation, influencing our local library to expand its feminist publications, and a new liberty to express myself on any issue. Those days of feminist focus are over for me now, although on occasional Sundays the pastor/friend of our adopted church and I engage in verbal battle. I have come to believe that the arts, more than any other medium, are the primary influence for reaching the heart which is, after all, the springboard for fundamental change."[14]

~

"My growth in 'being woman' has come about slowly, until the recent past. I marvel at how inculturated I was without ever having realized it. More and more my womanliness takes on an awe and appreciation that, had I experienced it early in my career as teacher, I would have taught, elicited in all my female students."[15]

~

"My town, religiously, seems to fall into two areas: conservative fundamentalist and agnostic. Church attendance is pitiful on a per capita basis. As a Christian liberal feminist, this is a lonely place. I have been here for two years and have found no 'sisters' to talk, laugh, cry, bitch, lunch, or play with. The 'ladies' at the church just don't cut it! They are just too much older, although some of them have a refreshing liberal viewpoint."[16]

~

"Women and religion are at a crossroads. If women are not taken seriously and their talents recognized, I think there will be serious consequences. I've had three daughters and they are _not_ drawn to current religious traditions. They see no place for women. They see women within the Roman tradition differing significantly on matters of human sexuality and issues affecting women. Why join such confusion?"[17]

~

"My relationship with God/spirituality/whatever is the most important aspect of my life, and I have to leave it to gasp out its last breaths because, as it stands now, there is no one, including myself, I can look to as teacher/priest, and the search is too frustrating to continue alone."[18]

~

"I hate to see women become 'good old boys.' I would like to see women using more energy in reaching out to other women in practical and celebrative ways."[19]

~

"As a child, I watched my favorite aunt, a born storyteller and excellent public speaker, sit there in frustration while her husband painfully stuttered through presentations of their mission work in churches where the male had to speak at the morning service."[20]

~

"I think that mixed groups of near equal numbers of men and women are most helpful to work at women's issues. Men often do not understand the pain of being discounted, nor do women understand the limitations put on men through rigid role expectations. We need to hear one another. Although presently I am the only pastor in charge of a small rural parish, I have experienced amazing put-downs prior to this, _not_ related to _me_ and my capabilities or shortcomings, but solely to the fact that I was a woman, rejected for certain functions by people who never met me, because I am a woman."[21]

~

"Women should be allowed to use their God-given talents in any role they feel called to perform. I am not a feminist, but am committed to equal rights and opportunities for all people."[22]

~

"I am out of the mainline church and have felt much greater freedom to develop my own theology and spiritual path. I am active in the function of our worship. When I am in mainline churches, I sense the strong pull to conform and feed the system before one's self. The pull toward a male expression of faith is very great, often too much to resist."[23]

~

"If a woman is good at getting things accomplished, she is seen as pushy rather than exercising leadership skills, in spite of a higher tendency on our part to gather support and share decision-making. There seems to be an assumption on the part of the lay leadership that a woman will be easy to push around."[24]

~

"Recently I have become concerned that I, and perhaps others, are being so controlled by our anger, resentment, pain at the unjust treatment of women in the church by our male hierarchy, clergy, and unenlightened women that we are becoming unjust ourselves."[25]

~

"I look forward to the day Hispanic women stop being so submissive in ecumenical matters and challenge the system that more often than not doesn't allow them to develop their potential as leaders in the church or any other entity."[26]

~

"All organized religion brutalizes women. Most make monsters out of our sons."[27]

~

"Spending eight years as a Sister has had tremendous impact on my life. I have a deep spirituality, but I can't seem to find a group here in _____ to identify with. I am a lesbian, fifty-one years of age, and wanting very much to find that spark that seems to have been smothered in my dealing with the church and convent. I'm not bitter, but very hurt that this happened in a spiritual setting that is supposed to nurture love."[28]

~

"Personally, at my age, I am not threatened or really interested in more leadership in church. However, I am very concerned about young and middle-aged women. The Catholic Church is scared of women."[29]

~

"Women's full participation in every aspect of our lives, including organized religion, is vital to the improvement of our world. Religions which limit women's participation shouldn't preach that they believe God is just and loving, but that their God is prejudiced, biased, discriminatory."[30]

~

"It was through a dear friend and former college sorority sister that I came to Christian feminism. I felt as though I had been 'born again' *again* when I saw *God's* truth, not man's. Praise God! His wider, fuller world was opened to me and it indeed saved my life!"[31]

~

"I am frequently discouraged about making any progress. Younger women seem not to have the need to push this battle for women's acknowledged equality and I see us slipping back. Lord-God-Father-Judge was a punitive protector at best, and I feel a real urgency to give women the option of nurturer, healer, comforter. I also wonder about the number of women who have been significantly abused, physically or sexually, who are involved in the spiritual renewal movement, and the connection between that abuse and God images."[32]

~

"I strongly believe that this time in our culture, both from the prompting of the Spirit and the evident societal needs, is pushing and urging women to stand up and claim our talents and strength to better the world situation. Women priests and married priests need to be here now so that we can be an honest and valid example to all the world in loving people the best way to alleviate hunger, homelessness, and all the other evils of abuse so evident in society right now. We really need it *now!*"[33]

~

"Women are not below men on my Lord's totem pole. I cannot worship a God who would create me as inferior. I'm not real keen on theology that focuses on humanity's need for forgiveness of sins rather than on the need for helping people find wholeness and healing. Treating me as though I am 'sinful' and blaming me for my 'sin' fails to recognize that adults are often grown children who were victims."[34]

~

"I find it increasingly frustrating that there seem to be so few models for women in ministry/leadership. So many women seem to accommodate the male model and many successfully. I find the male model very unsatisfying."[35]

~

"I'm caught in the struggle about whether or not a woman can be a Christian and not be oppressed. It's difficult to have a radical feminist theology and remain in the hierarchical, patriarchal structures of established religion. In the Methodist tradition, my experience of God and my spirituality within that framework are being stifled and confined. I'm not feeling spiritual growth as a result of my 'religion.' It seems to come more as a result of personal, God-given experience. I find myself trying to 'fit' my experience into my religion, but it's too big!"[36]

~

"There is, in my opinion, *so* much more than a building, a ritual, a hierarchy, a dogma to spirituality, such as the interconnectedness, the possibilities, the divine in everything — sunset, tenderness, change, hope—being tuned to the beauty, responsibility of life citizenship."[37]

~

"How I long for dialogue about women and the church, and women's spirituality in general. I feel isolated much of the time, my time and energy so consumed by two small children. Had you included in your questions a column for time spent *thinking* about social/political/ environmental/feminist issues, I could happily circle 'MUCH,' but as it is, my *time* is woefully self/family involved."[38]

~

"I am a member of a reconciling congregation and spend much time working for change within the United Methodist Church. I am sensing a backlash in church and society in opposition to the minimal gains of women, blacks, Hispanics, etc., anyone other than white, straight male. Conservative, anti-liberation churches are growing; risk-taking churches are not. It's going to be very difficult for women to maintain what little gain we've made, both in church and society. The 'ole boys' are after us! If gains are made in business, then watch out for regression and oppression in other areas. The boys will see to it that they maintain some turf and power."[39]

~

"I am seventy-five years old and most other women of this age group that I am associated with could care less about improving women's status. They have not ever been interested or concerned. Also I find too many young women who are not concerned. I was astounded to realize that I do not give any time to social and political action. All I do is read, be concerned, and talk!"[40]

~

"As the church becomes more conservative and self-protecting, one of the by-products is a decline in *all* minority concerns. It is my experience that the last concern to be addressed is 'women' and the first to be dropped is also 'women.' "[41]

~

"In my twenties, thirties, and early forties, I was extremely active in several national movements focused on increasing women's status and influence in the Roman Catholic Church. Growing increasingly impatient with the pace of change, instead I made a conscious and absorbing commitment to work for change for women in higher education. Because of extensive responsibilities and commitments now in higher education, my connection with 'women-church' hangs by a thread in the pattern of lives woven together."[42]

~

"When a pastor disapproves of ordaining women, women seldom hear that it is an option. In my case, being already ordained and now active as a lay person, I am never asked to preach, assist at communion, or share worship leadership in any way. I believe this is partly because I am a woman, and partly because I am not one of those in the church who thinks the pastor is infallible."[43]

~

"I believe militant, flaming feminism is destructive. I agree that equal rights and opportunities are important for women, but I am convinced that if it is gained at the expense of the well-being of men, we will have created a monster in our society."[44]

~

"I continue to feel excluded from liturgy which uses all masculine images of God, especially when there is not a woman priest at the altar. I had the wonderful experience of having a female priest for two years and it changed my worship experience and my life. I was represented and welcomed at the altar as never before — or since."[45]

~

"Thank you for the chance to honestly share my feelings! The patriarchy literally engulfs and disempowers us as women, try as we do to break free."[46]

~

"After much soul-searching I left my family's Baptist tradition and became an Episcopalian. Episcopalians have a long way to go, but locally I am in a better environment for women. My priest is a wonderful feminist. One reason I gave up the fight in the Southern Baptist Church is that I wanted my daughter in a positive environment for women. I believe women need networking in an ecumenical context. I have received material from Presbyterians, Roman Catholics, Episcopalians, Southern Baptists, Methodists, American Baptists. Denominational differences fade in the face of a common goal."[47]

~

"I am reminded of the true equality, nonhierarchical structure, that exists within the Religious Society of Friends. While I have worked as a therapist with Catholic religious and am aware of the rigid role-set and lack of full participation of women in the life of the church, I have been mainly spared the pain of sexism in my religion. I do seek 'intuitive' and visionary experiences outside of meeting for worship. Some of these pursuits, such as dancing and drumming, tend to attract more women than men, though that too appears to be changing."[48]

~

"How do women with small children who stay home to raise them fit into all this? Talk about feeling alienated! Whew! I'd have a lot more to say if I weren't so tired."[49]

~

"Women must work harder at celebrating each other. There are women in more traditional lifestyles with a profound witness to offer. Let's not forget them. Women have made some great strides, but there's a ways to go. Let us do more than replace men with women; let's usher in a new way to live in mutual respect."[50]

~

"I have lived with the male chauvinistic attitude most of my professional life (after medical school) and just assumed it was 'the norm' until recently, thirty years too late!"[51]

~

"As a fifty-year-old single parent with a doctorate, I am amazed at how often I still feel unskilled, 'lacking,' and nondirected. I believe this relates back to my socialization as a female in an agricultural home with two older brothers and a distant father/controlling mother combination. I often wonder, 'When does it all end?' I am so grateful for my female contacts who understand and support me. And I have worked hard that my daughter not have the same feelings!"[52]

~

"I suspect that much of the hostility I encounter comes as a result of my being a woman. However, folks are far too sophisticated on the whole to express that directly. Besides all that, I have been appointed to serve a conflicted, guilt-ridden, dying set of churches, so that is actually pretty peripheral. As a Christian and as a Christian feminist, I question my own desire to climb the hierarchical ladder. The Jesus I know came among us as 'one who serves.' Shouldn't that be my goal as well?"[53]

~

"I believe many women find their challenge and strength for growth in their religious tradition, and then, when their consciousness of themselves and their calling or ministry is enlivened, the religious group or setting has no use for it, or only a narrow, traditional use. Many leave or feel resentment or use their calling in unfulfilling ways."[54]

~

"I am exhausted from trying to do a good job at being a mother, wife, pastor, and responsible citizen. Most of the time I cope with my roles quite well, but as my career stresses have increased (from a move to a bigger church) and my children get older (and are involved in scheduled activities), it is more and more of a stretch. How to find balance? How to avoid feeling guilty all the time?"[55]

~

"I find it interesting that most women in ministry that I know have multiple degrees, for example, two or three master's degrees. They seem overly educated for the positions which they are able to acquire. They also seem grossly underpaid."[56]

~

"My hope is that as women come to understand and develop their own special gifts and are given an equal voice in the church or religious setting, the church (or gathering) may become more democratic, less autocratic; more creative in liturgy or worship, for home as well as church; more concerned for the suffering in the world; more concerned for political pressure in matters that affect the life of the planet; more ready to work for peace, within the group as well as without, learning to allow others to hold different points of view and convictions, more open to respect for other religions; a group with a mature assessment of evil, i.e., a force for love in the world."[57]

~

"I think it's all hopeless. We must dump Christianity and start over — or go back to the Goddess."[58]

~

"I am a strong feminist and have great difficulty remaining connected to patriarchal religion. Conversely, I have greater difficulty breaking a life-long traditional pattern/habit of mainline church participation. My regular social life is outside of my church and none of my social circle is 'churched.' I guess I'm saying that I'd rather not fight the Monday through Saturday battles on Sunday as well. So, many times I don't. Sexist language, male images, noninclusiveness in general: we need to find a way to remove these barriers. Our generic faith struggle is hard enough all by itself. The Goddess doesn't live in my church. I find her more often with my agnostic/atheist friends."[59]

~

"These issues have caused me more pain and unhappiness than just about anything else in my personal experience of life. I feel so disenfranchised and yet desirous of having a community of people with which I can share my spiritual longings and thoughts. So far, no luck. I've been outside the boundaries of my religious heritage for three or four years now, but have not been successful in finding an adequate replacement. I'm still looking."[60]

~

"The struggle women face in the church is a reflection of the struggle we see on a more cosmic scale of entrenchment in systems — economic, political, etc. — that no longer work and in fact are destructive. The stakes are high around this issue, for our very survival is reflected in it, as a people, as a planet."[61]

~

"I have a great deal of responsibility and independent decision-making authority in my career and it is hard to switch to the 'Sunday mode' where women are relegated to the back of the church. When I hear real progress in inclusive language, when I am able to discard my own automatic response to describe God as 'He,' perhaps I'll feel better about church."[62]

~

"It's been very lonely. I am very loyal to my church — I find much meaning and depth in Lutheran theology and tradition. But it's largely a white male tradition that doesn't acknowledge much of 'me.' "[63]

~

"I am a convert to the Latter-day Saints religion for almost twenty years. My activity has wavered in the last three or so years, but I have kept going primarily for my family. The Mormon faith is extremely autocratic. I have repeatedly been made to feel less valuable because of my femaleness, although the general explanation is that we are put upon a pedestal. Feminists like me are very oppressed."[64]

~

"I will not believe in a god who does not believe in me."[65]

~

"I dream of women unifying and demanding that women be ordained, that only inclusive language be used, that equality of persons be a matter of the justice agenda, and that we be taken seriously. I'm getting tired. I am present bodily at worship services (good for my job), but the psychological beating is taking its toll."[66]

~

"I belong to a religious congregation because of sisterhood, not because of the patriarchal church. I don't believe in priesthood or ordination of any kind whose context is patriarchal. Women are searching for new ways of being religious — relating to the Sacred and ritualizing gifted, sacred moments, rediscovering the Sacred who/which reflects nonviolence and harmony for the human family."[67]

~

"There is little understanding of the way many women today are seeking to live our faith from our experiences as women. There is little understanding of the need for inclusive language; there is almost no understanding of the need for a variety of metaphors/symbols/names for the Divine. Generally for me, the language of expressions of faith used within our congregation is far from my experience. Yet when I am with secular feminists, there is often either a disdain for faith or the feeling that faith is irrelevant. When I am with women who worship the Divine exclusively as Goddess, there is little understanding of how women can choose to stay within the Christian church."[68]

~

"I am a well-read, well-informed, committed, issue-oriented radical feminist priest in _____. I struggle between, 'Please, oh, for a nice separatist community,' and 'Someone must help the grassroots blossom.' It is very isolating academically in rural areas. The issues of integrity and 'Can I survive within the male structures on every level?' are very real for women in rural ministry. I have a book bill like the national debt. It really is like being a pioneer woman all over again. There are the rich, juicy, academic havens with all the writers I've read cover to cover. And then there is the grassroots day in and day out struggle. Sometimes it's energizing and at other times defeating. Books and tapes are truly sustenance, so thanks to all of you who make soul food for desert places."[69]

~

"I love my religion and many members of the congregations with whom I have associated, but I feel women have been placed in a very unfair position. I struggle with this concept constantly: why does he have authority and leadership over me? Because he has a penis? The reasoning is ridiculous. I have worked hard to develop a level of spirituality within myself. This spirituality could not blossom and grow within the confines of my church because I harbor feelings of resentment and insufficiencies. I am establishing a spiritual connection with God or Higher Power that does not wear all the conditions and requirements — and prejudices — of the God I have been taught within the church."[70]

~

"We are a long way from recognizing the equality of men and women. I believe women could help effect change in hierarchical structures in church, family, and in society. As women we do have to be conscious of the ways we use power and exercise authority. We have been affected by the structures we seek to change."[71]

~

"I feel like an exception to everything these days. I seem to be at a really different place from most of the women I know. I long to have 'church,' but I no longer will allow myself to be 'battered' by the institutional church. I continue to listen to women. I remain an ordained minister and continue to preach or do whatever I can to feed other women. There is Good News for us, but I feel very hungry myself."[72]

~

"For about forty years I have studied and encouraged women to use the gifts God has given them. I have planned retreats where the issue was studied and enlightenment happened, but it also brought criticism. I would like to see more openness to studying women in leadership in our denomination in the Pacific Coast area."[73]

~

"I must confess that I often feel and fear that all the time spent in study and reading, which I enjoy so much for its own sake, has been a kind of self-indulgence, and my opportunities to share what I have learned have been very minimal. I have no problem with 'men' used as a generic term, nor any great sense of competition with men, although I worked hard for ERA. What troubles me deeply is the failure of our generation, men and women, to raise the consciousness of each other and the next generation to a realization that if we are what we profess, *all* God's children, then we must want for and work for equality of opportunity for all peoples everywhere, and that means radical redistribution of the world's resources at home and abroad. Therefore, to that extent to which both men and women focus on personal power rather than upon all the changes needed to empower, spiritually and materially, the powerless and underprivileged, to that extent we fail to do God's will on earth."[74]

~

"I think that women should not ask for permission, but simply *do*. Whatever it is the Holy Spirit calls you to do, *do it!* I am a priest by my baptism into Jesus and grace of the Holy Spirit. We don't need women in Roman collars and robes, titled, working to be bishop, cardinal, and politicizing to be pope. We need women filled with the Holy Spirit to *be* Jesus where they *are*."[75]

~

"Basically I believe there is a Heavenly Father and a Heavenly Mother. There cannot be one without the other! She loves us and guides us, though I'm not sure why she is spoken of so little. I have three small children. They are my career for the next fifteen to twenty years. No job could take me away from them. I resent women who feel that being female is not good enough, that the only way they feel important is to want or have what men traditionally have, for example, administrative responsibility in the church. I also resent women who feel being female lets them off the hook as far as becoming educated and responsible for themselves is concerned. I'm sure our Father and Mother want all women to reach for the highest that is in them — and higher — and live the gospel of Christ in harmony and inner peace. We must each find ourselves by taking our minds off ourselves a little bit and reaching out to others a little more."[76]

~

"I find the 'good old boy' network alive and well and have crashed their closed club because of my present position of leadership. It's a stupid 'club'!"[77]

~

"Do you suppose you could find me a new job? It's hell out here in the trenches. Just kidding...sort of!"[78]

~

"I wish I had more mentors, and yet I am at an age where I should be one. I feel a bit at a loss spiritually in this area, and yet my job and fear of not finding work I like in another city has kept me here. I know I need a spiritual community for growth and direction in my life, especially now. I feel very dry. When I was in college and in seminary, discussions and access to helpful personal groups was there. It's been a long time. I feel at a loss of where to turn to make my life more meaningful and fulfilled."[79]

~

"I spent many years carrying much anger about the role of women in our church. I can no longer afford to exist that way. I now consider myself ordained by God's Spirit and I do what I need to do when the occasion presents itself. I don't fight anymore. I'm too tired. But there is still anger that surfaces on occasion. It's not the best way to be, but I don't know how to deal with the anger at this time."[80]

~

"It's mighty slow going, making an impact on both women and men. Many refuse to recognize that problems exist, that nonsexist language is an important consideration, that sexist 'humor' is offensive, that

women are second-class citizens, that our churches sin in this regard, that hierarchical structures are destructive, devastating, painful
to half the population. If it weren't for the model we have in Jesus
and the support of our sisters in suffering, hope would go down the
drain."[81]

~

"A male priest having to come to preside at prayer in an all-women's
community seems totally ridiculous and limits my ability to invest
myself in the prayer. I struggle with living in a religious community
that I love but that seems to have a different image of God's church."[82]

~

"I am an evangelical Christian, although an alienated one. I look
forward to the time that women and men can share service to the
people of God in complementarity. Much dialogue, sincerely done,
will precede this possibility."[83]

~

"I do not want to be a separatist. I do not want only the women of
the congregation to be able to relate to me and to my kind of spirituality. It does seem to be the case sometimes. I want to be able to find
the common ground and the growing edges for all of us, while still
respecting and dealing with the differences."[84]

~

"Women in leadership positions in the churches are diminishing the
relevance of denominational differences. There is a spirituality and
vitality among both Protestant and Roman Catholic women which
delights in service and worship and witness but considers hierarchies
and the pronouncements of synods to be largely abstract and irrelevant. When I am asked why I don't try for a conference minister slot
I laugh and say my tolerance for meetings is too low. I would rather
go the other way, toward direct service to the poor, and I am leaving
my parish to do just that."[85]

~

"I resigned from my position as acting director at the Catholic center
because I did not think I could take another year of the emotional
abuse I received from the priest on staff. He decided he wanted to
be in charge. My colleagues from seminary, my directees, people who
attend the retreats I give tell me I am incredibly good at what I do.
I have all this love to give, but the Catholic Church does not want
it, and I cannot go away. I wait and hope and trust that God knows
where I am, and I am doing what I am supposed to do, as insignificant
as it seems."[86]

~

"I think the greatest tragedy is that it is women who largely support the sexist system in Christianity, and that they are also misogynist. There is a great deal to be done to free women's spirits and minds."[87]

~

"I find I am tolerated by most men, admired by a few men, but seldom confronted! If my input or decisions are not to their liking, I am ignored. Women applaud what I do. A few younger women are following my example, but older women are incapable of changing their habits of staying in the background."[88]

~

"I think things have improved but have a long way to go. The South is way behind on inclusive language. I think women could save the church and society if we got our act together. Sisterhood keeps me going."[89]

~

"I think there is a dreadful waste of human potential when people are denied a chance to serve God in formal ways just because they are women. When will we learn that traditions are just that. They are not necessarily mandates from the Lord. Having worked as an engineer for fourteen years, I know I have certain strengths and weaknesses as an employee. Few of these are gender based. Being female is always a curse and an opportunity."[90]

~

"At this point in my life, I'm really not interested in any kind of religion or religious practices. I've gone through so many — Catholic home, school, and church, religious community, ecumenical, Vatican II renewal, Mother God, wicca, symbols and metaphors (old and new). I'm tired of it all. When I was a child, a girl, a young adult, it all was very meaningful and I touched God. Now I touch God just by living and doing the ordinary, simple, common, normal things. I'm amazed and in awe of everything and everyone and don't need to symbolize or ritualize it. All that is is already a symbol, a metaphor for the divine, the mystery of life. When I say, 'Where are you?' to God, I just look around me, and feel, and say — 'This is God.' And then I become present to it — whatever, whoever it is — and I find God."[91]

~

"I believe that we women must go our own ways and let patriarchy and its institutions, *all* of them — religious, political, economic — die of their own dead weight! The sooner we let go, the sooner they die. We can do ritual and spirituality, and we don't need males to do it."[92]

~

"How grateful I am to be a Friend! My experience of Friends (about eighteen years) has been one of continual empowerment and growth. I've been encouraged to do things I didn't know I could do and I've found that Friends listen to and hear me and seek my ideas. My experience in the denominational university where I teach has been just the opposite. It's as if someone is pushing on my head, keeping me down and surrounding me with walls, boxing me in. In that system, I'm not heard."[93]

~

"Since working with incarcerated women, my faith has gotten stronger. I have actually seen miracles happen, sometimes on a daily basis. I have seen the women's prayers answered. In my own work, I have been tested many times over. I learned to let Jesus be my protector through the Goddess. I pray to the female side of God and she never lets me down. Sometimes I feel guilty that I don't attend Mass as often as I should, but when I go to work inside the jail, every day seems like a spiritual experience in the people that I touch and that touch me."[94]

~

"Ten years ago I was very active in church. I have suffered losses. A twenty-four-year marriage came to an end, and then my sixteen-year-old daughter was abducted. Her damaged bike was found, but police have not been able to find her body. We believe she is in heaven, alive and healed. With both my divorce — 'Christians, and especially conservative evangelical pastors and their wives, *don't* get divorced" — and the loss of my daughter — for over one year, the church pastor and others were *sure* she was naughty and ran away — I have come to realize that the (my) organized church did not support me as I had ignorantly assumed they would. Many Christians seem to be judgmental and so intent on being 'right' that they often show little or none of the compassion and love that my God has and is showing me. Because of this I have spent the last nine years renewing myself and so have not been active in the church organization. However, I do daily give verbal praise to God who has given me the strength and courage to get up each day. I attend church most every Sunday, but no longer feel the sense of community that I had when I had the role of pastor's wife and when I had credibility because of my kids. Middle-aged women with grown children are invisible in my church as well as in many other areas of society."[95]

~

"I was raised in the Mormon Church and about two years ago I experienced a severe unraveling of my beliefs. It occurred to me that if God was truly as He had been represented to me — male — severely patriarchal and Mormon, then I didn't want Him. I would rather go to hell. In a way I have gone through my own personal hell trying to discover who God is, what being a woman means, what my life means. I don't go to church anymore, although I feel branded as a Mormon for life."[96]

~

"I am by now what is disparagingly called a 'cafeteria Catholic,' cheering on the idea of liberation theology, enjoying the camaraderie of parish friends, feeling a part of the mystical body of Christ, but dropping whole chunks of the Nicene creed."[97]

~

"Making slow progress, decently and in order, in the Presbyterian patriarchy, thanks especially to some very bright, stubborn, witty women."[98]

~

"I find as I 'mature' (a nice euphemism for growing old!) that while I am still in support of feminist issues in the church, I do not need to be militant about them. I find when I state my case, my beliefs, that people listen if I am articulate and 'reasonable.' "[99]

~

"There's no doubt in my mind that a new age is dawning. I've decided to wait actively, living as freely and fully as possible, trusting that my personal actions will help move us toward this new awareness. Patriarchy is dead, but its death struggle is causing much pain."[100]

~

"I worked in parish ministry for fourteen years and I have already worked through a lot of personal anger regarding male domination in the churches. At one time I wanted to be ordained. Now I have lost hope that the structure will change in my lifetime. I live a contemplative life in the world now. The peace and nonviolence within makes it difficult for me to identify with 'militant' feminists. My own life pain and my experience of the male church and male politics have made room in me for depth and utter longing that all may be one, that there be no longer male/female, powerful/powerless, rich/poor, violent/nonviolent, white/color, etc. Native American spirituality gives me nourishment and meaning as I move to become one with all the earth. At this point in my life, I am unable to read the scriptures which I prayed and journaled over for thirty years!"[101]

~

"I'm sure some of my negativity toward Christianity now arises from being threatened with exposure — due to my lesbianism — at my prior place of employment, a 'Christian clinic,' forcing my resignation. This was done 'in love,' of course, by an evangelical woman with whom I was involved, and her explanation was peppered with biblical 'proof texts.' It was such a *personal,* hateful thing done in the name of 'righteousness' and 'God' that I've not been able to embrace that god or that system of 'righteousness' since. I am just beginning to trust my own thoughts and feelings about a higher power and my relationship to it enough to try again to connect with others and their spiritual journeys. I can't imagine, however, that this ever will be in any type of evangelical or fundamental Christian church."[102]

~

"The lack of ritual/symbol that can speak to me as woman accounts for my withdrawal from religion and my increased attention to spiritual maturity. Co-dependency in religion is appalling."[103]

~

"There should be a strategy that empowers the needy rather than one that merely addresses the symptoms of their need."[104]

~

"I don't know how we women can ever change the male system by attempting to make 'them' include 'us.' Perhaps we need to ritualize our own births, livings, dyings, and risings. Our inclusiveness of all who long for union could be the revolution."[105]

~

"As we try to move toward a more equitable system of partnership, it will be difficult, but our daughters will benefit from the price we pay. I have experienced both sexual and physical abuse at the hands of men who believed their gender somehow 'entitled' them to be pleased and served by women. Somehow 'helpmeet' has been twisted and misinterpreted to serve the interests of the dominant group. I am presently in therapy to try to deal with the rage I have held for a long time. I believe these issues are significant as we try to create a society that nurtures and supports individual growth and freedom and mutual respect, not only for humans, but all living things."[106]

~

"Women will have to become more confident to re-educate men and other women, to show that sharing the leadership is peaceful, loving, engaging, and supportive. These characteristics are profoundly and traditionally female."[107]

~

"One of the great sins of the church is the continuing co-dependency role which is really fostered in women. There is little or no recognition that sinfulness in women is more often related to being too submissive — humility that is self-abasement, pride disguised as martyrdom. I would never say that we would use power better than men — we are just as fallible — but we wield power in a way that is so destructive to ourselves. How I wish I had been taught as a little girl to take a few risks, to be more assertive. One gets so self-righteous being a 'good little girl." At sixty-plus, I'm working very hard to just be human."[108]

~

"I am a woman born thirty years too soon. When my husband (a minister) retired, I realized how empty my spiritual and intellectual life was. We don't live where I can find a Woman-Church, but I feel in many ways, considering my age and the era I lived through, that I have helped and been helped by many women. I find them in my writers group, my art league, and my fellow retired ministers' wives who, at sixty-five-plus, begin to ask: what does God require of me for my remaining years? What did God have in mind when She created me? Where have I been all this time! What do I really believe about God, the Bible, the church? I have read voluminously, and have written my own theological statements, but it is lonesome."[109]

~

"My involvement in religion has always been as a layperson and has had a social action/equity focus. My daughter and I share feminist goals, but my daughter is not very involved in organized religion. Care and concern for the environment occupies a major focus in my life, occupying a major block of volunteer time. I was recognized by the U.N. Association as one of the outstanding women in my state for my volunteer work for women's equality. My greatest interest and skill is in linking people together in networks and support — linking issues such as aging, environment, women's issues, and personal support."[110]

~

"I was interested in my response to filling out this survey. I began to feel guilty — that I'm not doing more, that my group isn't more democratic, that I'm not advocating more for women, that I'm not working in a soup kitchen, etc. Guilt: the great trap for women!"[111]

~

"This kind of 'connecting' is valuable in creating a sense of 'being in the struggle of recognizing and claiming our truth' *together*."[112]

~

"Recognizing that women are not the only oppressed, simply the more oppressed, is key to sharing the faith experience with men."[113]

~

"I think of the Easter reading from Mark: As the women were on their way to the tomb, with spices in hand, they said to one another: 'Who will roll away the stone?' Conscious of the major obstacle ahead, they continued on their way, with every confidence their purpose would be accomplished. As we confidently move along that path together, what surprises await our arrival?"[114]

~ ~ ~

You have heard some of the women in this study tell, in their own words, a bit of their story. You will be hearing from more.

~ ~ ~

Defecting in Place **is a national study on feminist women and the church.**

It is apparent from the preceding statements that women in the church are no longer subservient or silent. Many are finding their voice and, in the process, are beginning to say what they feel. They are speaking out, not only in private, but in the public forum, and consequently have become a major challenge to the institutional church. Evidence indicates that many church-going women have been "heard into speech" within small feminist circles concerned about spirituality and personal spiritual growth.[115] Such groups, and the women within these groups, are the focus of this study.

This project began in the state of Connecticut where, with the support of an initial planning grant from Lilly Endowment, we uncovered a wide range of local feminist spirituality groups previously unknown to us. Based on an analysis of interviews with women in these groups and with the assistance of women theologians and sociologists at two day-long consultations, we designed a national study also funded by Lilly Endowment, which began in December of 1990. Our purpose: to learn more about why feminist women leave or stay with churches and how their participation in feminist spirituality groups or more traditional church women's groups affects their involvement in the church and their congregational participation.

With the help of the women sociologists named as consultants and advisors to this study, substantial time was spent preparing an interview guide and designing and pretesting a sixteen-page questionnaire. The next task was to locate feminist women who were likely to be affiliated with a church, either as a church-goer or as a nominal member, and who were also part of a women's spirituality group. We knew that such feminists are sometimes outside of local congregations. Furthermore, to ensure that our sample would also include those women who support feminist values or reflect a feminist perspective yet insist that they are not feminist, the term "feminist" was intentionally omitted from the questionnaire. Names were drawn from the mailing lists of feminist journals and centers, from lists provided by our consultants and advisors, and from other women on seminary and university faculties and in denominational offices. A notice was placed in several publications of interest to our target group. Names were also provided by a snowball sample taken from lists included in returned questionnaires.[116]

Midway through the study, the project investigators, consultants, and advisors came together for a weekend in northwestern Connecticut to evaluate the data. It was a time of sisterhood and sharing, of telling our stories, of liturgical celebration, of modeling what our study was about — women empowering women into a new level of consciousness in an affirmative and supportive context as a step toward systemic change. Central to this experience of "women-church" were the narratives of those who responded to our survey and our analytical data. During hours of serious and solid exchange, we grappled with critical issues and struggled to articulate our task. As theologians spoke of transformative models and sociologists of comparative analyses, the women of color in the group pushed us to find ways to increase minority representation in the sample. Following that meeting we did a supplementary mailing targeted to strategic constituencies, with acceptable results.[117]

~

The women in this study form a select national sample of women concerned about religion and spirituality.

Although we directed our study to those feminist women who belong to women's groups because both our experience and feminist theory support the importance of group affiliation in the process of seeking change, at no time were other voices or experiences ignored. The women who speak in the narrative section of this chapter are representative of the women who make up this study, women from diverse contexts who reflect a variety of positions both within and outside the church.

A total of 3,746 women responded to our survey, about a 55 percent return from those who received questionnaires. Responses were also received from 112 men. While the women range in age from under thirty to over seventy, most are between thirty-five and fifty-five years of age.

Tables 1 and 2 (see pp. 261, 262) indicate that the women in this sample are well distributed geographically throughout the United States. They come from every state, including Alaska and Hawaii, and statistically all regions are well represented.

By design one-third of the sample are Roman Catholic and one-half are Protestant. Four out of five Protestant respondents belong to traditionally "oldline"[118] denominations, namely, Episcopal, Lutheran, Presbyterian, Methodist, United Church of Christ, and Disciples of Christ. The rest of the Protestant sample belong to a number of other denominations.[119]

While the majority of the women in this sample are white, the study also includes smaller samples of Asian American (numbering 49), African American (63), and Hispanic/Latina (173) women.[120] Eighty respondents identified themselves as lesbians.

The women in this sample are highly educated. Nearly two-thirds have graduate degrees and approximately three-fifths have some graduate education after college. Many are leaders in their communities and in their churches. About half the sample are married and an additional 11 percent are in a committed relationship. One-third of the women surveyed have a child or children still at home. Four out of five respondents work at least part-time, and 58 percent of the sample are employed full-time. Nineteen percent are ordained and 13 percent are Roman Catholic Sisters with religious vows.

Apart from the numerical survey data that the questionnaire has provided, an open-ended invitation to share "any comments about women in the church either in general or in reference to yourself" at the end of the questionnaire resulted in several thousand women speaking from the heart about issues of particular concern. These narratives are central to our reflections about feminist women and the church and to the conclusions we draw from this study. They are used extensively throughout our report.

~

A majority of the women in this study are feminists.

Approximately 80 percent of those surveyed responded in ways that are more or less feminist.[121] That a majority of the women in our sample are feminist should come as no surprise, for we sought a feminist sample from feminist sources. What is surprising is that approximately 20 percent of the women in this feminist sample do not test out as feminist. The implications of this statistic will be examined in subsequent chapters.

Many of the women who responded are feminist by their own self-definition. Others would be considered feminist by others by reason of their perspective, or because they have spoken or acted in support of a feminist issue or feminist values. Although women were not asked in the questionnaire whether they saw themselves as "feminist," their classification as such is based on their answers to a series of attitudinal questions that indicate a feminist bias.

The majority of women in this survey took attitudinal positions generally considered "feminist." For example, perceptions that women are blocked from access to leadership positions in church and society to a greater extent than men and the conviction that women *should* seek top leadership positions are typically feminist perspectives. A core feminist value, that inclusive language[122] should be used in church services not only to refer to parishioners, but also to God, is held by a majority of the women surveyed, who also see God as

in part female and within women. Positions on women's ordination
and the conviction that female leaders tend to share power more than
male leaders are also feminist indicators.

Not all feminist women agree on what is generally considered
feminist. This accounts in part for the very split response among
women in this sample on the value of "affirmative action," or whether
women should be given hiring priority over men with equal abilities.
Women who strongly believe in one feminist value may be lukewarm
or even opposed to other feminist values. Both the numerical data and
comments made by women support this generalization.

Even those women who agree in principle may differ in what
they feel should be done. Women may be *transformative feminists*, or
transformists, who promote systemic change throughout the church
in leadership, liturgy, and theology. A transformative feminist perspective is illustrated by this comment quoted at the beginning of the
chapter: "Let us do more than replace men with women; let's usher
in a new way to live in mutual respect." Some of the transformative feminists may become "exiting feminists," who give up on the
church altogether, or as a woman quoted earlier said: "We must dump
Christianity and start over — or go back to the Goddess." However,
the majority of transformative feminists in our study want to retain
the Christian tradition. As various women interviewed have put it,
"Keep Jesus, but dump the patriarchy." The following perspective is
representative of many who, in seeking transformation, are currently
"defecting in place":

> "I focus my energy and my consciousness on the people and the
> hope that I see in their lives, their faith, and their commitment.
> I believe that there is still hope for the churches' transformation
> and I see the Spirit at work in subversive ways."

While some feminists are committed to radical systemic change,
others are more or less *reformative feminists*, or *reformists*, who want
some changes in the present structure, changes that are more inclusive of women, but who prefer to keep the prevailing denominational
and congregational structures intact. A reformative perspective is expressed by those who would "maintain what little gain we've made
both in church and society," or by those who are satisfied simply
because "the number of women clergy placed continues to inch up,
if slowly." Interviews, comments, and survey responses indicate that
the majority of women in this study would be broadly classified as
reformist.

A smaller number of women in our sample can be classified as *conformists*, mainly because they seem to be content to leave the system

just as it is. This perspective is illustrated by the following response: "Granted my church is patriarchal [but]...who or what sex runs the church as an organization is not important to me. My personal relationship with God the Father and His Son, Jesus Christ, is what really counts with me." Conformists are likely in the majority among all women currently in churches. However, in our study they are a minority due to the described study focus and the way our sample was obtained. Ambivalent responses indicate, however, that many of the conformist women in our study are wavering. As we move toward the twenty-first century, more of these women will probably be espousing a feminist perspective.

While our analysis indicates that a majority of the women in this study are feminist to some degree, the question remains: how would these women identify themselves?

Although we did not use the term "feminist" in the mailed questionnaire in order to avoid unnecessarily antagonizing women who might react to the word and therefore refuse to participate in this study, we did ask in many of the telephone interviews whether the woman considered herself a "feminist" and whether other women in her spiritual support group and/or the group itself would self-identify as "feminist."

The interview findings suggest that women can be (1) *explicitly feminist* (self-identified feminists) because, either by word or action, they lay claim to being feminist regardless of how one defines that term; or (2) *implicitly feminist* (unidentified feminists) because they take some feminist action or support a feminist issue or reflect a feminist attitude, such as wanting female images of God included in church services, yet do not think of themselves as feminists and may even deny that they are. Transformists are most likely to be explicitly feminist. So are many of the reformists, while other reformists and many of the "wavering" conformists are apt to be implicitly feminist.

It must be said again that the women in this study are not representative of the majority of women in Christian congregations. We did not do a random sample, but rather an exploratory study using purposive and snowball techniques to find feminist women in the church. The strength of this study is that it can depict how feminist women who are in or who have recently left denominations and congregations feel and react to what they see in the church. Although feminist women are likely to be a minority among all churched women, these feminist women are often leaders in their communities and in their churches and therefore can exert an influence disproportionate to their numbers. They have the potential to effect change, particularly if they work together.

A number of these feminist women who were surveyed as well as those who were interviewed express a sense of being "alone" in their parish or congregation. They may be accurate in feeling that they alone, unlike others in their congregation, are having a difficult time accepting religious patriarchy and the sometimes stifling insensitivity they perceive in church services, leadership, structures, and systems. However, they may be simply unaware that there are other women in their congregation who feel the way they do. One of the assumptions underlying this project is that feminists in parishes and congregations have not "come out" because the climate has not been conducive and support has not been visible. We hope that this study will help other feminist women find their voice so that they might find one another.

~

The women in this study speak candidly: about religion and how it relates to their lives, about wanting something more in terms of the spiritual and/or spirituality.

In words that reflect deep personal pain, women give voice to their frustration with institutional religion. Some are angry at being "discounted" or "put-down," and in their estimation, "used." Many have come to an awareness that they have been oppressed and marginalized, that they have not been treated fairly, that they have not been fully included, that they have not even been heard. Some have given up and gotten out, but the majority are hanging in there, often at the expense of an emerging spiritual awareness that they are coming to on their own. Not all are so thoroughly disenchanted. About one-fifth of the women surveyed seem fairly satisfied with the way things are in their churches, although most of these women also want some changes made.

We heard expressions of a "profound longing" for something more in terms of spirituality. What many seem to describe is a journey into awareness. Women said they are searching. They are not always sure what they are looking for, but they know it when they find it. What they find is described as "too big" for religion and is generally not condoned by religion, but more often condemned by it. A number of women want "to find that spark" that has been missing from their religious experience, and they are finding it with other women. They are also finding themselves and are learning to rejoice in and celebrate their womanhood as reflective of God's image, as life-giving gift of God/dess.

The women in this study are talking about a hands-on approach to faith and tradition. On the one hand is religion, and on the other is spirituality.[123] They are fully in the present, yet are affected by past conditioning as they yearn for a more liberated future. Weaving through their narratives of disillusionment with religious structures is an amazing resilience of spirit and a tenacious hope that dares to assert "a new age is dawning." Hurt is tempered by humor. There is truth-telling despite the cost. Some will say that the women profiled here are indeed "valiant women" and that their courage is inspiring. Others will recoil at their assertiveness, and some may even be scandalized by their verbalized rebellion. Most will probably dismiss their experience as the consequence of those in a secular age who have lost or are losing faith. Quite the opposite.

The women in this study are women of faith, women who are seeking a deeper integration between religious expectations and the relationship they are cultivating with the God of their faith experience. The following chapters examine the challenge this poses to the institutional church.

Chapter 2

Women in Protestant and Related Traditions

Women from a cross-section of Protestant and other traditions tell about their relationship to their churches.

~ ~ ~

"I've been known in our church for my 'feminist' views. All I want is some semblance of equality in decision-making! I'm also tired of coordinating banquets and making cookies."[1]

~

"I have been a very active participant in my denomination for more than forty years and only these past few have not attended my local church regularly. This is a result of sexual misconduct of a former pastor. Even though five long-time churchwomen brought it to the church's attention, we were not believed."[2]

~

"It's one thing to allow a strong female into the pulpit *now and then*, but, apparently for some, quite another thing to take direction from a strong female pastor day to day, month to month, year to year. Direction which might have been easily accepted from a male pastor has been met with all kinds of negative reaction."[3]

~

"I am getting sick and tired of hearing from all the clergy, 'I value your input. I'm so glad you spoke up,' etc., but nothing changes and I feel I have not been heard. The Book of Order comes first, and then the Bible, or so it seems. I long for spontaneous, loving, caring, joyful worship. So what if it is not done in order. Let the Spirit direct our gatherings."[4]

~

"We may be on the cusp of real change — God transforming. It is a complex but exciting time. We are literally being asked to choose oppression or liberation. The feminist voice has mixed itself amid the warring theological voices and will not be lost. Truly God is blessing the church."[5]

~

"Quakers from the very beginning have had women and men fairly balanced in decision-making and influence in the life of local and broader meetings. The first feminists were Quakers, the first Quakers were feminists."[6]

~

"A woman from the church called today to express desire for a lay service early on Sunday mornings, to informally sing, share the Word and concerns, and pray together. Would we be seen as subversive? Probably."[7]

~

"I have no desire to hold the priesthood because I share in its blessings, and I am busy enough. Otherwise the men might not do anything."[8]

~

"My mother, a devout Episcopalian and full-time secretary for her church, has had to leave her job due to illness. She has worked full-time for this parish for a number of years. I knew working conditions were difficult for her, but I had no idea to what extent until last week. I believe that if a man were doing this secretary's job, or any other, that the pay would be higher, benefits greater, and the office state of the art."[9]

~

"I find it difficult to even think of returning to the available church congregations after my experience in university worship, which was one of great inclusivity. Such a community is difficult to find."[10]

~

"I've never thought that organized religion was very satisfying. The more I read works by feminist scholars, the more distant I feel from organized religion and can see the potential for eventually needing to reject my present church."[11]

~

"Time seems to stand still for women in the church. Leadership at all levels seems so far removed from the people of God they are supposed to be leading!"[12]

~

"My experience has been that when congregations experience a woman's pastoral ministry and leadership, they are 'won over.' "[13]

~

"An ordained female I know has more or less been forced out of her pastor position in part because many in her congregation cannot accept a woman as a strong leader. A comment in a complaint letter said: 'This church needs a strong leader. A woman pastor is too pushy.' "[14]

~

"You can have wonderful qualifications, much spirit and enthusiasm, and a good track record of past experiences and still be unemployed because the mindset of a search committee is to have a male minister with a family."[15]

~

"Women in my diocese are treated shabbily. Our bishop is against women being ordained priest and bishop. He can barely tolerate women deacons. He has brought in male clergy who support all of his views."[16]

~

"Women in the church, especially single 'older' women, are a forgotten entity, and pastors do not know how to respond to their needs. I have experienced this for twenty-eight years as a widow in a Lutheran congregation."[17]

~

"I am blessed to be part of a congregation that does not make me feel like I am constantly struggling to feel included and like a regular person."[18]

~

"The mission of the church is on the fringes, in chaplaincies that address the needs of the poor. Women have had to create employment, generate funding, and fight for support every year in budget hearings. The men still want to assert that the parish is the center of ministry, but it isn't. Renewal of the church is taking place in external ministries, in basements, in women meeting together to study and pray. The shape of the church is changing."[19]

~

"I was very active in a church with male/female co-pastors, women in leadership positions, active in peace and justice issues. It was a myth. The male pastor was sexually abusive to many women, including myself. He always had his way in decisions. He claimed to be a prophet, have special knowledge of God's will. God's will and 'spirit-led' were used to condone my own rape."[20]

~

"The role of women in my denomination is changing. More women, many of them second career people, are seeking ordination to full-time ministry. It remains difficult to find acceptance, however, among colleagues in ministry from other denominations, especially in the South. My child is harassed by children from other traditions because his mother 'thinks she is a minister.' "[21]

~

"We have always been the most powerful potential the church has. The church is full of women. It's time we began to exercise the power God has given us."[22]

~

"I called a local pastor and said, 'Look, I'm a busy person but I want to do something for the community. So if I'm going to spend time, use me. I'm ordained, I like to visit shut-ins and hospital cases and old people. I can do kids and youth groups. . . . I've done prisons and women's shelters and homeless shelters. Where do you want me?' He said, 'Let's do lunch.' He cancelled and said he'd call to reschedule. Never did."[23]

~

"I like the way Mormon men help with the kids. I like the church's emphasis on men 'dating' their wives. I like the support they give to women who want to be home with their kids. I like that we are taught to think and to have a good secular education. Women had the vote in Utah before women in the U.S. did. Why should I want to be liberated when I already have my freedom?"[24]

~

"I struggle with continuing to support an institutional church that is more exclusive than inclusive; more concerned with numbers and dollars than people; claims to seek justice, yet within its walls, reeks of injustice. Corporate worship in the congregations in my area has been leaving me drained, angry, misunderstood, and wondering where God is in the midst of it all. I do not question that I am called to the ordained ministry. I do question how I am to live out that call today!"[25]

~

"The ongoing question for me as an ordained clergywoman is, 'Will the institutional church be transformed by new winds of the spirit blowing, or am I slowly being co-opted into an institutional mainte-nance supporter?' I maintain a parallel track and recommend it for other women, that is, I participate in a bimonthly women's ritual/ study group and I am part of the institutional church. It's kept me sane for three years."[26]

~

"There are five Episcopal churches in the area. Three have women at the helm. They seem to be so much more willing to speak of Christ as presence. My parish is thawing from a staid, dead, empty, cold old church to a vital, spiritually based, connected instrument of God."[27]

~

"I belong to a church that has had a woman as its minister for the last five years. The church has grown under her leadership. It has been imbued with a vitality and excitement it had lacked before she came. The first day she conducted a worship in our church, I wept during the whole service. It was as if someone had said to me, 'You're okay. This is your church, your God!' "[28]

~

"As I think about the future of women in the church, I am afraid. I am afraid that the day will come when I will have to leave the church, because it will have grown too hostile for me. I love the church and I love my work in it as a pastor, but I'm afraid I will wake up some morning to find my ordination rescinded. The world is not a friendly place for women, perhaps especially for religious women. But wouldn't the world be different if it was women's visions that shaped it?"[29]

~

"My husband and I are a clergy couple. We have served as co-pastors in three parishes and are now retiring. A *very* few still introduce me as the 'pastor's wife.' No one introduces my husband as the 'pastor's husband.' "[30]

~

"I am disabled and use a wheelchair. Two bishops have said I am 'unemployable,' yet I have an honors record in seminary. The faculty and fellow students have affirmed my vocation over and over again. I have a long list of committee appointments, etc., and I've been a contributing force in the seminary community. The issue is hierarchy, i.e., white males. The congregations are great. I administer the chalice, read, preach, with wonderful affirmation. Not one complaint about my chair. I am director of religious education and again, nothing but affirmation. The bishop stands fast. Does he/do they understand the gospel they preach? Jesus would get worse treatment now than in 30 A.D.!"[31]

~

"Slowly but surely, women are being felt and heard in the sanctuary and halls of the church."[32]

~

"I had worried so about how I would be accepted among these highly individualistic and rugged westerners in a diocese that had ordained only a handful of women and in a parish where 98 percent of the congregation had never even seen a woman priest before. I expected rejection, I prepared myself for it, and what I received was absolute acceptance as a priest, from the very first day, from both women and men. They had never heard of inclusive language before I arrived, yet they readily accept and embrace feminine imagery for God, and especially feminist interpretation of biblical texts."[33]

~

"When I pray to God as Mother and they to God as Father, I trust we are each and all heard and there is joy in the differing voices. I no longer look to the church for wholeness and perfection. It is often as dysfunctional as society, sometimes worse."[34]

~

"Sometimes I question the sanity of women fighting to get into the institution — and those of us who stay! I guess my problem is that I expect people to actually take the gospel as seriously as possible, and that seems to be of peripheral concern to most Christians."[35]

~

"My concern is that only a *few Christian* Asian American women are emerging in leadership roles on a regional/national level. There are precious gifts and perspectives they can contribute to the larger church and to Caucasian women as *all* struggle for an inclusiveness in our respective denominations. Don't accept the first 'no' for an answer! The first 'no' is supposed to show the 'modest' response as done by most Asian persons. You must be *persuasive, supportive,* and try at least *three* times!"[36]

~

"I think my spiritual identity is moving away from the church, largely because the church seems preoccupied with fighting over who 'owns' it, or who is 'in' or 'out' and why. I find that activity life-destroying and the God of that activity demonic, a God I do not 'worship,' let alone desire to serve."[37]

~

"Having served the church some thirty years, I have no pension, simply social security. Churches need to be educated about this."[38]

~

"On the not-so-good days, the question is: What do we do with a church that hates us? Wants to see us dead? On the better days the question/hope is: Can the church fix itself to be a place of justice, love, and nurture? Today I have hope."[39]

~

"One clear conviction I have about God is that God is not about denominational lines."[40]

~

"I find that some of my female pastor friends are as frustrated as I was, while a parish minister, over the unwieldy way the work of the ministry has grown. It demands too many nights away from home. I got out. The work needs to be rethought, reconfigured, or else mothers of young children, not to mention anyone who needs 'down-time' at home, will leave the ministry."[41]

~

"I find that intelligent, active laywomen often don't take their feminism to church. I don't think they can face the spiritual pain of what the church's misogyny has done to them."[42]

~

"Being a 'pioneer woman' has not always been pleasant, but I have been grateful for the support of other women. At the same time the greatest opposition to me as a woman professional in the church came from other women. Those scars are deep. Generally, I would describe my feelings about my relationship with the church as lonely yet hopeful. I firmly believe a Reformation far greater than the original one is now taking place."[43]

~

"My perspective has changed since I joined the Unitarians because women's roles in this congregation are appreciated and fostered. I was a member of a religious congregation for twenty-nine years. My Catholic tradition is deep, but I am no longer interested in what the Catholic Church stands for or what it is attempting to do today. Women should strive for self-determination and help educate *all* women to the fact that we can make our own spirituality and worship our own God, whoever or whatever that might be."[44]

~

"When my partner of seven years chose to end her life, I felt alienated from the church. I 'dated' many churches before finding one pastored by a woman who touched my spirit with her messages."[45]

~

"The most guilt-producing area for me is being a mother/wife and pastor and not being as 'available' to my church position due to needs of young daughters and husband. Salary inequity between male and female clergy is also outrageous."[46]

~

"I am a woman pastor in my fifth year. I feel I have 'made it' politically in my area as far as the church is concerned, but it's about to wear me out! I'm beginning to wonder if this is what I really do want. I *can* do it, fit in, have leadership positions, etc., but I'm not sure that's what I want for me. I am a wife, a mom, a growing creative person, and I'm happy to have achieved what I have but am ready to do something else that really appreciates *me* and my gifts. My support group of caring, Christian women has been a great asset to my life this year."[47]

~

"It's heartbreaking when out lesbians lose jobs within the church structure simply because they're lesbian. Our group works fiercely and sometimes angrily to diminish this deplorable situation."[48]

~

"Women continue to shoulder an enormous part of the work of the church and share less of the power."[49]

~

"Just a line to say *thank you!* I don't ever remember anyone that actually asked for my opinion."[50]

~

"The past two years I have worked both within the church and in secular women's centers at the county level that provide rape crisis and domestic violence services. For so many women who come for services, their faith plays a big part in what's happened and how they choose to deal with their lives. Speaking very broadly, the church has generally been a negative factor for a majority of these women. It has perpetrated the silence around the pervasive violence toward women."[51]

~

"The church is a difficult place for women. It meets some of my professional/vocational needs, but few of my personal needs. This is especially true for a single woman."[52]

~

"I am an unprogrammed Friend who appreciates that women can get to be the 'Quaker pope.' "[53]

~

"Women have a chance to do it right, not just imitate some men. Become proactive on behalf of all the unaccepted, unloved, marginalized, excluded, that all might come to wholeness together, not one group at a time."[54]

~

"I was someone deeply involved in church since birth until three years ago. I was a pastor's kid. I was a pastor's wife. Church to me now seems so man-dominated and full of illness. I'm not sure I'll ever want to go back to the institutional church. I miss the music and the community but do not miss the pain of never fitting into the 'Martha' role, never being allowed to forget it...."[55]

~ ~ ~

A majority of the Protestant women in this study, ordained and lay, feel alienated from the institutional church.

Three out of five women in the sample who claim an affiliation with a Protestant denomination[56] say they "often feel alienated from the institutional church" (see Table 3, p. 263). A clergywoman expresses what many feel:

"It is increasingly clear to me that were I not a priest of the church, I would not participate regularly in any one parish or congregation that I know of."

In this study the word "alienation" refers to both feelings and an attitude toward the institutional church. "Alienation" denotes the opposite of "in harmony with" or "in full accord with" and conveys both disapproval and discontent. This describes the alienated sample precisely. Feelings or attitudes of alienation sometimes lead to actions that further alienation. For example, a woman who "feels alienated" because of the use of exclusive language in worship may stop going to church on Sunday. There are, of course, degrees of alienation. Complete alienation ordinarily results in termination of membership in a congregation, or even the denomination or possibly any Christian tradition. For most of the women in our study, "often feeling alienated from the institutional church" seldom means they have given up completely on their present congregation or their denomination.

"A great deal of work needs to be done to make a place for women who now feel alienated from the patriarchal churches," writes one woman respondent. Part of that work, she feels, is dealing directly with the "backlash from terrified men" who confront feminist convictions with "heresy trials and study committees," which only serve to alienate women further.

The reasons for women's alienation surfaced again and again in our study.

"I am discouraged about the church's resistance to change, openness, newness. I often feel alone, unsupported, unappreciated. Hanging onto my sense of call is a continuing struggle. Hanging onto and claiming the Bible as sacred scripture is also a continuing challenge."

~

"I don't think that churches in general offer much to young adults. Once one graduates from high school, it is about ten years before programing for their age seems to resume. Between school and work and an apathetic church, it is hard to connect with a congregation."

~

"I have been a member of several different denominations during my faith journey and have not been totally smitten by any of them. My expectations have become fewer and fewer, and even the few which remain have not, for the most part, been fulfilled."

~

"Our current pastor has had many problems relating inappropriately to women in past congregations, we have recently learned, and although this was known to those 'in power,' he was sent to us anyway. We are fast becoming a dysfunctional body. Some women have spoken up, and we are told to 'trust the system.'"

~

"Clergy spouses are an oppressed group if there ever was one in the church. My husband is looking for another church so I automatically am 'searching for a different congregation.' This has very little to do with my spiritual needs."

Many women feel let down by their churches. They feel deprived, discounted, and stifled in areas of significance to them. One such area of concern to women is their own spiritual life.

Women in eleven different denominations living in twenty states located all across the country wrote that they are not being spiritually fed by their churches. Both clergywomen and laywomen spoke of being spiritually starved or spiritually confined in congregations that are "largely irrelevant to my spiritual growth" and sometimes even a source of psychic injury. One woman expressed what many feel: "I love the church. I have no anger. Just a growing emptiness." Many are taking responsibility for their own spiritual lives and looking elsewhere to satisfy their spiritual needs. "I love my church and its heritage," writes one woman, "but find my spirituality far more enhanced by ACOA [Adult Children of Alcoholics]." Other sources of spiritual growth for women are "my psychotherapist," "my spiritual director," "my women's group," "my work in prison ministry," "my family," "reading," and "close friends." These women and so many others "no longer look to the church for all my spiritual needs." The comments of two women capture the feelings of others in the sample.

"I consider myself a very spiritual person...and have not found church helpful in nurturing the spiritual aspects of individuals or my journey toward wholeness."

~

"In my experience the local church is largely irrelevant to spiritual growth. I believe that God is at work very much outside the church at this time. The church is too restricted by maintaining itself institutionally."

Another woman explains her decision to honor her inner spirit:

"I have found friends (women and men) with whom I can connect on a deep level. Some are church members, some are not. Some are clergy, most are not. Some are Christian and some are not. When the spiritual quest is present, the outer form makes little or no difference."

Like so many women searching for an authentic spiritual life, her concern is not only for herself. "If at sixty-five years of age I am having these difficulties in the organized church," she continues, "how much more difficult must it be for young women who are on their own spiritual path to stay and find a place in the church." The same concern is seen from another perspective:

"I think the issues to be addressed are deeper than male/ female issues. They are human, spiritual issues basic to Western Christian thought. Until we understand the larger spiritual issues involved in our lives together on this earth, we will create church institutions that are self-serving, exclusive, and instruments of political or social forces."

Convinced that it is the Spirit within who is helping them shape their spiritual lives, women are making choices they would never have dared to make just a decade or two earlier. A Mormon woman describes how she and some of her feminist friends are quietly carrying on a spiritual ministry on the margins of church life.

"Many women 'assume' spiritual gifts and opportunities which are not necessarily 'given' to them by the church authorities. Many women exercise their 'personal gifts' of healing, blessing, and leadership in 'clandestine' or 'alternative' groups or organizations. Some *take* the right of the 'laying on of hands' to give blessings to friends and loved ones."

The church traditionally addresses the spiritual through Sunday worship and other religious services, yet many women find these experiences disturbing. For some, they are actually destructive and are the reason why some women have stopped going to church.

"...participating in my church worship made me feel dead, sad....I knew I couldn't keep going. I can't risk my own spiritual death."

~

"Attending traditional religious services drains me and elicits feelings of anger and frustration. I tend to avoid them."

Many women pointed to exclusive language in worship as a psychologically alienating factor. One woman explains:

"I believe exclusive language is abusive and destructive. I believe it harms both men and women, boys and girls. It leads to superiority/inferiority feelings and narrow, limited concepts of God....I go to church on Sunday and it takes me all week to recover."

The issue of inclusion reaches far beyond language. For a number of women, the church's tendency to ignore and exclude is a source of alienation.

"I believe the church must begin to affirm our relationship with the earth and all other human beings before it will become a place and process where we truly *worship* together."

It is difficult for many women to entrust their spiritual development to a church that makes little effort to reach out to and welcome those who are poor, those who are ethnic minorities, and others who are in need. They say their congregations avoid addressing issues that affect us all, issues women consider vital to spiritual integrity. "Where is the church in saving our environment? Where is the church in peace and social justice concerns?" These women "don't see 'the church' as living up to its role in society." Their demands are clear.

"It is crucial for the churches to respond to women's concerns such as economic survival, racism, cultural difference, violence against women, and sexuality with more compassion and understanding—and more importantly, with structural and ideological change....Without this change, the churches will continue to become more irrelevant to the majority of Christian women in America."

Some women are strongly critical of the church's response to single women, lesbian women, and women of color, and challenge its attitudes with regard to marital status, sexual orientation, and race. Many lesbian women told us of personally painful experiences with their congregations and denominations.

"I decided to come out fully cognizant of the fact that I would never be elected an elder as an out lesbian. When I sought some pastoral help in dealing with being at once single and so very much exposed, one minister told me, 'Probably a good thing you're single. It's easier on the congregation that way.'"

~

"I am an out lesbian who was elected and ordained a deacon. At the congregational level I endured a horrible election process. Recently charges were filed against our congregation. I'm not sure, with all this stress, why I keep going to church."

~

"I am a variety of contradictions — lesbian, Christian, traditional, and often feel alone in my spiritual journey. I long for a church where I can be as accepted as my heterosexual sisters."

With regard to the issue of inclusion, criticism of the institutional church extends to church-going women. "How can we work together to face the homophobia among us and in the church?" The woman who poses this question also calls for "more work on the relationship between white women and women of color. What are our common and different agendas? How do we trust or not trust each other?"

Some women find the institutional formality an obstacle to personal growth. For them, the spontaneous, Spirit-filled gatherings and informal, innovative rituals of feminist spirituality groups are far more nurturing and sustaining. They have trouble finding support for their feminist perspective within their congregation. Many choose not to reveal their radical feminism to their congregation. Perhaps this is why they often do not have the support of other feminist women who may also be anonymously present and consequently grow more and more alienated because they feel isolated and utterly alone. Lack of support surfaced as an issue in a variety of ways:

"The institutional church has not been supportive of my work toward ordination except on a technical basis. I deduced from some subtle verbal comments that I was seen as a foreigner, even though my great-grandparents were the first of my family to come to the U.S. I found deep-rooted, probably unconscious, racism because of my physical appearance. Although the racism does not shock me, it *has* discouraged me from pursuing ordination."

~

"I love my church very deeply but feel a deep division among women members. Most are traditional, conservative, and uninterested in rocking the church boat. ... It is difficult for many women to speak out — or even *think* out."

~

"I have worked in five local churches for the past twenty years as a Christian educator, in addition to teaching in a university. The last church job I left after four years because the pastor told me he wouldn't work with a woman. I got support to stay from the congregation, but very little support or protection from the institution to whom I've been loyal for forty years of my life."

Underlying all of the discontent is the unrelenting reality of an institutionalized sexism that is supported and fostered by patriarchal structures. Patriarchy, the "institutionalized system of male dominance," continues to deprive women of access to power in the church.[57] This deprivation is acutely felt.

> "Women, in general, have the attributes that humankind aspires to and relates to religion. It is unfortunate and unforgivable that women have been kept in either a secondary role or no role in the church."

Because of a prevailing patriarchal culture, women's experience is still discounted and women are still excluded from full participation in church life as well as from the interpretation of that life as it relates to the whole of human existence. Here are two graphic examples of what patriarchy has done to women.

> "Women in my church are hard-working, self-sacrificing, and often obedient to a fault! Although more and more women are becoming more aware of, and possibly involved in, women's issues, most 'kiss the chains that bind them'! They are willing to accept and expect patriarchal bonds, and the patriarchy continues to define, to rule, and to limit women's roles."

> ~

> "It saddens me that so many women in my primary congregation are afraid to take leadership roles. They lack self-esteem and hang on to old beliefs regarding women's places in the church."

Some other examples of how women feel:

> "It grieves me to think about raising my boys at a sexist church, but there doesn't seem to be a lot of other good choices."

> ~

> "I have a lot of frustration with the patriarchal paralysis in the church. I understand that change comes with time and a great cost, but I often feel like I am in a quiet battle in which women are losing. What has kept me in ministry/church so far has been my passion for the women who know there is something more for them, but don't know where to look but the church."

> ~

> "I am convinced that the structure of the system is completely corrupt. And I am convinced that the corruption is supported and justified by the theology of a male savior focus. As long as the redeemer/savior/head of the church is male, women are going to be second-class citizens. In Mary Daly's words, 'As long as God is male, male is god.'"

> ~

"I understand women's need for a 'Mother God.' However, I don't personally feel this need. I do, however, desire equality *now*. I feel women have a stronger role to play in church and should be in on decision-making."

~

"What can we do to convince 'white men' particularly that in order to change the world according to the scriptures, they have to be willing to give up some of their power and money to be able to give the underprivileged some of the privileges that God wants for all."

Women are rebelling against patriarchy in all of its many forms. Some are making hard choices:

"I have essentially left the institutional church, i.e., voted with my feet. My anger and rage at white, sexist, elitist men in the church is so great it ruins any positive aspects. I miss the church and would like to go back to it someday."

One of the concerns about women in organized religion is that "it tends to keep them in submissive roles, which is not healthy emotionally or spiritually." One woman writes:

"The area of my concern is for women in the church who do the chores of the church, that is, dinners, receptions, coffee hours, bazaars, painting, cleaning, and on and on. I know one woman whose devotion is displayed by scrubbing the communion rail to keep it white. She is the epitome of the women who work to keep the church a place conducive for worship in the traditional manner. One woman asked, 'What is this business of the Virgin Mary? I can't ask the pastor (male) and my husband doesn't know anything.'"

An especially vulnerable group of women are those who are called upon to fulfill the role of "the pastor's wife." An enormous gap exists between traditional expectation and contemporary realities.[58] The following comment illustrates this point:

"My church experiences now are almost all negative as far as my mental, emotional, and spiritual life is concerned. Numerous other clergy wives feel as I do. It's tragic to have watched myself and my husband and so many of our friends being destroyed by the church that views us from an eighteenth-century perspective."

Paternalistic attitudes and patterns of behavior have kept women passive and, as more than one woman has admitted, have made women "dependents and co-dependents in process addiction" in the churches. "Those of us who daily accept indignities as 'the price we must pay' simply add to the problem." The issue of abuse was mentioned again and again by women in our survey.

"I am from a family where religion has always been very important. I am the third clergy wife in four generations. I am also in recovery from family abuse — sexual and emotional. I was raised to take care of men, gain my personal power only from men, and to worship a male God. The personal pain, grief, and contradictions which have resulted for me as I have become more and more feminist have been incredible.... But more important for me than the pain is the joy, the freedom, and, finally, the authenticity I have experienced since I began to break free from my women-hating roots. I have found a God I can finally relate to with all of who I am."

One of many sexually abused women wrote:

"I was emotionally and sexually involved with a pastor of the church, an experience that was exploitative and abusive and experienced as incestuous by me in terms of the impact it has had on my life and faith. That experience was repeated when I sought counsel from another pastor.... In spite of everything [I] hold fast to the hope that God is much more than my experiences of the church."

These are some of the many reasons why a majority of the women in our sample feel alienated from the institutional church. Denominational affiliation makes surprisingly little difference. In our study, 62 percent of the women who are Disciples of Christ "often feel alienated," 61 percent of the Presbyterians, 60 percent of the Episcopalians, 59 percent of the Methodists, 59 percent of the Southern Baptists, 58 percent of the American Baptists, 58 percent of the Lutherans, and 56 percent of the women who belong to the United Church of Christ. Clergywomen (60 percent) did not differ significantly from laywomen (63 percent) in these denominations. However, 86 percent of those self-identified lesbians affiliated with a Protestant denomination say they often feel alienated from the institutional church. Among Unitarian Universalists, who are neither Protestant nor Christian and who are considered to be one of the more liberal and egalitarian religious bodies, 58 percent of the women surveyed expressed feelings of alienation.

In our study, the women least likely to feel alienated are women in the more theologically conservative Church of the Latter-day Saints (or Mormons), a tradition that considers itself Christian but not Protestant. The data show that 47 percent say they are "often alienated from the institutional church." Most Mormon women, similar to women in other conservative churches, do not feel alienated precisely because they agree with their denomination's understanding of God as primarily a male entity and either like or simply accept that men control church leadership. What is surprising, however, is that so many Morman women, 47 percent of those surveyed, *do* express feelings of alienation.

~

A number of Protestant women admit that there is a gap between denominational rhetoric concerning equal inclusion of women in the church and the reality they confront daily in their particular congregations.

"I have plenty of opportunities for inclusion on the higher institutional and judicatory levels of my denomination. After all, that is where gender inclusion is visible, and thus almost symbolic. The greater exclusion which I have experienced, and blatant sexism, is on the grassroots level, within the local church."

~

"My experience as an associate minister in a large, urban congregation was that despite changes in language (inclusive) and outward enthusiasm to include women in church life and leadership, there is a real hesitation to make structural changes that would accomplish those ends."

~

"In my denomination all polity supports women, but the problem is that many individual churches are not willing to hire women pastors."

~

"In my denomination, women do have equal access to all offices. However, I am not so naive as to believe there are no subtle ways to limit that access so that women never achieve equal power."

~

"While women have 'paper equality' in the church, *practice* is quite different. This, of course, does not apply to 'open' lesbian women who, along with gay brothers, are very much 'second-class citizens' officially in the denomination and treated as sinners in need of repentance for their sexuality by most of the members."

Although many women in this study are proud of the benefits women have achieved, which include the growing numbers of women ordained in their denominations and the leadership positions they now hold within their congregations, many still perceive that women are far from attaining equality with men. Many feel it is a question of double standards:

"Mixed messages are sent to females. As children they are taught to listen for God's call, but as adults are told that God doesn't call women to certain roles in the church."

This disparity between rhetoric and reality is deeply embedded and widespread. Says one respondent:

"Though given increasing equity in my denomination, I still feel the prevailing belief is that women can come in and do these things (leadership, clergy, etc.) until the men emerge to fill the spaces currently occupied by women."

Lay women say that women are not heard or valued to the same extent as men. This is equally true in both conservative and liberal traditions:

"Women speak and pray in our general church meetings, but we are not included in the decision-making arenas. Female stories and experiences and histories are rare in church lesson manuals. Female articles are usually shorter, and all we write and say is edited by men."

~

"I find it is very difficult to be really heard. Most men in the church think they are inclusive and understanding and assume any problems are ones you should or could solve by changing the way you feel or forgetting your concerns."

Women are becoming more and more sensitive to the subtle or not so subtle forms of discrimination they encounter in congregational life.

"I realize more women are attending seminary than ever before and the church is slowly calling women to fill pulpits, but — girls and young women are still not encouraged to become pastors."

~

"As a black woman, I am of the opinion that my chances for a call are almost zero. Our church is trying to change but is having a lot of difficulty in the white male giving up power."

Women also complain that they are not the ones who make the major decisions within the congregation. This is true for clergywomen as well as for lay.

> "Even in our congregation, where responsibilities from session leadership, to Sunday school teaching, to ushering and committee membership are split evenly between men and women, I still feel that women defer to men in decision-making. Women tend to carry out decisions, but men seem to make them. In myself I see the same tendency, even though I don't like it."

> ~

> "I minister in a rural area. Change is threatening, as much to women as to men. Women do much of the church work and hold many positions of leadership, but when it comes to finances and major decisions, men still run the show."

Underlying their feelings of alienation is the frustration many church-going women feel at being so near and yet so far from genuine inclusion.

~

Clergywomen still struggle for equity and equality within their denominations.

Despite the growing number of ordained women in all ordaining denominations, women are not so easily accepted on an equal basis with men.

> "Yes, women are now ordained as ministers, but many male ministers put stumbling blocks in the female ministers' paths, sometimes subtly. There are still many young males, as well as older ministers, who are prejudiced against female ministers. Some refuse to take holy communion from a female minister."

Gains have been made, nevertheless, and women seem to be winning the people over, a congregation at a time.[59]

> "My experience as a clergywoman is that my presence is threatening at first — some people leave the church because they don't believe a woman should be a minister — but as time goes on, opinions change. Churches seem to be much more open to pastoral leadership from a woman after they have experienced it."

Clergywomen are one of the main reasons why so many alienated women remain with their congregations. As pastors and role models, as symbols, so to speak, of what is yet possible within the institution, they continue to bring hope, solace, and spiritual healing to a generation of disaffected women. Two women express how they feel.

"I remember the first time I heard a woman preach, and the first time I experienced a woman officiating at the communion table for the Lord's Supper. It suddenly occurred to me that I was part of the church, not just the ladies' auxiliary of the church. What a wonderful new feeling."

~

"It is a very special privilege for me to have a woman pastor. I feel privileged to have known three, and I am currently contemplating moving to another church because they just hired a full-time woman pastor with whom I can identify."

Many women feel that "those who 'minister' to others best are almost always women." This impact female clergy have on other women and on a congregation of women and men is often threatening to their male peers. One of our respondents points this out:

"Male clergy are very protective of their 'turf.' As clergy, women appear to outpace the men in creativity, willingness to try new modes of serving, and support for people in our efforts to do the work of carrying out Jesus' commands...."

Sometimes, however, clergywomen are a disappointment to women, particularly when it seems they have been co-opted by the system and choose to perpetuate the male model. Several women express this view:

"I worked *hard* for the ordination of *women,* but I have been most disappointed with the women I know here who have been ordained. For the most part, they are just as patriarchal (if not more so) as the men."

~

"Even though great strides have been made, our seminaries and theological schools are still male-oriented and male-dominated. Women clergy are brain-washed on the importance of the male image and preach the same way, using the same images and following the same patterns. We have a long way to go to free women in the church."

The major problem expressed by clergywomen in our study is finding full-time employment. One of the women, pointing out the distinction between Protestants and Catholics on the issue of ordination, writes: "As Mary Daly once said: 'You Protestants have it backward. You get ordained and then fight for a job. We get a job and then worry about being ordained.'" Another respondent who is over eighty years of age reflects on the many changes that have taken place in the church during her lifetime and regrets that among the many women who are ordained, "the majority have a difficult time, particularly when they want to make a change and move to another church." The challenge is not to get "stuck" forever in an entry-level position:

"A major problem for clergywomen is receiving a second call, especially if one has gone to a rural area (and low pay) for a first call."

~

"Women ministers are still placed in lose-lose situations and, as second career people, enter at low pay ranges, which affects pensions. We are not 'moving up' and hence are stuck in 'dead-end jobs.'"

Indeed, the real issue in the Protestant churches is not women clergy but women pastors. Here clergywomen come up against a brick wall. Many of the clergywomen surveyed note their frustration.

"Our denomination is committed to placing women in pastoral positions in our churches. However, most of our churches are still very resistant and our polity leaves the local church in control. Consequently, we have few women pastors."

~

"Despite the increasing number of ordained women, they are still relegated to subordinate positions or shunted off to small struggling churches which can't afford to pay them a living wage...."

~

"There is still the 'glass ceiling' in terms of women and senior pastorates, especially in the larger churches. It becomes an economic issue when the big salaries go only to men."

~

"In my denomination, women still face discrimination when it comes to moving up to senior pastorates or large churches. Many very capable colleagues have left parish ministry for places where their gifts may be more fully utilized and affirmed."

There is evidence that poorer churches, especially in rural areas, are more eager to accept women pastors because they know that they can get a better pastor for their money. In fact, this motivation for hiring a woman was revealed quite blatantly to one of the clergywomen in our study:

"Some churches are aware that there are a lot of excellent clergy-women who are underemployed or unemployed. One church even said: 'We know that we can only afford to pay the minimum recommended salary package so we're looking for a woman. We know that at that salary level the men who will consider interviewing to be our pastor would be mediocre. With what we can afford to pay, we'll get more for our money if we hire a woman.'"

It may indeed be advantageous to small churches to be able to attract gifted clergywomen who cannot get a call — or a pastorate — elsewhere, a fact observed by another clergywoman:

"Small churches which often received the 'leftover' men from a seminary class who left soon to move up to a nice suburban church are now getting more women. These women are often mature, not at the bottom of the class, and are good pastors, preachers, teachers. I am beginning to see a positive impact on the small churches — revitalization of program, outlook, and a quality of life they have been yearning for in years past. Some rural, small churches are beginning to want women ministers instead of men."

As good as this may be for the receiving communities, it still leaves the clergywoman at a disadvantage, both financially and professionally. Although men tend also to have more trouble moving to bigger churches with higher clergy salaries now than fifteen or twenty years ago, the better positions still go to the ordained men.[60] Clergywomen today are particularly concerned about earning a living wage, a concern not likely to be alleviated in light of their disappointing salaries.

This study reveals that clergywomen unemployment is directly related to feelings of alienation from the institutional church. Clergywomen who are not employed by a congregation are among the most alienated Protestant women. Data indicate that 71 percent of the clergywomen surveyed who are *not* working in a local church as pastor or assistant/associate minister say they "often feel alienated" from the church. Further, significant correlations show that the lower the income of the clergywoman, the more likely she is to feel alienated from the institutional church. This finding supports the assumption that clergywomen's alienation is related in part to financial issues.

~

Most of the women who say they feel alienated from the institutional church are still members of local churches.

A majority of Protestant women who say they feel alienated from the institutional church are still affiliated members (see Table 4, p. 264). In fact, 82 percent of all clergywomen who admit to feeling alienated are part of a congregation. Among alienated laywomen, 66 percent of those in the more liberal denominations and 84 percent of those in more conservative traditions are still very much a part of the church. The question is, *why do they stay?* Here is what the women themselves are saying:

> "Sometimes I feel on the fringes because of my theological understandings of God and my anger at the disrespect and injustice often heaped upon women by unaware men *and* women. It has been difficult for me to stay with the church at times, and yet it is one institution where much that I value is proclaimed. So I continue and hope for transforming change."

> ~

> "Why do I stay? To walk away from ordination would be, I'm convinced, a betrayal of God, of myself, and of those whose lives I do touch. And it would identify my call from God too closely with the vagaries of the system."

> ~

> "I need (at this time) both the large church picture and a smaller sanctuary type community. To paraphrase Mother Jones, I 'pray with the oppressed and fight like hell for those who aren't even aware of, or are afraid of, their oppression.' "

Whether out of loyalty or determination, or because of habit or friendships or family ties, or simply because there is nowhere else to go to be part of that which the church represents, these women have decided to remain affiliated, many in fact for the long haul, others at least for the present.

For laywomen, whether in liberal or conservative traditions, what happens in the congregation is often the determining factor in whether a woman stays or leaves the church. If her local church is meaningful and satisfying, at least some of the time, more than likely she will remain affiliated with the church despite her anger, frustration, disappointment, even significant disagreement with denominational policies and exclusive practices concerning women and their role in the church. Survey analyses indicate that among churchgoers, the more that women like their local church, the less alienated they feel from the institutional church. Positive indicators are:

- when women feel their participation is "appreciated"

- when worship and parish programs are "relevant" to their lives

- when women are "pleased with the direction" the congregation is taking

- when they feel "joy and satisfaction" from their "work for and participation in this congregation"

Content analyses of women's comments give some indication as to why a majority of feminist and alienated Protestant women are still members of local churches even if they are dissatisfied with their congregation.

Despite sexism, exclusive language, and insufficient spiritual nourishment, *some women still feel that the congregation is a community where they have received and can continue to receive essential encouragement and support* from other persons:

"I am not happy always with either my local congregation or the denomination, but I don't think I will ever leave it. When I have had particularly distressing times in my life, my church people have supported me and stayed with me."

~

"Over the years I have found much sisterhood in the church — loved working with women to do what needed doing. I live with anger, as 'the church' has discounted women. . . . "

~

"Even though I can at times feel very discouraged about church, its slow, begrudging acceptance of 'the least of these' — gays, street people, refugees, children — the very ones it declares to be the chosen of the Lord! — every time in my chaotic life that I've needed 'the beloved community,' it is there for me. I often feel like a relic, a part of the faithful remnant. Am I?"

Many of the same women also feel that *their church has been a part of the life of their family for a very long time, and there is value in remaining within the stable religious and community framework it provides.* One woman who says she feels limited in her church, which is quite conservative, has no intention of leaving because "that is where my lifetime connections are." Two women from different denominations write:

"It's been hard to stay in the institutional church, but for me right now it would be harder to leave. The church is where I find home and family. . . . I also have highly developed survival skills and a strong desire to help the people in the institution grow and change, and thereby change the institution."

~

"I stay in the church because it has offered me a good spiritual map. It is a helpful organization for my family, and it is a huge part of my life."

Women for whom the congregation or denomination has provided a long-standing identity as well as a place of worship and social experience shared with family members and perhaps all or nearly all of their friends are especially likely to find breaking away from such a tradition terrifying. For these women, leaving the church usually means severing many valued social ties and entering into a period of uncertainty and loss as they search for something else. One woman illustrates the dilemma of choice:

"I find myself drawn to other styles of worship and other belief systems, at least portions of them, and yet at this point I cannot imagine actually breaking away from 'my' church. Partly it is fear that makes me flinch away from what might, after all, turn out to be a leap from the known frying pan into the unknown fire where, besides being just as uncomfortable spiritually, I would be lonely as well."

As the above narrative also illustrates, *some women stay in churches that they really do not like or where they really are not happy simply because they have not found a church that is better and are dubious whether any churches are.* The following comment stresses this point:

"I believed in the doctrines of my church, but the treatment of women completely changed me and encouraged me to question everything.... But I don't want to drop out because of my parents and the long-term connections and friends I have. Besides, I drop out to go where? I don't see anyplace else so great for women."

For some women, *a church can provide the organization and resources for doing social outreach programs that are not possible for a small group of individuals.* One woman explains:

"I struggle with my own anger and frustration at the indifference and shallow denial prevalent within the hierarchical structure of the church. I just haven't found a replacement that offers the rich grounding and structure that enables effective and broad social action programs."

Comments from women surveyed indicate that a large number of women remain in congregations and denominations that support practices contrary to their own values because they feel that churches are no worse than other social institutions. Put another way, *churches are as good as and often much better than secular organizations or society in general.* Two women from different denominations comment:

> "I don't buy most of mainline theology ... yet I have great connection to the myth and the tradition. It's part of me. I'm part of it. I've found much love and security in this "churched" community. The secular world is much more sexist and cruel than the church. At least that's been my experience."

~

> "For a while I was very angry with the church and quit attending. Now I realize our entire culture oppresses women. I really do not know if I will be as involved with the church as I once was, but now I know I can't leave it completely."

Some women have lowered their expectations regarding what the church can do or be for them. One woman writes:

> "Some of my sisters in Christ are so hurt by the continued repression of women that they have left the church. Such is not the case for me. I have limited expectations of *any* institution or system."

A number of women continue with the church for a variety of reasons, some of which are purely personal. For some of the women, their reasons are clear. For others, they stay simply because — well, because.

> "I am a fifth generation Mormon of pioneer heritage. Something of the stubborn strength of my foremothers makes me dig in my toes and refuse to be rejected.... The net result frequently leaves me feeling hypocritical or manipulative as I attempt to express just enough of my feelings and opinions to foster dialogue and change, whenever possible, at a local level, without expressing so much of my opinions as to destroy my credibility entirely...."

~

> "My decision to stay within the boundaries of the institutional church continues to be a moment by moment choice, despite ordination and marriage to a pastor. I love my pastoral work, but I am not certain the structure of the church will allow significant reform in the long run."

~

"My feminist perspective informs and enhances my faith, but it also alienates me from the church. I remain committed to the church because I see the potential for the church to change. Yet it's a challenge to maintain long-term vision and hope. . . . "

While it seems most women will stay with the church, as has been shown throughout this chapter, other women will leave; in fact, many have already left. Some do not believe the church can change or that it is worth the struggle. Some, after years in the trenches laboring for renewal and reform, are tired or burned out. Listen to the words of those who are at a turning point or are leaving or have left:

"I thought when I started working for the church that I could change the church. I have seen little change and I am growing weary. I am in the process of leaving my church over issues of gender and orientation."

~

"As a woman in the church, as a clergywoman, I feel now, after nearly twenty years in ministry, that my choices are to be sick or mediocre if I plan to remain inside the institutional church. These are not choices I will make, so I'm getting out."

~

"I have moved further and further away from the institutional church and from Christianity. My final break with the church came three years ago after a lesbian friend committed suicide, partly due to her struggle against the church's policy on nonordination of gays and lesbians."

~

"My heart breaks as I talk to friends who are leaving the church, both those with master's degrees in continuing education and in divinity. They are totally frustrated with the church. There is no spiritual depth, no intimacy with parishioners or fellow professionals."

Alienated women who remain in the church can understand the painful choices of other women. Individually, or as part of a feminist spirituality group, feminist women seek to support one another in the decision each one feels called to make to remain faithful to God and true to herself. One woman tells how she sees it:

"I have been a bridge between those who have remained in the church and those who left as I have attempted to remain open to both. Those who left have always been instrumental in my own spiritual growth and a challenge to me as I remained connected to the denomination. I find them more exciting to be with and see them struggling more to find meaning in areas of spirituality that seem very fearful to those within the churches."

Feminists who leave the church and others who stay often share a vision of God's "new creation" and are committed to similar goals. On the other hand, among women who stay, even among those who are alienated, goals and vision may differ. While some of the women who stay are committed to institutional renewal and reform, a growing number of alienated feminists are seeking systemic transformation. Some are convinced this can only happen from within.

> "...how shabbily women are still treated and how completely convinced many of my sisters are that their current status is biblical....I want to change things from within, not as an outsider. I love the church. Essentially I'm a crusader without a leader or a defined cause. There are many of us out here looking for something more fulfilling than serving lunch!"

> ~

> "I see myself and my women's group as part of a wider social movement. We are part of a transformational process as individuals outside and inside the church institution."

In this study, clergywomen and liberal Protestant laywomen who feel particularly alienated tend to take the more feminist positions on issues of concern to women. When the institutional church ignores the feminist agenda, it fosters alienation, not only among feminists, but also among other women sympathetic to some feminist values and to the reforms feminists support.

Although alienating policies contribute to how women feel about the church, the source of women's alienation is something far deeper and more pervasive. Authoritarian leadership, offensive language, and exclusive images and practices are symptomatic of a systemic patriarchy that presumes that its hierarchical infrastructure, androcentric canon, and male-dominated rites are sacrosanct. As the narratives presented throughout this chapter indicate, more and more women are convinced that a church so controlled by male privilege and male power is not what God intends.

As feminists in particular work for change, they often pursue common objectives even as they support different goals. Whether simply seeking changes in polity and praxis to reform rites and revitalize structures or committed to transforming traditional religion through massive systemic change, women today struggle to keep faith with God and with the tradition as they preach a liberating *ekklesia* in the midst of ecclesiastical rigidity.

Protestant feminists are linked to a cause that transcends denomination. They also share much in common with protesting Roman Catholic feminists, as the following chapter will show. For all of their pain and disillusionment, it is truly amazing that alienated women are still hanging in there with the institutional church. One woman speaks for many in this chapter as she offers these concluding words:

"We women have inched forward over the past decade. However, we have a long way to go. I consider it a real tribute to women's faith and spirituality that we remain the majority of church-going people."

Chapter 3

Women in the
Roman Catholic Church

Listen to the voices of Catholic women as they talk about themselves and their tradition.

~ ~ ~

"As a Roman Catholic woman, I live with the pain of belonging to a church institution probably unparalleled in its structural sexism and its commitment to an authoritative hierarchy (and too often an implicit theology) that is exclusive and oppressive. I have felt silenced, ignored, invisible, unimportant. But as I'm always telling anyone who'll listen — it's not their church, it's not Rome's church, it's *our* church. We don't have to fight for a place in the church, because lay women and lay men *are* the church, the body of Christ. It is my conviction that this is so, manifest in my own life in a deep love for the sacramental tradition and ritual of the Roman Catholic Church that keeps me at home there. I question this decision sometimes, or more accurately, register its costs, but I'm not happy away from the church. I am comfortable with this church because I've lived through my anger, my embattlement, and because I'm comfortable rejecting its nondoctrinal positions which conflict with my own convictions. Perhaps I'm naive, but I'd like my children to at least begin their spiritual lives with a less complicated and problematic relation to the church than I'll be able to provide."[1]

~

"This may be the last bastion of total male domination in the Western world. The altar has become the sepulcher for thinly veiled misogyny. Even though the church can no longer control the consciousness of its followers, it shows no inclination toward self-examination. The institutional church may want to retreat into the nineteenth century, but the membership seems bent on entering the twenty-first century with new spiritual priorities."[2]

~

"Many women such as myself struggle to remain within 'the church' while at the same time critically needing women-church for acceptance, spirituality, etc. This presents a dilemma. I want to change the current patriarchal structure and framework of church, yet I don't want 'leaving' to be the only solution."[3]

~

"I am a Roman Catholic woman and very disillusioned and discouraged about the status of women in the Catholic Church."[4]

~

"Women in the church are not seen or heard."[5]

~

"I am amazed at my own changes of attitude over the years. Whereas once, when young, I accepted everything the institutional Catholic Church proclaimed, now, years later, I've gradually evolved into deciding most matters for myself. I question much of what comes from the papacy and curia. Women are still far from assuming their rightful position in the church. I support liberation theology and the ordination of women in the Catholic Church, but I haven't reached the point of putting myself on the line for these issues."[6]

~

"As I get stronger and more clear about who I am, I find the church less and less able to meet my spiritual needs. I long for a community of spiritual sisters."[7]

~

"In my Roman Catholic experience of more than seventy years, had I not grown up in a family where I was an equal with the males and always encouraged to be myself and *allowed* to be myself in every respect, I would have ended up being totally crushed by having great self-esteem under one pastor, then being devalued by a succeeding priest. God knows what He is doing in allowing women a few more years on the average than men. It's the secret of the church's survival, those 'little old ladies' hanging in there! The Holy Spirit *loves* them and their tenacity."[8]

~

"I reject a patriarchal God, church, and hierarchy — and am rejected by them. With other women, in unstructured, nature-focused gatherings, I find my way, am sustained, nourished, encouraged for the next stage of the journey. Sometimes I am able to join in church-based worship, but only because it is not a typical 'parish.' "[9]

~

"I have seen many women nurtured into ministries only to have their gift rejected according to a pastor's whim. It seems as though laypersons are necessary only to relieve the pastor/priest's heavy workload. It remains a challenge to me personally to work through this frustration while still remaining within the church."[10]

~

"I find that the church is a noninviting environment for women. Going to church only makes me angry and more distant from God because it is so male-centered. I feel that I am more Christian if I remain outside of an organized religion because organized religions are biased."[11]

~

"I was educated for sixteen years in the Catholic educational system, followed by many years of non–church attendance. Several years ago I realized I truly missed the formal communal worship. I have read, prayed, discussed, observed. I feel extremely alienated from the church as it is today and also sense a growing anger by men toward women in the establishment. I would love to attend a religious/ spiritual group for women but have not found one. So I went 'parish hunting' and have recently found a parish where I am comfortable. While it will be a sacrifice for my family, having to commute a fair distance, I believe it will be beneficial to us. In the past week I have spoken to two friends who feel similarly. There is a great deal of anger 'out there.' It is remarkable to me that women have remained as religious as they have. God isn't the problem — the church is."[12]

~

"Three years ago I entered the RCIA [Rite of Christian Initiation for Adults]. Two years ago I was confirmed in the Roman Catholic Church. The RCIA was beautiful — caring, loving, without regard for the gender of the individual. I had no idea that when I would be turned loose in the church I would find *no* place to fit. Everything seemed to be run by men who were inaccessible or invisible. Women were crawling over each other to please these men, never succeeding of course. It was so alien to the RCIA I didn't know what to do. I tried to participate for approximately a year. It wasn't safe for me, so since then I made a decision just to go to church and find my community elsewhere."[13]

~

"Woman are underpaid, underutilized, undervalued. Even when we work in collaborative situations, the system still keeps us unequal. I don't think the system is capable of changing."[14]

~

"The Catholic Church hierarchy has ill-served the people of the church by the lack of use of women's gifts. The shortage of priests, which results in people's needs not being ministered to adequately, shouts loudly that people other than male celibates should be allowed ordination for the good of the people of God."[15]

~

"I feel very alienated from church. Church lacks warmth and is distant from people's lives, especially women and families. Many pastors are afraid to go beyond their parish confines."[16]

~

"Women are functioning as pastoral associates, directors of religious education, chaplains, and parish administrators. However, I see these 'positions' as ministry by default. Where a man cannot be found, a woman is allowed to function. It is not, in my estimation, a discernment of charisms."[17]

~

"I have enough comments about women in the church to fill an entire book. Out of my experience of working full-time with a women's organization in nine countries for twenty years, I can only conclude that it is women who can and will lead the church toward its true mission. The system must change and it is women who will have the courage to demand the change. The clergy cannot do it because the system has nearly destroyed them."[18]

~

"I think young people, especially women, would be more likely to remain committed to the Catholic Church if they had more of a say in it. I think a number of women are turned off because only men can be priests, especially since the clergy is always lamenting the shortage of new priests. I know a number of Catholics who attend churches of other denominations because they don't feel their spiritual needs are being met in the Catholic Church."[19]

~

"I feel our male-dominated church needs to be changed to allow women the same rights within our churches as we have, supposedly, in other areas. Even if my generation doesn't need or want changes, I feel we owe it to those coming after us, our daughters and granddaughters and younger friends, to open doors; in the least recognize the potential for all women so they can be free to worship in a church that values women and will utilize their ideas, ideals, vision, and talents. There is so much potential and knowledge to tap into that can glorify God and bring freshness and a new life and spirit to our churches."[20]

~

"I personally feel much greater freedom within my religious congregation of Roman Catholic women than I do within the Roman Catholic Church. The clerical mentality remains quite oppressive and I decided many years ago to work for systemic change in non–church-related areas for women. Although it has been a great struggle, I feel there is at least some hope in those areas, whereas church will be the last bastion of change for women."[21]

~

"I am a lesbian woman waiting to hear if I am accepted as an administrator at a Catholic college, and if so, what do I disclose and discuss with the president prior to accepting a position. I love my Catholic faith but sometimes wonder if I can continue in the institutional church, which discriminates against me as a woman and lesbian. I think I stay only because of the support I get from dear friends who are straight or celibate, who understand and appreciate my deep spirituality, and are willing to journey with me in my anger and sorrow, as well as my joy."[22]

~

"The congregation to which I belong is an ecumenical Sunday gathering, quite unique, very sensitive to women. It includes women preachers and other ways of using women's gifts. I wonder sometimes if I'd be worshiping if this opportunity was denied."[23]

~

"Just ignore everything the pope and Ratzinger say. Each has to do whatever he/she is called to do. We are the church and the theologians are our spokespersons."[24]

~

"My four children are not members of any church. That is the case with every one of my friends. The Catholic Church is rotting from within, but the hierarchy do not choose to acknowledge that fact. It is a very sad thing to see. I believe in the teachings of Jesus as the way to live one's life to the fullest. However, these teachings are in no way reflected in the hierarchy of the Catholic Church. That is the crux of the problem. Something like 'do as I say, not as I do'!"[25]

~

"As the mother of two daughters and two sons, I am worried. I feel that I can't count on any of them being involved with the church. As for myself, I keep going but I don't feel very good about the liturgy or the church's policies."[26]

~

"In the past, I was very active in racial justice issues, democratic politics, the needs of the poor, Church Women United, and I played the organ and guitar for the Catholic Church as a volunteer for twenty-five years. Now I am a paid organist for a small United Methodist church. I enjoy their woman minister. Since their communion is open, I receive communion with them monthly. There is great appreciation and fellowship in the small Methodist congregation. I continue Mass and communion once or twice a week at our larger Catholic parish, without much feedback. I feel disappointment following the great joy and expectation felt at the time of the Second Vatican Council. I want and plan to 'stay in the Catholic Church,' but find more inspiration elsewhere at this time."[27]

~

"Our diocese has just recently begun a program to train Parish Life Coordinators to administer parishes in the absence of a pastor. We are experiencing a rather severe shortage of priests. So far, those trained are women. There are also a number of women pastoral associates in our diocese. In our parish women eucharistic ministers preside at communion services, evening and morning prayer, and wake services. I feel the extent of women's participation in the parish is contingent on the attitude of the pastor."[28]

~

"No matter how hard you work or how you 'slice it,' it is a male-oriented church and the women have to help the women . . . and the men, etc. While the leadership seems to be in the hands of the men, it is the women who 'move' the church. They are its 'heart'!"[29]

~

"It is a struggle to be publicly committed to a church with which I disagree on so many issues."[30]

~

"At times I have a hard time justifying my membership in the institutional church when I would not participate in another institution which discriminates against groups of people because of race, national origin, or sex."[31]

~

"The church's rigid stand on sexuality has alienated the great majority of our young people. They are way ahead of the church in seeing sexuality as a beautiful gift from God. It is an ongoing tragedy that they have dismissed the church as a force in their lives because of its unyielding stance about sex, mostly anti-female in essence. People of our generation (over thirty-five) have the wisdom and sense-of-self to *ignore* the church on its sexuality teaching and stay within the structure to gain the needed community, sacramental presence, etc. Our young people have sadly 'thrown the baby out with the bath water.' "[32]

~

"Many times I feel suffocated for spiritual nourishment and find it piecemeal. My spiritual experience is that of being 'in exile.' "[33]

~

"Women have many gifts that are not recognized or are underutilized in the church. Church hierarchy gives 'lip service' to women's contributions while acknowledgments as well as salary increases or other monetary benefits are given to men. The patriarchal system is at times demeaning and humiliating. I make these comments after almost twenty years of working within church structure. Now while working in the private sector for a nonprofit agency, I feel God's presence more personally as I work with and encounter female ex-offenders on a daily basis. I see the face and love of Jesus in the women's faces. I share their trials and struggles, their joy and frustrations too."[34]

~

"Women have maintained religion and religious values in the family for centuries, but their place in society and the church has not been recognized. Men in general have not participated as much in church. They only want to give orders but not to serve, i.e., roll up their sleeves and do any job. I see many priests who have a position of leadership but lack people skills to be effective leaders. The church may be afraid to recognize women because they are fearful of losing their power. They equate power with money, just so much of it around, instead of with love. The more you love, the more you can love."[35]

~

"Fifteen years ago my consciousness of women's issues was raised by a committee I chaired with my husband to study the role of women in the Catholic Church. I saw the work of our committee whitewashed, questioned, and ultimately 'shelved' by the bishop because he was afraid that dissemination of our report would be politically risky. In actuality it was a study that was quite sanguine, but he said it 'implied' advocating ordination of women. Since then I have determined that I would not waste any more of my time nor effort on supporting the church on any level except my local parish level. I am still a Catholic and I refuse to be driven away from the community I claim as my home."[36]

~

"Except for my intense commitment to adolescents, I am no longer regularly involved in any church-related or humanitarian group efforts, although I do support both financially. I am a relatively aggressive and self-confident female who has encountered few gender-related barriers at work but who has disagreed with the institutional church on both feminist and other issues for years. My confrontations have been quiet and individual. I recognize I would be an asset to group endeavors but, at the moment, I remain a bit too self-centered to stir. This survey has emphasized my self-determined detachment and made me uneasy. Who knows if that is a 'first step'?"[37]

~

"I have no desire for ordination myself, but I see it as a painful tragedy that women are excluded from ordained ministry in the Roman Catholic Church and treated so badly in other churches even when ordained. I would not currently even desire to participate in a church service, considering the current usual structure in a Catholic parish. I do, however, find that participating with the young abused and neglected children that I work with to be meaningful. We strive as a group to figure out how God is with us in life. I lead the services when the priest is away."[38]

~

"If women were given leadership roles in the church, youth would be more active in the church. Church to me right now is when I connect spiritually with others."[39]

~

"Women have no positive role in the Roman Catholic Church as currently structured and as the pope is trying to move things. It is very difficult to raise children and teach them about God, faith, and spirituality without talking about disagreements with traditional doctrine. There is truth and beauty to be found even in my very conservative parish. It is like pulling one or two bright shiny threads out of a fabric of dingy, muddy brown. I feel so isolated in my Christian eco-feminist views within my parish and my church."[40]

~

"I think where powerful things are happening in the church is with *individual* women who listen to God, follow a call, and start ministries or a center or some related good. However, this is working *around* the system. I believe the system needs changing to give equality to women."[41]

~

"I am sixty-three. The patriarchal, institutional church has failed me. I was a devout Roman Catholic once, yet now I see no hope for women in this church. *If* women became equals, they would have to change the church or knuckle under. If they knuckle under, what's the point? As for change — I can't see all the patriarchs giving up their power. This struggle is larger than an institution. We need to become a cooperative society to survive, and I just don't see men giving up their dominant position."[42]

~

"My attitudes toward church I feel move toward a Christian pagan, if there is such a category. What surprises me is that I find many like myself. Also, those I find are members of religious orders — women into nature rituals, Goddess worship, as well as Eucharistic sharing. It gives me hope."[43]

~

"I was raised a Roman Catholic and consider myself a very spiritual person. I pray and meditate daily and give every day and every event, good or bad, to God. But I am so disillusioned with the church and their attitude on women and women's issues that I seldom attend church services. It seems hypocritical. I grew so tired of weekly anti-choice rhetoric during the sermon and in all the parish newsletters that I quit going to weekly service about four years ago. My spirituality now is very personal, primarily between God and me. I try to exemplify it in my positive attitude and treatment of other people."[44]

~

"We are a treasure still buried that needs to dig itself out. I wonder if we can gather, at least monthly, to celebrate God in our lives in our own way without waiting for any present church to set up what we need. Let us create new models of church while being faithful to what we hear from God in us individually and as a group, rather than waiting for men to give us permission. Let us invite men as observer participants, that is, invite men to trade places with us. I am not against men, just too much male rule, as though men are really better than women. I'm for equality. I feel/think it's needed for real growth and the maturity of the human species."[45]

~

"Though I view the Roman Catholic Church as very patriarchal, I feel called to remain within the church and be a voice crying for change."[46]

~

"I have been involved in spiritual growth in a deliberate way since 1975. I did not question my Roman Catholic religion before that time. I took formal lay training and was mentored by a woman with a lot of religious training as a lay person. I am now having a real struggle attending Mass. Though I love the Eucharist and believe in the church as community, I feel undervalued as a woman in the church. I often feel so angry that I imagine myself standing to scream out my frustration. I believe I will quit going before that happens."[47]

~

"I am rooted in the Christian Catholic religious tradition, but I also recognize the feminist concerns that urge an attempt at some sort of reconciliation within the Roman Catholic Church. There is a strong passion for the Catholic tradition deep within me. This passion supports my continued graduate studies in theology. I am a feminist and find that I am diametrically opposed to Roman patriarchal structures and methodologies."[48]

~

"The Catholic Church continues in its discrimination against women, women's sexuality, and issues surrounding equality with men. I often wonder why, after forty-eight years, do I still remain a Catholic? I guess the bottom line is 'I won't go and Rome can't throw me out.' I live my life in the light of the gospel and theologians who teach liberation and creation spirituality. I can't listen to the prattle coming from Rome. It does not relate to my spiritual needs, study, or life experience. I'll stand before God as my judge — not men. I believe that women from all denominations should work together to foster ecumenism and heal the wounds in the body of Christ."[49]

~

"I really question the value of women seeking ordination in the Roman Catholic Church as it is currently organized. I'd rather see women put their energies into alternative activities to foster their spirituality. Let the intransigence of current church leadership self-destruct and then help in the renewal and reconstruction, with a big maybe."[50]

~

"I strongly disagree with much of the Vatican/hierarchy rulings and am vocal in dissenting. However, I feel it will take many, many years for any changes and I pray I can hang in as 'loyal opposition.' I receive great spiritual comfort from daily liturgy (rather than Sunday Mass 'productions') and there is a special 'church' community who are my family. Small groups get together to pray, read, discuss, help, console, bitch, and grow. In the last ten years I've experienced a lot of this, which I choose to attribute to the Holy Spirit's leading. These groups are filled with women (and an occasional male). I find greater, more honest spirituality in twelve-step programs than in church. I love the sacrament of the Eucharist and I know it sustains me. The sexist language really upsets me, so I lector three times a week and change it, my 'burrowing from within,' so to speak. I do not seek a separate woman-church but full inclusion in the Catholic Church. That's my daily prayer — one day at a time."[51]

~

"What women seek is not ordination into an anachronistic structure but empowerment in new forms of liturgy and community."[52]

~

"Unless the Catholic Church does more outreach to the entire parish, I feel parishioners will decline. Older single people (thirty to sixty years of age) are *the* most neglected groups. And some of these people are the loneliest. Although I consider myself a Catholic, many would not consider me one. I do not favor all of the man-made rules, but I love the spirituality."[53]

~

"There is deep discontent among many, although not all, Catholic women. There is much sympathy for our situation among the clergy and some bishops, although most remain rather quiet because of the official position from Rome."[54]

~

"Now that 'communism is dead,' the new enemy to the Vatican is 'feminism — false feminism.' My nightmare is that Rome 'wakes up' and ordains some conservative vowed nuns in habits who would plug into the existing system of clericalism and take the vow of obedience to the pope."[55]

~

"I support equal rights/equality for all people, but only if it means changing hierarchical and patriarchal systems at the same time. Ordination for women in the Roman Catholic Church, without changing structure, could be as oppressive as the current situation. One can find oppressive, hit-you-below-the-belt women as well as men in church. I look for systems that promote justice, fairness, and life-enhancing practices."[56]

~

"Only by way of exception women function, lead, and work in leadership positions in society, in church. Sad to say, many women are satisfied with this token or paternalistic participation. Thus the continued need to bring women into greater consciousness and awareness of their reality, and then to create a new reality that does not foster dependency or co-dependency."[57]

~

"Although I am Roman Catholic because I am a daily communicant, there are tenets of the Catholic Church that I do not believe in, such as papal infallibility and celibate priesthood."[58]

~

"As a Catholic, I have little hope of affecting hierarchical change, at least while the present pope is alive. I'm in a double bind. Can't change the power structure without becoming a part. Can't become a part *until* I become male. I feel estranged from my church. So often the liturgy, spirituality fails to speak to my experiences as woman."[59]

~

"As a Roman Catholic who has worked for some years in an ecumenical setting, I'd have to say that the experience of women in my denomination is quite different from the experience of women in many other denominations. The overt/legal difficulties for Roman Catholic women include the exclusion from ordination, the connection between ordination and governance (authority to make decisions), and a strong centralized government which has difficulty accommodating national and/or cultural differences. A frequent question put to Catholic women is, 'How can you stay in that church?' On the positive side, the RC Church has changed more in the past thirty years than it had in the previous four hundred years. Much of the change has been generated by dedicated, articulate, and determined women. Keeping this in mind makes all the frustration tolerable — most of the time."[60]

~

"I've been searching for another church with my values, where I would be acknowledged as a woman. My counselor tells me there are many such women as myself searching for a theology that affirms women. My personal relationship with God remains wonderful. God is always saying I'm loved, cherished, holy, sacred, forgiven, pure, innocent, etc. I don't spend nearly the amount of time praying and meditating that the men priests do. Why isn't God telling the men about us women??? About how much he thinks of us??? It's a mystery to me."[61]

~

"Two of us tried unsuccessfully to begin a women's commission in our diocese. We worked for months with a group of women to determine the needs of women in our community and then wrote a proposal for the commission. Our bishop wouldn't meet with us on this. We met with his representative. We met three times over a two-month period. The final answer is no! We then continued with our parish women's group which has expanded to enough women to make four small groups, two daytime groups and two evening groups. It seems to me that if the church doesn't provide meaningful avenues for growth for women, we are called to develop them or discover them for ourselves, to pastor one another and encourage each other to use what God has given us to build up the body of Christ, always integrating and interfacing with the entire community of faith, not separating from it."[62]

~

"Five years ago I was quite confident about many things. But these days, as I approach age sixty, answers are fewer and I live with questions no one around me seems to be asking. I have always known myself to be outside the church, even though I was baptized in one. Though I worked for years in the church as director of religious education and teacher, in social justice groups, ministry, cursillo, etc., church structure is irrelevant to me now, as it is to poor and homeless women who are my friends. In fact, I share more in common with these poor women than I do with women in the church groups I've belonged to, and in that group of 'outcasts' we have spoken more truthfully about our experiences as women in relationship to God than was ever allowed in groups of church women. I don't belong to a particular congregation anymore, but I do attend Sunday liturgy at the Catholic university in our small town. I go because it is the start of a nice day with my husband, and because it is the least objectionable liturgy in the area. Until three years ago I was fed by the writings of women scholars in the church, but I don't read them anymore. What nourishes me now are the poetry and fiction of First and Third World women and the stories poor women tell about their lives. There is a God at work in them that I want to know."[63]

~

"If I weren't in a religious community of women I don't think I could persist in the Catholic Church. In some ways I think my loyalty is more to my community than to 'the church.' Yet I have to remind myself that *I am* the church. I was taught this by my community years ago in the novitiate. I am alienated from the official church, but not alienated from the church I am. That makes a big difference."[64]

~

"I still attend church weekly because I believe in the strength and grace gained by worshiping together. The only way I can continue in the Roman Catholic Church is by believing that the church is more than or bigger than the male hierarchy. I do not want to leave the church, but I fear my anger could lead me elsewhere. Or maybe my anger will lead me to work for change *within* the structure."[65]

~

"It is extremely difficult to work as a woman in the RC Church. Two experiences I had recently — the pastor, thanking volunteer parishioners at our end-of-the-year banquet, said: 'Father _____, Father _____, and myself would like to thank you for the work you have done in this parish.' Another lay woman and myself are an *integral* part of the staff, or, rather, do most of the work. I really felt like a nothing and intend to say it. I know this was not malicious. It's just the way things are. Then a newly ordained priest came last June and told me he wasn't working for me. I had a position that he wanted. The pastor wanted me to give it to him. I held onto it, not because I wanted it, but because of the justice issue involved. The young priest made it very difficult and often took things into his own hands. However, I held on. He leaves tomorrow. Perhaps he has learned that he can't step on all women."[66]

~

"During six years as part of a pastoral team with Order priests at my parish, I was encouraged to take on numerous leadership roles, including serving two years as president of the parish council, finance committee, and Archdiocesan Peace and Justice Commission, and as a commissioned lay minister. A new broom swept clean, not just the role of women which was previously supported, but over all. The new conservative, chauvinist leader was focused on achieving a task at the expense of others, particularly women. I and other women were excluded from the inner circle. Some women returned to subservient roles, doing altar linens, Ladies Guild tag sales, etc., while others disassociated from the church and searched for self-fulfillment and spiritual direction/growth in other communities and agencies. This May, however, women received a gift from God. This conservative priest asked a woman to give the homily from a feminist perspective and suddenly acknowledged the maleness/femaleness of God. Breakthrough! There's hope. It was a peak experience. It was bliss!"[67]

~

"I have had a faith-crisis within the past year. I've always been Catholic and feel very at home in a progressive congregation. Last year I was threatened with excommunication after I stood at the altar and prayed with the priest during a liturgy. He was disciplined. I'm still struggling with the full implications of this experience for me."[68]

~

"The church 'system' in operation today is not one that I want to support. I do find my own religious community life-giving and am able to worship and celebrate Eucharist with female leaders and a chaplain very sensitive to inclusivity and justice/peace issues."[69]

~

"In the years I did parish work I found it frustrating because I did more than the priest was ever willing to do, but I was always subject to his whim. Strong and capable women threaten men who hide behind their titles."[70]

~

"How can a church speak of right to life and then deny its female members the opportunity to develop to their fullest potential those talents and abilities given to them by God? The hierarchy expects me to take them seriously when they speak of freedom from oppression for all, and yet, I have to stand in my classroom and tell the boys that they *can* and the girls that they *can't* be altar servers."[71]

~

"All I want is to go to Mass and feel that women are part of the celebration of the gospel!"[72]

~

"New paradigms are needed for church community as well as the rest of society. Single women, women of color, and lesbians, especially, 'don't fit.' "[73]

~

"It is the work of women which allows for the church to be seen as effective. If women stopped giving, making church relevant, it would no longer exist — just empty buildings without vitality. Women's involvement makes the church credible."[74]

~

"I believe there is a direct relationship between treatment and respect of women in the church, and justice. I am not hungry or physically abused, but I wonder if my accepting a secondary role, language that ignores me as a woman, elimination from some areas, does not encourage other behaviors that are demeaning to women. What am I accepting when I continue as an active participant and member of such a church? One? Holy? Catholic?"[75]

~

"One solution to the so-called shortage of priests would be to approve married priests among men and deacons (ordained) among women. A future step would be acceptance of women for the priesthood, but it will take time for the hierarchical men to go to their eternal reward!"[76]

~

"In the Roman Catholic Church — officially — we are still second-class citizens. However, in 'enlightened' post–Vatican II parishes (and in many religious communities) we are really able to help move the evolutionary clock forward quite effectively!"[77]

~

"Being in the church, as a woman, is a continual process of incarnation, death, and resurrection. About every three days I want to leave the institution. When I consider the depth of its teachings on social doctrine, justice, etc. (not necessarily its dogmatic teaching), I recognize there is no institution that holds more hope for the future of humanity. Also, there's no place for me to go."[78]

~

"I got a B.A. in theology, thinking I wanted to be a minister within the Catholic Church. After two years as a youth director, I quit the church for good. I continue to use my gift of ministry, but not in a religious setting. I work in human services with adults with mental illness. My goal now is to secure a leadership position where I can use my gifts for bringing people together and inspiring them to do great things together."[79]

~

"In my experience, informal groups meeting in private homes without official church sanction do the most good in terms of hearing women's stories, encouraging women to find a voice, assisting them in finding ways to be heard and in overall re-education, especially in the areas of theology, biblical study, spiritual maturity, and self-knowledge."[80]

~

"My husband and I completed a three-and-a-half-year diaconate formation program. We both did the _same_ classwork, homework, exams, and practicum. For this _he_ was _ordained_ a deacon, and I got a lay minister's certificate. We both did a lot of prior soul-searching. We are now on the diaconate staff and spend at least one long monthly weekend guiding the formation of twenty deacon aspirant couples. In my parish, I serve in adult education and preside and preach at least twice weekly at a weekday service. My husband preaches at all parish weekend Masses monthly. Rather than taking a more 'militant' stance for women in the church, we both use many opportunities to gently call forward consciousness-raising to the injustices of sexism within the church. Our attitudes influenced the decisions of two of our sons _not_ to be Catholic priests."[81]

~

"For too long women in the church, Roman and universal, have been oppressed. As a newly 'out' lesbian, I am becoming aware of oppression in a much more personal way. The fact that the hierarchy considers me 'morally deviant' tells loads about its attitudes."[82]

~

"I am a survivor of ritual abuse at the hands of the Catholic Church. I have experienced first-hand the effects of abuse of power in a male-dominated system. I was exorcised for sexual abuse — 'woman is the temptress' — when I was about four years old. The result is that I spend most of my life as a disempowered female in matters of church. Much of my life is spent reconciling with church and abuse of power, somewhat successfully. It is important for me to hold onto the God the Father image because I have a strong desire to make that a healthy relationship (my father was my perpetrator) before I 'might' move in other directions."[83]

~

"As a Catholic I am _fed up_ with the church. I am sick and tired of being told that ordination shouldn't be an important issue to me, that I should just _accept_ it as it is — and this is the advice of a _liberal_ priest in a *liberal* church! I will be married in June in a Lutheran church because I refuse to raise my sons and daughters in a sexist church. The priest just doesn't understand!"[84]

~

"I was raised Roman Catholic and in fact was a nun for two and a half years. But as I became more and more aware of how the Catholic Church is dominated by men and oppressive to women, I just quit going to formal church services. This was especially true once I had a daughter. It just seemed screamingly unjust to tell her that her brother could become a priest but she couldn't. I never quit my spiritual search or dedication to prayer and spiritual growth. That is not something I 'do' but who I am. I missed celebrating the Eucharist tremendously. In the last two years I have become active in my local Episcopal community. It is wonderful to have a community again and to be celebrating Eucharist every week. It really moved me to tears the first time I went to a Mass celebrated by a woman priest. It seemed so right. But a large part of my heart is still Roman Catholic. It makes me ache to see a few men try to hold back the growth of a whole church because they're afraid of losing their power base. I do think the Spirit is quite alive and moving us all. Maybe She has something totally new that She's calling us toward."[85]

~

"Many women in my acquaintance are very well informed on spiritual issues and appear to be quietly participating in a deepening spiritual journey through study, scripture sharing, prayer, and community formation. They will be prepared to be well-informed leaders in the church, when and if the opportunity arises."[86]

~

"Not being allowed to participate fully in the RC Church is the major reason I have stopped going. I do not want my sons and daughters (ages sixteen, fifteen, twelve, and nine) to be exposed to the exclusive maleness of the church. I do not intend to join another denomination."[87]

~

"I prefer to call myself an American Catholic. I have a real problem with the present pope and Roman leadership in general. Also I feel *very* strongly that women should be ordained deacons and priests in my religion. I feel I have a call to the diaconate and cannot believe that a loving God would deny the response to her/his own call."[88]

~

"If I were ever asked to justify my lack of participation in the church, I would say that I practice 'ecclesiastical disobedience' — my

conscience would not allow me to participate in the sexist/racist institutional church. I often say that it would be tantamount to a black
person joining the Ku Klux Klan."[89]

~

"Women allow and encourage me, as I do them, to find/discern my
own deepest inner truth and power and be open to the surprise and
mystery of God within and without. 'Church' is evolving tremendously for me, much broader than formal church/congregation. I
could not exist solely in 'formal church' but can keep a marginalized,
participating stance to be 'free' in a healthy choice yet committed
way."[90]

~

"I participated in the local group/diocesan preparation for the Catholic Church's pastoral on women. I was surprised at the anger and
frustration that permeated the meetings. Women feel used to do
most of the 'chores' of the church but abused in that they receive
no position of power or authority in return. I believe the Catholic
Church will have to ordain women before a church theology that is
women-kind, women-friendly will be officially developed."[91]

~

"I think that most religions that exist take themselves far too seriously."[92]

~

"I still consider myself Catholic and I will not renounce my baptism, so the organizational church (for which I have high disregard)
is 'stuck' with me. I was heavily involved with Dignity for nine years,
hoping the hierarchical church would deal with gays and lesbians in
the spirit of Archbishop Hunthausen (pre-1984). I now believe my
spirituality has evolved beyond any organized structure, and it incorporates respect for, if not belief in, some Native American beliefs and
some principles and concepts of Eastern religion. I paid my dues for
nearly thirty years and now concentrate on celebrating my life rather
than trying to change the world."[93]

~

"At present I am Catholic, denomination-wise, but in an ever-evolving
way that is becoming much less 'Roman.' I see the formal Roman
Catholic Church so violating and out-of-touch with daily reality that
I'm not sure what shape my Catholicism/ecumenism will be in five
or ten years from now. I will not allow any group to tell me if I am
'church' or not. That is my choice. Grassroot movements are changing
and shaping a newness that will bring a fullness that the dry bones,
power-clinging, formal churches are tragically incapable of. I don't

know details about 'where' we are going or how we will be in the future but sense 'all shall be well,' even in the midst of great pain and transition. A radical conversion is brewing worldwide."[94]

~

"As a Catholic I am repeatedly challenged by the papacy and hierarchy, greater annoyances now because they so distract from my prayer life. I say the daily office and observe a gradual withdrawal from the institutional church to the enriching privacy of my own prayer. Also, being gay is not easy in Catholicism."[95]

~

"Perhaps as the number of priests declines there will be a realization that women can and do deserve to have positions of authority/service in the church."[96]

~

"I feel like I've said all I can say so often that I'm weary of it. Suffice it to say that the Roman Catholic Church, as it stands mired in patriarchy, is not redeemable, so I've stepped out to use my energies in areas of justice and peace, and to search with other women for ways to celebrate life and make the future better for my granddaughters."[97]

~

"I am very disappointed with the Catholic Church and organized religion in general for its lack of relevance to women and children. It's a man's world and a man's perspective. Youth programs are terribly weak, and my five- and seven-year-old children protest going."[98]

~

"I hope that your data will be able to identify how women are managing to grow and develop in spite of the male-dominated hierarchy, and how more and more are not because of it. Somehow our brothers must wake up to their arrogance and pride. If they do, then we might be able to journey together."[99]

~

"I am discouraged about women and church. Mostly I don't care anymore, don't care to continue to work for change. I call myself Roman Catholic, but I rarely go to church. I give my money to other organizations. Once I was very involved and wanted to be ordained. I don't know what could change my mind or make me want to get involved. I can live well without the church — I do better avoiding places and people who display so much sexism and homophobia. Those are poison to my spiritual well-being."[100]

~

"I believe a transformation has begun, not within the established structures but beyond them. It spills over into them but will not be contained within them. It feels as if our spirits have outgrown the 'church.' "[101]

~

"Seven or eight years ago I was much more active in my parish and on a diocesan level than I am today. I am in a period of stepping back and rejuvenating after 'burnout' and some bad experiences when several pastor changes occurred over a three-year period in my parish. The parish is more stabilized now as we have received a parish coordinator who is a woman with hopes, dreams, and style of leadership similar to those the parish was accustomed to. As for my own spirituality, it waxes and wanes, but with a basic core of belief in God."[102]

~

"I have gone from a very devout Catholic deeply involved in liturgy to someone who rarely even attends Mass. As my feminist consciousness has grown, I find myself feeling very uncomfortable in a patriarchal church whose past and present continue to oppress women. Recently I attended a Mass at which babies were still being baptized 'in the name of the Father, Son, and Holy Spirit.' Only the latter was someone I could relate to. I felt like a stranger in a familiar land. Seven years ago my fifteen-year-old daughter was raped and murdered and the killer never identified. It was very hard to continue to believe in a God I had prayed to for protection for my children. For a time, religion and the church provided great solace. Finally, as the worst of the grief passed, so it seems did my need for the church. I do believe that there is an intelligent creative force responsible for us and our universe. I don't know if this creator has a personal interest in us. I believe each of us does have an underlying purpose to which we are called. I do believe that we do survive in some spiritual sense. I have been awestruck and convinced of transcendence by the experience of nature and the touch of love that has come to me through friends. The depth of love I experienced upon holding my children in my arms was transcendence. If there is a personal God(dess), I will only find my way through 'awe-full' experiences and loving relationships. I wish I could still find that in 'the church.' "[103]

~

"In all my years as a Roman Catholic, a Dominican Sister, a wife, and mother of eight children, I have continued to grow in my hunger for God and desire to see the church grow as a guide in people's lives. Ordination of women was not a major issue with me until recent years when the 'closed pulpit' and presence only of male representatives in sacramental reconciliation has been painfully disturbing to me and many with whom I work. As DRE, the issue of an unjust wage for my education and experience is still difficult for me. In any other institution it would be unheard of, but in the name of 'religion' it has been covered up to protect the pastor."[104]

~

"The voices of women are needed to end the church's silence about the violence and sins against women. The one-sided sexual morality of anti-abortion and anti-contraception needs to be examined through the eyes of women. One of my greatest concerns is the impact of the institutional sexism on the young, college-age women I meet in the university classroom. Many have a deep religious faith but find their churches, Catholic and Protestant, irrelevant."[105]

~

"I have one foot in and one foot out of the Judaeo-Christian tradition. I feel freer that way. I participate only when I can do so authentically. I still struggle to bring about change in the structure, but I'm not waiting around for it to change. I'm about creating alternatives. I love the church and grieve the loss of so much of it, but it feels better than staying completely in a reality that does violence to me."[106]

~

"I do not think in my lifetime I will ever cease to struggle against the patriarchy of the church or to be wounded by the images of women (what they 'should' be) which the church has given us. Quite frequently I am tempted to quit the struggle with the Catholic Church. My faith in and personal relationship with God is certainly not dependent on the institutional church, but it does provide me with community, ritual, and a sense of history and my place in it. I think the problem with all of the Christian churches is that they espouse a religion *about* Jesus and not the religion *of* Jesus."[107]

~

"Women in the Catholic Church are a resource of great magnitude, for the most part untapped. I've seen more people alienated and hurt by the current male-dominated leadership through lack of sensitivity, lack of hospitality, and poor interpersonal skills with lay people. Rigidity in roles, i.e., "playing pastor" and wanting no personal relationship with staff members save for crisis situations doesn't image the church of the New Testament. Jesus was a defender of the oppressed, not a counter of the collection basket!"[108]

~

"I have moved from considerable activity, both social and political, in my work and out-of-work structure. I've been in the habit, in jail, and with the poor and needy for the better part of fifteen years. I am concerned, aware, and sophisticated in the issues you are examining, but I am currently out of gas and bored with it all. I am beginning to think the most important thing in my life is to have 'God' inside and operate my life out of that relationship, that dialogue. It makes for a good compass, good companionship, and good laughs. To hell with the church."[109]

~

"I believe that the role of women in the church is the most important issue facing the church today. I fear that if the situation does not change soon, then the only choice that remains is to leave the church and to seek wholeness elsewhere."[110]

~

"Sometimes I feel I am defeating my own best interests if I help keep the system working."[111]

~

"Even though I spend much time in consciousness-raising of women's issues among adult women and college students, the alienation from the institutional church is overwhelming at times. I see hope in the increasing awareness of the 'woman in the pew,' and I see my work as subverting the structures of the institutional church. Sometimes I am so hungry for nourishment and support. It's lonely always breaking ground. I miss ritual and structural support for my convictions, yet I am 'spoiled' because I have the theological and education skills to think for myself, to call stuff 'bullshit' when that's what it is. Oppressive ecclesial and social structures don't stop me. They just make it more difficult. The feminist spirituality group we started this year has blossomed into four groups already. There is a hunger and an expectation the hunger will be satisfied. Women are looking to women."[112]

~

"Recently I was not rehired as youth minister for the parish. The new pastor felt maintenance of the buildings was more important than ministry to the youth. Why is it that the male clergy become like dictators and destroy in a few weeks what it took years to develop? Am I hurt and bitter? Yes. I hurt not only for myself but for the youth who are now confused over this and begin to wonder if the 'church' really cares about them. I often wonder why people, especially women, remain Catholic when they are oppressed. For me, it gets hard to celebrate Eucharist when I know the politics of the church."[113]

~

"I am *angry* with the institutional Roman Catholic Church and its way of dealing with women. We are systematically shut out of the power which makes the decisions for the people. As a result, we have very sexist policies and doctrines: birth control, overemphasis on sex in general, overemphasis on abortion, double standard on celibacy, homophobia. There is a need for open dialogue with feminist theologians and the larger church."[114]

~

"I fear the struggle for justice for women in the church will be a long one. However, to be silent, or worse, to be indifferent when facing injustice is sinful."[115]

~

"Anger is rising as the Catholic Church turns a deaf ear to the rights of women within church structure. This patriarchal, hierarchical structure is holding tightly to its power."[116]

~

"For twenty-five years I have worked in the Roman Catholic Church, often giving as many as thirty hours a week as a volunteer. I have also worked as a teacher in a Catholic school and as a director of Christian education for Catholics at a military base. I've been parish council chairperson, youth minister, CCD teacher, CCD teacher trainer and workshop leader, RENEW leader, editor of our parish newsletter, co-ordinator for the diocesan family camp-out (a weeklong retreat for several hundred), and, with my husband, diocesan coordinator for the marriage preparation weekends for several years. I've been a speaker for several ecumenical groups and renewals. For this whole period I have found strength and inspiration from small ecumenical women's prayer and sharing groups. Several years ago while participating in a lay ministry formation program that also trained men for the diaconate, I had an unpleasant awakening! I realized many of the men had no desire or gift for preaching, less religious education than I, less experience of ministry, less commitment to prayer, etc., yet *they* but not I were able to be ordained deacons. It precipitated what I call my 'Catholic menopause.' Perhaps I should call it my 'Catholic women-pause'! I decided that, as a fifty-year-old woman, I had outgrown my need for father figures and needed to find my own inner authority, authenticity, and a place to articulate and share my inner experience of God. The search has been painful and productive, and though not finished, has begun to focus on preaching the good news as I have experienced it through my dialogue with God in scripture and life experience. Unfortunately, this has brought me outside the Catholic Church, not only for spiritual support, but now for ministry. In the scheme of things, I am not very significant, but there are many more women coming to the same place and there will be more and more each year. That is going to be a tragedy."[117]

~

"In our church many of us Hispanics volunteer our time, hours and hours on end, but when it comes to hiring someone for a job, they usually hire an Anglo. We desperately need a bilingual person in our office, but after years of telling them, they always come up with the same answer: there's no money. Then they hire whomever they want, usually a nonspeaker of Spanish. Our parish is about 50 percent or more Hispanics, many of whom do not speak English."[118]

~

"So much of my pain comes from women telling women things that keep us in bondage to old ideas, old values which *don't* value us as thinking, capable people. My own pain increases when I realize that I taught the same stuff to others. I hurt when I see broken women trying to find control by going back to the traditional (male as superior) position of the church. They have sacrificed the young girls to some tortured idea of church where boys are OK and girls are limited."[119]

~

"I never questioned the church. Now I belong on a day-by-day basis. I keep asking, 'Why am I still a religious? Why am I still a member of the Catholic Church?' Those questions are very real and I know that I am not the only one who struggles with them. Knowing that helps to keep me going and searching for the path that my life needs to take. Since I work within a church setting, I frequently meet situations where women, myself included, are put down or taken for granted. The reason I stay is because I also work with elementary schools and I feel that I can help the cause of women through my influence with those schools. We have a long way to go because prejudice is a very difficult thing to overcome."[120]

~

"The role of women religious in the Catholic Church needs to be analyzed. I feel that many times we have been used as buffers between the clergy/hierarchy and the laity. We are not ordained and have no say regarding decisions in the church. There are only two kinds of people in the Catholic Church, the ordained and the nonordained."[121]

~

"I sometimes feel I have dropped out of the church. My Hispanic part keeps me in the Catholic Church. My woman part totally disowns the Catholic Church. I do feel the Catholic Church works for the 'poor,' in general for many Hispanics. Yet once the poor are middle-class, women are locked out."[122]

~

"I am blessed to be a participant and a supporter of women's groups who feel as I do. There is hope. Abandoning our faith community is not the answer. Patience and working toward change is. I believe that there are not enough men, well-intentioned or not, to hold back what can only be the power of the Spirit."[123]

~

"In many ways the 'church' is a countersign to the values it professes."[124]

~

"Most of those who do volunteer ministry in the church where I am are women. They do the ministry but are not included in the planning or in decision-making."[125]

~

"Women have to take over the power from men and men have to let it go. We need not wait any longer to do something for/in the church."[126]

~

"Because I worship in a small community not affiliated with the archdiocese, I am free not to be angry. I am no longer controlled by church authority; therefore I am freer to act, to challenge the church."[127]

~

"Women in the Roman Catholic Church are still second-class citizens. I have a lot of trouble with the patriarchal structure of the church. In my parish my lover and I are accepted. We are known as a couple and I'm sure many realize our lifestyle. We have been open with our pastor and he has been supportive, but this is not generally the case. If I was back in a parish which was lead by a priest who rejected me, I wouldn't go to church. To me, going to Mass helps me remember my roots and gives me a prayerful space. I am exploring old religions, trying to identify God for me. I see myself as a spiritual person, but religion at this time is a frustration. I've struggled to find myself, come to grips with a history of abuse, and find God."[128]

~

"Many younger women just don't care about 'church,' meaning authority and structures. We go in search of caring and understanding priests who treat us as human beings worthy of consideration. I applaud the priests and bishops who speak up for women, sometimes at the cost of a 'promotion.' But I admire even more the women who are speaking for themselves in a world dominated by men and masculine models. Over the past ten years I've evolved from a regular attender of liturgies to one who almost never attends, since God is no longer present for me at those types of services. During the years I've been with the Navajo people, I've attended several of their ceremonies and God is there — with the *anawim* — and I feel, touch, and *know* the Holy One during those times of real prayer and community. As a woman religious, it's painful and lonely. However, I am convinced, after many years, that the churches must be emptied before men will hear us. Many are sympathetic, but it's the same as with the poor — there are many well-meaning Christian people who would like to 'do' for the poor, and screw it up every time, since they cannot do that in reality because they have never known hunger or the lack of options that illiteracy and alcoholic behavior spawn. The same for the well-meaning and sympathetic men in the Catholic Church. They have never been 'un-named, spurned, or battered' by the institutional system which even now has become more dangerous to those who question 'faith principles' in the light of our lived reality. Living here with the Navajo people, especially the women, has taught me much of God and the people, so the Mass — in the real sense — the remembrance of Christ's birth, agony, death, and resurrection, continually unfolds in earthen hogans with no water, light, or amenities but with a holy, reverent people who have not forgotten the God who lives in all things and makes all things holy."[129]

~

"I have traveled, as woman in church, from cleaning the altar to now being able to share reflections from the altar. My oldest daughter, a faithful and talented woman and doctor, has kissed off the RC Church to belong to a Presbyterian community. I applaud her. My second daughter is a youth minister in a Catholic Church. I applaud her. My third daughter is at a crisis point in knowing herself and has abandoned 'church' but not God while she is in counseling. I applaud her. My fourth daughter has just graduated from university and loves *all* spiritualities and abhors all institutions. I applaud her. I thank God and my inherent faithfulness to the women before me who helped shape me into a strong woman today despite the abundant paternalism I have had to live through. I believe my grandchildren, and especially my granddaughters, will inherit another world if feminists and people of creative spirituality continue to motivate and inspire men and women."[130]

~

"This is the painful question I wrestle with: for women, is there a real connection with God, the Divine, through church?"[131]

~

"I was raised as a Jew in a Jewish community and was married at eighteen by a rabbi. My very closest neighbors were orthodox. I'm fifty-eight now. About eight years ago, after many experiments with other spiritual paths, I added Catholicism to my 'religion' — was baptized, confirmed, and taken in by and took on the church. I became hyperactive and worked in the CCD, became a lector, Eucharistic minister, parish council member, and through this learned a lot about the way the church works, and most of all became very aware of women and our relationship to the institution. *It's terrible!* Almost every Sunday I agonize through the woman-excluding Mass. It is the height of absurdity to me that we spend our energies on projects from the archdiocese, priest, vicariate, and especially Rome when we are in a time of such terrible need in our communities and all of us so overextended, men and women alike. The men complain, the women smile and go on doing everything, and then leave the church because of birth control, abortion, divorce, exclusion, and exploitation."[132]

~

"I think some of us live and function in *two* churches. I participate in the institutional part of the RC Church because of sacramental life and the people in my parish. I also consider myself a member of the disciples of Jesus who gave us a way to live and to be. This is increasingly important to me as the institutional power people become more oppressive to women. My belief is that the discipleship of Jesus is primary and will eventually triumph. I support women's ordination because I *hope* (beyond rationality!) that it may restore the church to the people, or help to do so."[133]

~

"I no longer want women to become part of the institutional church since I think they would be forced to buy into the system. I would prefer that women withdraw and allow this oppressive system to destroy itself."[134]

~

"While my parish is quite open to involvement by lay women and men, the diocese is an Old Boys' Club. It is at that level that I find the support for such things as 'pro-life' to be 'anti-woman.' Accordingly, I direct my financial support to alternatives such as Catholic Relief Services and Mary's Pence."[135]

~

"What real concern for spirituality, peace, and justice is evident is usually, in my experience, due to women. While some men participate, most in our parish leave this to the 'women-folk.' Another inequity! What *do* they think about?"[136]

~

"I keep choosing to remain in a religious community of women, and thus to remain in the institutional church, yet I get more and more angry at lack of involvement in decisions on all levels and more at a loss as to how to deal with the paucity of depth in many priests and church leaders. I am longing for meaningful rituals, and in praying with the women with whom I live and work, we do share many such rituals, and support each other. More and more 'laws' of the church make no sense to me. I find myself struggling not to slide back into old routines/ways because of their deceptive call to stability and clear 'answers.' I am longing to belong to a group that matches my longings and experiences and dreams but have settled for what others can share, or having no one to share at times. Although I am consciously a woman committed as a member of religious life, I am unable to swallow the old image that was negative and the old symbols associated with the externals. Running deeply below both the church and religious life, I believe, is a strong, redemptive, and powerful source of power and growth and life, and it is in that 'stream' that I base myself and my actions."[137]

~

"The way that I have resolved the tension I feel in not being accepted by the institutional church to which I belong is by looking for and finding a pastoral situation in which I am accepted generally, but it's not always easy."[138]

~

"I believe that women in the Roman Catholic Church are not treated fairly, but I also believe that there is a huge deficiency of *real* support for women as heads of household."[139]

~

"In the last three months I have chanced upon a tiny chapel where Mass is celebrated most intimately, where women 'minister' when Father (who is very old and infirm) can't be there. At age sixty-three I have discovered through experience that God and I (and you) are one and life is a dance! May we encircle the globe in joyous love."[140]

~

"I am very concerned about women's position of discrimination in the Catholic Church. I have considered switching churches but have decided to stay and fight for the time being. About twenty-five women in our diocese worked to get a women's commission started, but our bishop wouldn't even meet with us to discuss it. Only trust in the ultimate power of the Holy Spirit to change the institution keeps me in the Catholic Church."[141]

~

"I have in the past been very active in adult education/evangelization/RCIA, but I 'hit the wall' over injustice toward women and the laity in the RC Church about seven years ago. So my best friends continue to be Catholic women striving for justice, but I simply have had to move on to the rest of my life."[142]

~

"I look forward to the day when all baptized persons will share equal status and will be called by the community to share the gifts they have for the good of all. I look forward to a church of inclusion rather than exclusion, when all of us will be challenged by the gospel. I look forward to a day when the patriarchal system will dissipate and God's people can collaborate to create a world where all are free, where we can talk with each other in circles rather than triangles. I look forward to claiming more of my own personal authority so I can influence all that I hope for myself, women, men — all our church. I am a woman of faith who is struggling and challenged by these times, but I also have hope in my heart."[143]

~

"I have worked for over twelve years in the structural church to reach out to women and received very little encouragement. The church by its indifference has given me a gift of self I expect they had hoped to destroy. I no longer feel the need to have them approve or understand. I know my daughters will not put up with that type of structure, and they will teach their children. Women pass on religion through the generations. We are the church."[144]

~

"In general I find that I am pulling away from the church. The double standards and the way the Catholic priests I have dealt with seem out of touch with feminine reality — yet they *use* women to do *all* the dirty work and put men on advisory and planning committees! What hurts more than the priests asking for that is all the takers who never question it. Even when I have raised the issue, I am the one who is seen as uncooperative and trouble-making, which I suppose is true! It is just too depressing. Yet I continue to attend regularly and support the local church. As for the archdiocese, I stopped *all* support a couple of years ago when I called to make an appointment with the archbishop and was told I had to write a letter describing what I wanted to talk to him about, and then he would decide whether it was important enough to see me! I decided on the spot he didn't need my money. The current pastor told me the archbishop had warned him about me, that I am a heretic! My theology I got from theology classes sponsored by the archdiocese!"[145]

~

"Right now I struggle with my own spirituality and the responsibility I feel for my children, fourteen and sixteen. Is it right to keep submerging my needs and stay in a community 'for them' which does not address, honor, celebrate my theological beliefs? I'm tired of institutional structures that require more giving. I give all week on the job, at home, and never feel affirmed that my work in education, which is my ministry, is enough. The 'sisterhood' gives so much to each person. I guess this is my church."[146]

~

"If I could, I would leave the Roman Catholic Church. I am unable to do this; it's in the bone, so to speak. So I remain in, on my own terms. I cannot fully participate because of my beliefs on abortion (I am anti-abortion but pro-choice. Yes, I've had an abortion myself) and on marriage (I have just this year walked out of a marriage of thirty-seven years). I attend daily Mass as part of my own religious ritual. I say prayers at home, sometimes read the Office. I almost never go to Sunday Mass. I do not give the church per se money. I give money to the church-affiliated soup kitchen, but mostly I give money to Heifer Project International, which provides goats and other livestock to families all over the world. My process has been to try to integrate it all, to develop a spiritual practice which meets my needs, to live a life according to my own very unorthodox principles. All I really know is that finally, after many years of struggle, I have developed a walkable path which, however, would not bear much scrutiny by the institutional church."[147]

~

"I am a therapist at an interdenominational counseling agency. My own denomination causes me much pain and anger. So much life, healing, and creativity are stifled by decisions and people at the diocesan, national, and international levels that I feel overwhelmed. The leadership is willing to risk great losses and alienation to maintain centralized, patriarchal, celibate control. This obsession with control is so contrary to the spirit of Christianity as I understand it that I feel deeply betrayed by the church which initiated me into that spirit. I move between despair and rage and can hold onto my church only by a thin cord. I feel battered by the pope's caricature of American women as selfish and complaining, ignorant of the 'real suffering' in the world."[148]

~

"At this time I don't believe in ordination for anyone, men or women. Ordination is a dominator/dominated system, no matter who wears the Roman collar. One of the most difficult things for women to do is to stop supporting the structures that oppress them. As women become aware of how they cooperate in keeping those structures alive, they need strong support groups to strengthen them. I believe that it is imperative for women religious who have the resources and the time to be mindful of their lay sisters. Sharing stories of oppression is healing and supportive."[149]

~

"At one time I was a very active Catholic and served on many committees and spent hours and hours doing volunteer work for 'the church.' Now I have no desire to even attend Sunday liturgy. Many of my friends also feel this way. I feel sad about the situation, but not upset, maybe 'let down' by the church. Very few priests use inclusive language! I guess I'd rather have more say in where I donate my time and money."[150]

~

"We still have more work to do in the Roman Catholic Church, more so the Mexican American women. We are still cooking and cleaning."[151]

~

"For now I choose to remain within the RC Church, but it is so hard. It gives me both the greatest joy and greatest pain in my life. I'm impatient for change."[152]

~

"I am very concerned about issues concerning women, especially within the church. I have come to understand very well how religious structures help form and shape social structures and attitudes. It is almost impossible to change social structures without a concomitant change in the religious structures. It has also become very clear to me what the extent of the problem of global injustice against women truly is. To try to solve the problems of poverty, homelessness, militarism, racism, without solving the problem of sexism, is like trying to put a puzzle together on a table with a wobbly leg. The effort is doomed to failure. I continue to stay with a group that blatantly discriminates against me in the name of God, that trivializes my concerns and dismisses me as 'excitable,' angry, radical, because I feel there is nowhere else to go. I stay because I believe I can effect some real change, but I am committed to stay only as long as I'm given the grace to do so. I experience much pain, anger, and disillusionment, but I am driven by a hope and a faith in something truly great about to break into human consciousness. I feel very lucky to be alive at this moment in human history. God is doing great things, and it is my strong desire to be a part of it all."[153]

~

"I was so well brought up for my role as submissive Catholic wife that I have only recently found myself questioning the patriarchal structures under which I have lived all my life. The questioning brought insight and much anger. I blame the church for the attitudes which kept me, my mother, and my sisters virtually enslaved, robbed us of self-esteem, made us feel unworthy and unloved and suspicious of love. I blame the church for my failing marriage, which never had a chance, because neither my Catholic husband nor I knew anything about love or sex or relationship. I am in therapy to try to find and reclaim my self, and I badly need a support group of women for interaction and validation of my experiences and pain. I am trying to leave the church, but it has such a hold on me, is so deeply embedded in my life, that I can't let it go without a great deal of guilt. Two thousand years of the male celibate hierarchy's sexual voyeurism have undermined my faith and trust in the rules and regulations of the leadership of the church. I believe most, if not all, the problems and hang-ups in my life are attributable, directly or indirectly, to the church, and yet I cannot bring myself to break with it. It is a cult of the worst kind."[154]

~

"How any male clergy can go to bed nights and sleep is beyond me — the overt sexism is rampant. How do they see 'sin' when it's so obvious women are excluded from equality in the church. I am not supportive of Catholicism, although I attend a Catholic church."[155]

~

"I am a loose-fitting Roman Catholic church-goer. Perhaps I am becoming a 'universal' Catholic. Maybe I am not Catholic. But that should be my choice. Today I am RC."[156]

~

"In my life, God refuses to be limited by a church, no matter how ancient or huge. I'm able to rage, suffer, and ignore the church by turn, and still walk in God's light."[157]

~

"I, and I think many other women, have a sort of love-hate relationship with the church. More often than not I'm unhappy with the system, the way authority is exercised, the way that women are excluded, etc. At the same time it is so much a part of me and I am so much a part of it that I can't imagine being separated from it. I focus my energy and my consciousness on the *people* and the hope that I see in their lives, their faith, and their commitment. I believe that there is still hope for the church's transformation, and I see the Spirit at work in subversive ways."[158]

~

"I consider the RC Church to have been a largely negative influence in my life — from a strict Catholic family (eight children) and an inadequate education in substandard Catholic schools. I often think that the RC Church had to convince me of how bad I was (original sin, self-denial) so that I would feel compelled to 'buy' what they were selling (sacraments, grace, redemption). I now believe in the innate goodness of a human being, and an immanent God/Goddess."[159]

~

"I am wrestling with my need to express my view that women must retain legal right and economic power to choose abortion, miserable choice though it may be. I am not yet willing to face conflict with anti-abortion friends and/or sanctions from my church. I'll have to resolve this some way, someday. I've let the church rob me of my legitimate voice. I feel the majority of Christians ought to be at work in the world, bringing their Christian way to bear on the work at hand. In my case, I've gone through a couple cycles of 'out-in-the-world' and a couple of (God help me!) 'fix the church.' I'll not work for the church for pay again. I'll search for ways to stay involved enough to feel a part, without being eaten alive. Am I angry? You bet! Am I conflicted? You bet! Am I committed to *living* Eucharist, sharing what we're given, in gratitude? You bet!"[160]

~

"I believe that the church's attitudes, theology, and spirituality on women have profound connections to the perpetuation of violence against women — rape, incest, and battering. In a sense, they are justified by the church viewing and treating women as inferior, as second-rate, 'as separate but equal'!"[161]

~

"We are facing a critical time in our Roman Catholic Church in relation to women. It is going to get worse before getting any better. For many women, they have gone beyond the point of no return. Increased education, particularly historical understanding of church, scripture, etc., has given women an intelligent point of view to evaluate present practices, theologies, and attitudes. There are several things of concern to me. Women who are trying to change the system are separated by faith, denomination, ethnicity/race, and class. I see very little, or ineffective, efforts to deal with these issues. We fail to realize that what we are trying to change has a historical edge and is thoroughly and efficiently organized. As a group, we are not."[162]

~

"I believe we women are, many times, our own worst enemy. We lack conviction and assertiveness when it comes to claiming and demanding our rights in the Roman Church. We need to stand together and present a united front."[163]

~

"I have come to believe that if the church is to move forward as a leader in social justice, the church must look first at itself in regard to social justice and women. The gains that women have made in the Catholic Church are mere tokenism. I just received my weekly Catholic paper for our diocese. I usually glance through it, then put it in the trash with the rest of my junk mail. One need look at almost any such local periodical to ascertain just how much of a voice women have in the church. You not only don't get to read articles by women with a feminist perspective, you don't even get to read articles by men which discuss women in an honest appraisal of the church and social justice. Karl Rahner referred to the Second Vatican Council as the third major movement of the church. I believe that the most important movement of the modern church is the movement toward genuine equality between men and women with honest open dialogue and shared leadership. I also believe that if Christ were to visit us like he did two thousand years ago, he would be as disillusioned with the church leadership now as he was then."[164]

~

"Women in the church have tremendous responsibility but no authority. I strongly recommend national women's days of 'remaining home' to stress how visible we really are, though treated as invisible and discounted."[165]

~

"Women, especially myself, are getting more and more alienated from the hierarchical church. I see more and more of my friends leaving the 'traditional' Roman Catholic Church because they can't 'stomach' the anti-feminist attitude of most male clergy members."[166]

~

"The patriarchal power and control is stifling our spirit. However, if there was hope for the Soviet Union, there is hope for our church as well. Just keep marching around the walls of Jericho and they'll come tumbling down someday."[167]

~

"The status of women in the Catholic Church is pathetic. It may as well be 400 A.D., not 1991. I am alienated and sad. I constantly struggle to stay in a church that relegates me to a small role. I believe it is sinful and I often think about leaving, but given the status of women in other denominations, where do I go? The maddening thing is, I believe many of the priests and nuns agree with me, so I feel a certain loyalty to my local parish, but none to the institutional church. I have three daughters and I wonder if they will stay the way I have since they have not been indoctrinated the way I was in the 1950s and 1960s and they are used to expecting equality in society. I pray I live to see the day women are ordained priests."[168]

~

"Except for the exclusive language which has driven me mad for thirty years, I'm not having a big problem with the Sunday liturgy. I have grave doubts about the deacon program. It has been my personal experience with a number of deacons that once they are commissioned, or whatever it is that is done to them, they make perfect nuisances of themselves. Furthermore, they are often boring, and we don't need any more of *that*. Conditions within the church are worsening. The seat of power is the bishop's seat. Today when you change bishops, you change directions. I don't do any work in the church. I give sparingly of my time and money. My friends are not confined to any one congregation or group, never have been. I do have a sense of shared history with the group of women who came together to form women-church. If the church was doing its job, we wouldn't need a women-church."[169]

~

"As a Catholic nun, I live with two other women. Our discussions and sharing are less formal and casual, but always available. So that's probably why I do not feel the need for a formal women's group or prayer group. Also, although viewed by many as pious and devoted to the church, as the years go on, my ties and devotion to church are less and less strong and more indifferent. Spirituality is more important than formal church involvement."[170]

~

"I am a former religious and am married to a resigned Catholic priest. We no longer give any money to the Catholic Church, but choose to exercise responsible stewardship by donating to progressive and social justice organizations. Due to some painful experiences and a growing sense of alienation, I have been on a self-imposed sabbatical from the institutional church for over a year. Perhaps it has been a mid-life conversion experience in recognizing the gap between organized religion and true spirituality. That awareness has helped me to recognize that gospel values are frequently modeled more faithfully in many other dimensions of my life than they are in my parish church. I feel that I *am* church and will thus always be a Catholic Christian at the core of my identity."[171]

~

"I have been accepted by RCIA but have not been able to join the Catholic Church in full communion because my husband is a lapsed Catholic who refuses to have our civil marriage blessed. Due to my work, my four children at home, my rural location, and my husband's suspicion of religion, my scope for action is limited. Most of my 'activities' consist of reading and occasionally of letter-writing at this point."[172]

~

"If you find an answer to this question, please let me know. Why do women stay with our churches when they treat us so poorly?"[173]

~

"I find it a constant struggle to stay in the church, but I stay and hope to be an instrument of change. I'm not sure I will stay always — it doesn't seem to get any better in our diocese with a conservative bishop."[174]

~

"Even though I am a nun, I avoid usual parish liturgies like the plague because they are so painful in their sexism and usually boring to boot. I prefer to worship with a Wednesday evening group (mixed gender — but we share equally in all aspects of the celebration) and a feminist group that meets every two or three weeks for rituals and a pot-luck supper."[175]

~

"Women religious are increasingly more uncomfortable and unable to work for the church. So where do we go next? What new frontier or trail is there to blaze?"[176]

~

"I think women are the agents of a major shift in the church, helping to replace the old hierarchical model with one of collaboration and cooperation. I believe that this model will ultimately triumph, but I think the process is very painful, and many of us may never see its realization."[177]

~

"I love the Catholic Church, as it has been such a large part of my life, especially growing up. However, it hurts me also, now that I am older and can see how patriarchal and prejudiced it is. For a while I thought maybe I should leave it, but after much thought, I have decided that I really want to stay with it — it is a part of me — but that I also need to work toward changing it for the better, since I am going to stay. I am sure there are many others in the church who feel the same pain from it, yet love for it, as I do. If we all work together, we may be able to change matters in the long run, I hope."[178]

~

"I get very impatient, but not alienated, by the Catholic Church's *official* stance on women in ministry. Nevertheless, I see this issue as a train that has already left the station. The only question is, how many obstacles and delays can be imposed before a consensus of the faithful drives it to its destination. When it arrives, a lot of us intend to be still on board. This is the church of my faith and sacramental life, and I trust never to be driven or discouraged out of it, but to keep moving with it and providing some of the impetus."[179]

~

"I believe that the institutional church does not speak to the feminine spirituality/mentality and therefore, for the most part if not altogether, is no longer meaningful to women. I believe that women have become church by creating community and serving the needs of each other and those of society. We, rather than church 'leaders,' have become the social and spiritual conscience of our times."[180]

~

"When you talk about women in the church, I see it as woman and all her places of interaction with others, such as home, neighborhood, job, etc. I don't see it as a woman and a 'building.' "[181]

~

"I spent four and a half months in a federal prison in 1988. We were co-ed on arrival in April; by September it was an all-female prison. My crime was 're-entry of a military installation after having been barred' for my peace and justice ministry. It was incredible to learn that the ministry goes on by women themselves. Very much the story of our culture on the outside of the walls too."[182]

~

"No matter how hard they try in Rome, the toothpaste will not go back in the tube — the times, they are a-changing. The Spirit is alive, well and restless — good things are ahead."[183]

~

"I believe women can find creative alternatives for ritual and prayer without giving up totally the connection with tradition. I think women creating their own forms/rituals will make a powerful contribution to the future understanding of 'church.' "[184]

~

"I hope, however, that if and when women can be ordained, they will not become a part of the power games that are present in the church today. It could mean that the Roman Catholic Church would become a church of the loving servant. That may mean a new kind of church altogether, a church of Jesus, rather than a church of power."[185]

~ ~ ~

Many women have been given a forum here because we know it takes a lot of voices saying the same thing over and over in order for women to be heard.

~ ~ ~

More women feel alienated in the Catholic Church than in any other denomination in this study.

The outpouring of pain and anger in the preceding pages gives a human face to this stark statistic: *Four out of five Roman Catholic women who participated in this study say they often feel alienated from the institutional church* (see Table 3, p. 263). Those feelings of alienation are intense.

"Sometimes I think the Roman Catholic Church has to die completely before new life can come. I see so much pain and injustice. I wish I had the power to change a piece of it."

There is remarkable agreement among Catholic Sisters and Catholic laywomen[186] on this issue: 82 percent of the Sisters and 81 percent of the laywomen surveyed often feel alienated from their church.

"The thinking women I know both within and without my religious community are finding it more and more difficult to identify with the institutional church. The more we can help women to formulate and articulate their needs and their questions, the less tolerant and accepting they will be of religious structures and/or practices which are oppressive."

These statistics are particularly significant when compared with the Protestant sample. There the proportion of women who feel alienated does not exceed 62 percent. Although the percentages differ sharply, some of the reasons for feeling alienated are the same for Catholics and Protestants.

Catholic women in this study, both religious and lay, *want their church to make use of inclusive language and to include female images and names for God in its liturgical worship.* Above all, they want their hymns and prayers to image God in ways that are more inclusive of women's experience and they want to name God in ways reflective of that experience. On the other hand, women want *both* male and female images of God to be part of their liturgies. In other words, gendered images of God should be balanced when used in worship. Women want inclusive language to be used, not only now and then, but in all liturgical and sacramental rites. They make it very clear that they would not find inclusive language disruptive to their worship. On the contrary, many women are finding traditional language an impediment to prayer. The majority would agree with this woman's comment:

"I think the sexist language of Roman Catholic ritual prayers and readings is absolutely *abominable*, especially 'men' and 'man' in everything."

Catholic women in this study, both religious and lay, want to participate fully in the church and therefore want equal access with men to decision-making responsibilities and to positions of leadership.

"As a woman who has spent the last three years preparing for a professional position in my church, I am repeatedly disappointed in the lack of opportunity that exists for women. At a time when my church is looking for ways to maintain parishes with a clergy shortage, there is no place for women to fill the need."

~

"My daughter is pursuing a doctorate in religious studies. She would be a caring, spiritual, and productive priest. Instead she will teach and/or write. I'm just completing two years of theology, spirituality, and ministry training. I feel most clergy are threatened by this. As long as the Vatican remains a 'tight little island' fiercely protected by the fraternity of curia, women will be treated as second-class citizens in church affairs. Such a waste!"

~

"Perhaps as the number of priests declines there will be a realization that women can and do deserve to have positions of authority/service in the church."

Clearly, Catholic women feel they lack sufficient or equal opportunities for participation in the liturgical life and ecclesiastical ministry of the church. They want access to those decision-making arenas from which they have been traditionally excluded, and they support affirmative action procedures with regard to hiring, promotion, and payment in order to achieve their desired goals. Above all, they want women priests.

Concerns about gender inclusiveness in language and in leadership mark the similarities between Catholic and Protestant women in this study. There are also differences. Although both groups are feeling alienated over similar issues, there seems to be a distinction in terms of degree. One of our staff members put it this way after completing a number of in-depth telephone interviews with Catholic women: "There is a much stronger and consistent anger, and I might even say rage, that comes through about the lack of recognition and inclusion and about the abuse that women in the Catholic Church experience." In other words, more Catholic women seem to be more intensely angry more of the time. They are also angry — and alienated — about some specific issues that are unique to Catholic culture.

Catholic women in this study find the Catholic male hierarchy's response to women alienating.

"We as a people and as individuals are being stifled for no better reason than being female."

~

"As a Catholic the church does not serve me as a woman — my needs are not met. Women are continually looked down upon. We are continually reminded that we are the same sex as Eve, who took the forbidden fruit, but it is never mentioned that we are the same sex as the Virgin Mary."

~

"Women in the Roman Catholic tradition have always been seen as either servants or problems...nor will Rome admit that women image God fully...."

Women are saying they find the institutional church to be "exclusive and oppressive," "demeaning and humiliating," "violating and out of touch," "a noninviting environment for women." They find it hard to get beyond the church's "sexist policies and doctrines." Many point to the celibate male system as being at the heart of the problem. "The male system of the Catholic tradition is very death-dealing," writes one of the women surveyed. "The church is so out of touch on birth control, sexuality, abortion, ordination of women, that we have little in common," writes another. The celibate system has deeply impacted the clergy's relationship — or lack of it — with women. One woman tells how she had "tried to remain connected to the church but found it increasingly impossible because of the diocesan attitude toward women." Many women shared devastating experiences they had had with bishops and priests. Several said they had tried to see their bishop either about a project or a need or a point of concern. In every case the response was, "Our bishop wouldn't meet with us. We met with his representative." Particularly painful for many women has been their experience within the parish, and notably with the parish priest. For example, "It is difficult to continue to sit and listen to the priest and scripture that tell me I am a second-class person. I often feel so angry...." There were many other comments along this line. "I worked in a parish for fourteen years and got fired because the priest didn't like me," one woman writes. Another says, "Our priest hardly speaks to me. Other women say, 'He doesn't like women.'" A third respondent recounts that "exchange of pastors has resulted in stopping major ministries, selling property, closing outreach programs — all without consultation." Her frustration, and that of many other women, is summed up in her closing words: "In terms of absolute power, it is a male clergy that holds it."

Many women are at a loss as to how to deal with the disempowering aspects of the church and its structures of authority. One woman laments: "I'm most discouraged at the church's lack of vision and practicality for how people really live in today's world."

Another woman shares how intensely she feels about hierarchical control. "Vatican arrogance and refusal to even listen to the pain endured by women whose economic, physical, and sexual abuse has been supported by centuries of Roman Catholic theology, philosophy, and practice enrages me." She is not alone. Many agree with the woman who says that women suffer at the hands of "dysfunctional authority figures who use their role as a means to control rather than *free* others in their relationship with God." Particularly upsetting for one woman is "the 'watchdog system' imposed on bishops and priests who might want to bring women into new areas of ministry and responsibility." This woman expresses the feelings of many when she says that "this obsession with control is so contrary to the spirit of Christianity." Such control silences alternative voices and renders invisible those who do not conform. The silence is a concern to many women. Church leaders are not speaking out on behalf of women, further isolating those women who feel compelled to speak out on behalf of themselves. "Silence in the area of women's issues in the church and in society is a scandalous sin of omission for many clergy." This and the following response reflect many women's views. "In many ways the 'church' is a countersign to the values it professes."

Catholic women in this study find their own feelings alienating. So many women continue to experience pain, anger, frustration at the discrimination they encounter at all levels within the church. They express this in a multitude of ways. "I am alienated." "I am battered." "I move between despair and rage." "I never feel affirmed." They struggle with these feelings engendered by a religious participation that should be helping to dispel negativity and be leading them to God.

> "What often scares me is my anger of the last two years. I have been trained to be 'nice,' and yet I can visualize myself walking out of a church service in protest. I would never have contemplated such an action five years ago."

Others say: "I'm in a love-hate relationship with the Roman Catholic Church and I'm miserable about this." "I feel disappointment." "I'm unhappy." " ...hurt and bitter." "I feel undervalued as a woman in the church." "I feel like a 'lost soul' much of the time." "I feel left out of the church." "I am fed up with the church." "I feel estranged from my church." "I feel very alienated from the church." "I feel that I am more Christian if I remain outside of an organized religion." One of the respondents points to the guilt that consumes her and so many women:

"I spend a lot of psychic energy reminding myself that I am a fully whole person, not worthy of excessive guilt, despite the subliminal and more obvious messages from the church."

One of the more painful experiences of women is expressed in the words of one who said she had stopped attending Mass on Sunday, then added: "My presence has not been missed." Women who are "longing for meaningful rituals" say that the "laws of the church make no sense to me." Yet a significant number are also saying, "I have hope in my heart."

Catholics care passionately about their faith and identify with their tradition. For all of the pain and anger, disenchantment and criticism, positive responses did surface. Quite a few women had good things to say about priests and parish life. One woman remains in the church because of "the presence of holy, fully whole men within the church who abhor the sexism as much as I." Another stays because of "a very open, creative pastor who is trying to build the parish on circles instead of pyramids." An analysis of Catholic women's comments indicates that the parish priest or pastor plays a significant role in an alienated woman's relationship to the parish and, sometimes, the tradition. One woman who is satisfied with her local community says, "The parish I am in is not typical" because "the pastor is open to the gifts of all the members and is willing to listen without judging comments based on male or female."

Liturgy is critically important to Catholics and to a majority of the women in our sample. For many, liturgy is the bond that unites them to the church. Rites that are welcoming and well done reach out to alienated women. "The RCIA was beautiful — caring, loving, without regard for the gender of the individual," one woman explains. "Recently my parish has taken a step out of the *very* dark ages," a woman is happy to report. "We have female altar servers... inclusive language.... These are wonderful steps forward." A young woman says: "I can worship in the community I work with because my co-chaplain is so good with language and inclusivity. We're willing to take risks, but we may also be fired." Another writes: "I love the Eucharist and believe in the church as community." Another rejoices: "Always I find somewhere a haven within the organized church to celebrate the Eucharist." One woman periodically travels a hundred miles "to attend a Mass at a church that is committed to community work, uses inclusive language, and has intelligent, relevant homilies." Again and again the women surveyed have said: "I love the church."

To be Catholic has meant, until fairly recently, something that was universally accepted and understood. For a significant proportion of those responding, and of the present Catholic population, Catholicism has defined who they are, not only to themselves, but to the world at large. But all of that is changing.[187]

Catholicism is no longer seen as monolithic or as a set of rules protected by threat of eternal damnation. It is first and foremost a community of faith indigenous to multiple cultures in which active participation by all its members has been mandated by Vatican II. Women have taken this mandate seriously. They had little or no problem when they stayed within the frame of conventional service roles, but when they began to push further, when they began to ask "why?" and "why not?" of what had always been taken for granted, when they began to think for themselves and then to articulate what they were perceiving, suddenly everything changed. The changes were not in the system. The changes were within women. These seeds of awareness eventually grew to be feelings of isolation and alienation.

Women have had to learn to handle the institution's complete dismissal of what are now their deepest concerns. The women in this study find themselves caught in a struggle between maintaining continuity with a cherished heritage while at the same time seeking to assure continuity with both a challenging present and an approaching future. They have found little support within the institution, which explains their criticism of the church.

~

This study reveals a strong feminist presence in the U.S. Catholic Church.

In this study, alienation is directly related to feminist values. That being so, we have here a very feminist Catholic sample. Four out of five Catholic women surveyed are feminist in some way.

> "Twenty years ago I was alone with my hurt and anger, wondering if I was crazy. Ten years ago I had discovered a few women who had experiences similar to mine. Eventually we began to study feminist theology and discovered scores of women with our experiences, pain, and anger. Today we are all radical feminists who wonder where we belong in the Christian church."

Ever since the close of Vatican II, the rise of feminist consciousness has been occurring in the Catholic Church. Often merging with other movements of conscientization and liberation, its progress has been slow but steady, made visible now and then in relation to specific issues or events. Theological images of a Spirit-church and the process of reinventing the church may have originated from other sources, yet these are among the many metaphors to which feminists have laid claim.

Differently defined feminists have different priorities, which leads them to select carefully the causes they support. In her book *Transforming Feminism*, Maria Riley describes "radical feminism" in terms of a theory of two cultures: a dominant patriarchal culture and an alternative women's culture that is emerging on the margins.[188] The same metaphor has been used to describe the broad social shifts within Catholicism. Eugene Kennedy also speaks of "two cultures," that of the institutional church and the church of the Spirit within it. After saying they are out of sync with each other, he poses a critical question. "Is the second culture of American Catholicism, whose members exert influence indirectly through their freedom from ecclesiastical control, subtly transforming the American Catholic Church in its own image and likeness?"[189] Kennedy is not speaking of feminism directly, yet this is precisely what fuels the fear of feminism in the American church, the fact that feminists profess a freedom from ecclesiastical control. One of our respondents writes: "I think some of us live in *two* churches." This study says she is right.

Without a doubt the threat of feminism lies in its understanding of authority. Sandra Schneiders explains that "human consciousness has undergone some kind of quantum leap during our lifetime" and a radical change has taken place with regard to institutional authority. In the American Catholic consciousness, obedience to legitimate authority has been eroded both in society and in the church. Schneiders faults the institutional church for this undermining of authority. Time and again the church has resisted the liberation movement of some subordinate group, limiting its self-determination.[190] The feminist movement is a case in point.

For many of the women in this study, and for many in the Catholic Church today, being feminist and being Catholic has become a struggle for spiritual survival. Feminist women are not fostering discontinuity within the communion of saints, as most keepers of the tradition have accused, but a continuity in the Spirit. They are responding to what they experience from within, which they perceive to be of God, and they seem to be having a terrible time making this understood. Women feel they have a responsibility to challenge the many ways their perspective is excluded when the church determines what constitutes the will of God for them. They feel they have a right to have some say in the way life is to be lived, the way prayers are to be prayed, the way God is to be praised. Not to be taken seriously, not even to be heard does violence to women in all aspects of their lives. In the first draft of their ill-fated pastoral letter on women's concerns, the U.S. bishops did listen to the voices of alienated women, citing them in their text. Subsequent drafts, however, silenced those voices, further alienating the very ones who had been the subjects of their concern.

Our study shows that many laywomen and Sisters find themselves pulled in two directions. They are concerned not to be "too feminist" for fear of being stereotyped, and yet they cannot passively support what may be for them the right religion but for all the wrong reasons. Such dichotomies reach deep into the soul and psyche, leaving a residue of frustration and pain. The desire for full inclusion on all levels of decision-making, ministry, and mission has put many women at odds with their church, but oddly enough, not with their tradition. To borrow a metaphor from Dean Hoge in his interpretation of change in American Catholicism, it might be said that feminism is also like a river rushing through floodgates opened by Vatican II. Although Hoge is not speaking of feminism here, his analogy applies. Feminists would agree with him when he says that John Paul II has "reclosed the floodgates" and that "pressures are building up again." There is no doubt that "the pope is taking practical steps to reverse the direction of the whole church... and he is prepared to accept unrest, alienation, and declines in numbers as the price he may have to pay."[191] Hoge does speak directly to the feminist presence in the church:

> The greatest tension today is on women's issues, where a network of religious women are the front line activists in a call for more respect, more autonomy, and a greater role in the church. If any Martin-Luther-like figures arise in the near future, they will probably be female, and they will not be easily silenced.[192]

In an act of profound courage, Bishop P. Francis Murphy chose a public forum to critique the proposed pastoral on women prior to the vote of the bishops and to support the feminist cause. He spoke of how "modern feminist thought, which, after all, comes in various forms, [can] begin to assist the magisterium in its reflections on the central and underlying issue — patriarchy — that supports the evil of sexism in the church and has a pervasive influence in our culture."[193] Aware of how central patriarchy is to the church, he tries to explain this to the bishops:

> In our failure to come to grips with the question of patriarchy, we bishops seem to be buttoning up a coat that has the top button in the wrong button hole. No matter how carefully we button the rest of the coat, it will not fit. We cannot adjust by skipping a button. We can't pretend it fits — no matter how nice the coat.[194]

Patriarchy is an anachronism. There are Catholic feminist women who know all about anachronism and about clothing that no longer fits. The most feminist women in this entire study are Catholic Sisters. As powerful as the reality is, the symbol of feminist Sisters is equally empowering. Here are women who have managed to leap across the limitations of centuries in less than thirty years.[195] The mandated reform of religious orders after Vatican II led to genuine renewal of religious life. Today the agenda of Catholic Sisters is one of transformation. They have developed a list of transformative elements that they hope to have accomplished by the year 2010. They say:

- Converted by the example of Jesus and the values of the gospel, we would serve a prophetic role in church and society by critiquing values and structures and calling for systemic change.

- Converted by the marginalized, we would invest resources in advocacy for structural change on behalf of the poor and oppressed and work to change the locus of power from models of domination to collaborative modes of power-sharing and decision-making.

- Understanding ourselves as church, we would assume our priestly role of shared leadership in the life and worship of the local church; and we would see ourselves as centers of the experience of God and of a spirituality of wholeness, global connectedness, and reverence for the earth.[196]

~

A majority of the Catholic women in this study are calling for the ordination of women as priests in the Roman Catholic Church.

Feminist consciousness has made it clear to women that just because things have always been this way does not mean this is the way they have to be. This perspective is what has intensified the debate concerning women priests.

> "Though I do not want to be a priest, I do not want other women deprived of it because of gender. I believe the church is cutting off its own foot by not allowing for women and married priests."

> ~

> "I believe that the work of women in ministerial roles today is laying the groundwork for that memorable day when *all* ministries, including ordination, will be open to *all* of us!"

> ~

> "Generally, I am thrilled by the "priest shortage." There is no shortage. They are just looking in all the wrong places at all the wrong people."

In this study, only 9 percent of the Catholics surveyed feel women should *not* seek ordination and 24 percent are ambivalent, meaning maybe yes and maybe no. A majority of 67 percent fully agree that Catholic women should be ordained. This statistic favoring ordination is identical to that of a 1992 Gallup survey of Catholic opinion that found that 67 percent of the Catholic population at large supports women priests. It also compares favorably with a 1993 ABC News poll taken prior to the U.S. visit of Pope John Paul II, which puts the figure of those wanting women priests at 62 percent. Polls conducted in recent years all show that those who favor women priests are in the majority and that their numbers are growing.[197]

Catholic feminists have maintained and strengthened their push for ordination for the past twenty years, encouraged by gains for women in Catholic parishes and in religious orders after Vatican II.[198] Papal statements reiterating the impossibility of women's ordination[199] are clearly a response to feminist pressure visible in the organized efforts of the Women's Ordination Conference,[200] in the spontaneous initiatives of the women-church network and a vast number of similar groups, and in the dialogue of scholars and practitioners. Many women in this study feel it is "a painful tragedy that women are excluded from ordained ministry." It can be said that the movement for women's ordination is growing because more and more women, by imaging God as female, clearly see themselves as created in God's image, as reflecting Christ's image. Therefore, they are rejecting the hierarchy's position that only a male can image Christ and act *in persona Christi* because only a man has a "natural resemblance" to Christ.[201] To this, one project participant responds, "The church's position on women's ordination is poor theology, poor pastoring, poor stewardship."

Influential in the shift from denial to acceptance of women as priests is the feminist vision of a just society with a church of mutual ministry, inclusive of gender, culture, race, lineage, social status, age, ability, and one's God-given sexuality. Little girls have begun to imagine themselves as "partners in the mystery of redemption,"[202] easily making the leap from altar girl to woman priest, something their grandmothers would never even have dared fantasize about. Proponents of women's ordination feel that women priests will make a difference, that women have what it takes to "reinvent" or "rebirth" the church. As one respondent wrote, "I support women's ordination because I hope that it may restore the church to the people, or help to do so."

A significant factor in the escalating support for women's ordination is the experience of women pastors. Among Catholic respondents, 15 women (9 laywomen and 6 Sisters) said that at one point during the last five years they held the position of "pastor" in charge of a congregation. During this time, 111 women (30 laywomen and 81 Sisters) saw themselves as associate/assistant pastors. Some of these women may have volunteered their services. However, currently 64 Catholic women in this study (26 laywomen and 38 Sisters) are paid by their parishes to serve as pastors, associate/assistant pastors, or parish administrators. These women typically function as priests except for the restrictions of sacramental ministry. Although not legally "pastors" in the Catholic Church, these women are often called pastors, not only by parishioners, but sometimes by bishops and priests.[203]

Of the 241 "priestless parishes" in the United States, approximately 74 percent are pastored by women, many of whom serve in rural and small-town areas.[204] The issue is broader than "priestless parishes." It encompasses "priestless liturgies." In a survey of all dioceses conducted several years ago by the Bishops' Committee on the Liturgy to determine how many were celebrating Sunday worship without priests, 167 of the 174 Latin Rite dioceses responded. In 51 of those dioceses, there were situations in which Sunday worship in the absence of a priest was occurring, either weekly or on occasion. Projections now several years old estimated that within five years 66 percent of the dioceses in the United States would have persons who are not priests administering or "pastoring" parishes.[205] In reality, the number of lay people in pastoral positions is declining under pressure from Rome. John Paul II recently warned the American bishops not to pursue this course, saying, "It is not a wise pastoral strategy to adopt plans which would assume as normal, let alone desirable, that a parish community be without a priest pastor."[206] Respondents report that women who retire are not being replaced and that some contracts are not being renewed.

One of the women pastors participating in this study meets several times a year for personal, professional, and spiritual support with a group of twenty other Catholic women pastors who once numbered thirty-five. She speaks of a positive impact in those parishes where pastoral leadership is female. Another pastor from a different region of the country says she meets annually with approximately thirty other female pastors. Her philosophy: "practice precedes legislation."

Parishioners in churches headed by women are becoming accustomed to the possibility of women ordained as priests. Many feel that because of this "different experience of church," the rules will have to change. Indeed, it is best not to underestimate the impact of women pastors. A female in a position of leadership who is teaching, preaching, taking charge, enabling, empowering, facilitating worship, and managing the affairs of the parish with a strong personal presence is a visual, visceral symbol of what feminism is about. Refreshing stories abound. At the installation and celebration of a Catholic Sister as pastor of a big city parish, a hand-scrawled poster from two children of the parish read, "Congratulations, Sister _____. We love you. How do you like being head of the church?" A portion of the next generation is growing up unencumbered by past prejudice. Many Catholics are sure to have experiences similar to that of UCC pastor Allison Stokes. She had asked a male minister to fill in for her while she was on vacation. His opening words were punctuated by the indignant response of a four-year-old girl sitting with her mother at the back of the church. "Mom, what is that man doing up there? Where is our minister?"

As women assume leadership roles and gain experience as pastors, many begin to question the limitations restricting their ministry. So do their parishioners. This study shows a direct correlation between both those women who work in pastoral positions, as head of a parish or in a collaborative role, and those who support women's ordination. Having a paid position in a parish or a professional ministry position in the diocese or in a diocesan agency increases the likelihood that women pastors or women in professional ministries will want to be ordained. Ordinarily age is not a factor, except for Sisters over sixty, who most likely would decline.

Not every woman in this study favors ordination for women. One woman writes: "We don't need women in Roman collars.... We need women filled with the Holy Spirit to be Jesus where they are." Another expresses what a growing number of feminists have concluded. "What women seek is not ordination into an anachronistic structure but empowerment in new forms of liturgy and community." Feminists eschew the hierarchical model. A woman who is presently a pastor says that ordaining women would mean "a masculine structure with feminine bodies in it."[207] While most of the women in the Catholic sample would agree that the system needs changing, they differ in how they would bring this about. Some say back off from everything and let the system crumble. Others say apply creativity to foster systemic change. While some say leave and some say stay, there are those who respond with a touch of humor. Putting a spin on tradition, a woman writes: "I can't imagine where I would be now if I had been born male. Maybe I'd be a bishop. Thank you, God, for having made me a woman!"

~

Catholic women who feel alienated from the church are, for the most part, remaining in the church.

The Catholic women in our sample told us they were Catholic. Some said they were ambivalent; some said they were on the verge of leaving, but nevertheless, they were Catholic. Those who identified themselves as former Catholics were placed with their new denomination, if any, or classified as unaffiliated and not counted among the Catholics. What this means is that of all alienated Catholics, 82 percent of the sample are still members of a parish, whether or not they go to church (see Table 4, p. 264).

Something crucial is implicit here — defining who is Catholic. What makes a person Catholic? Andrew Greeley says, quoting canon law: "You stop being a Catholic not when you break a rule, not when you disagree with the pope, but only when you formally and explicitly renounce your faith or join another religious denomination."[208] Implicitly, Catholics understand this. There have been and are so many people in a relationship with the church who are not in full communion with the church for whatever might be the reason, perhaps divorce and remarriage, or marriage outside the church. There are lapsed Catholics who have not renounced the church and are Catholic in name only. In these and all such cases, however, the church has done the defining, but that is true no longer.

Today, people say who they are, say whether or not they are Catholic, and what that means for them. Many of the women in our sample are Catholic just because they say so. One woman writes: "Although I consider myself a Catholic, many would not consider me one." Another woman puts it this way: "I am still a Catholic, and I refuse to be driven away from the community I claim as home." This self-identification is a shift in understanding that is reflected in the metaphor "defecting in place." To defect in place means to leave and to stay — to leave the old way of relating and to stay on one's own terms, to be present in a whole new way. "I've gradually evolved into deciding most matters for myself," says one Catholic respondent. Other women say: "I practice 'ecclesiastical disobedience.'" "I remain on my own terms." "I am no longer controlled by church authority; therefore I am freer to act, to challenge the church." Some say they maintain a "marginalized stance." Never before have so many Catholics agreed to disagree. Not too many years ago, they would simply have walked away. Protestant congregations are peopled with "former" or "recovering" Catholics. Many of the Catholics in this sample are in fact "defecting in place." They disagree with the church, are often alienated from the church, but nevertheless they are remaining. Why do they stay? "Because," says Andrew Greeley, "they like being

Catholic." And when asked what liking has to do with it, Greeley responded: "Everything."[209] Many in our study have similar reasons for staying in the church. "There is a strong passion for the Catholic tradition deep within me," says one. "It is in the bone, so to speak," says another. Still another: "Bottom line — it is home."

The women in our study show that there are a number of ways to be Catholic. Greeley again says that's not new. Catholicism "has always been pluralistic....It has defined its boundaries out as far as possible, to include everyone it can."[210] Not so in all times and places, not so in our times from the institution's point of view, but our highly educated sample understands the dynamics of interpretation, and this has set many women free. Among those who say they feel alienated, some are Catholic by association only. Others are actively engaged in some manner, reflecting a diversity of ways one can be a practicing Catholic and, as this study suggests, various ways of "defecting in place." One of the ways is by refusing to have anything to do with the parish. One simply belongs in spirit to the universal church. Another is deciding not to go to church on Sunday. Whether to protest exclusive language or to avoid incompetent preaching or simply to take a stand, staying away goes straight to the heart of patriarchal issues, for the Catholic Church still treats weekly participation as a moral obligation, saying Catholics *must* go to Mass on Sunday. One of the "defectors" puts it bluntly:

> "The Catholic Church tells you that you will go to hell if you
> don't go to church every week. Horseshit! God is not that cold
> to people if he's the loving, caring person the church says he is."

Approximately 30 percent of the Catholics in this study who say they feel alienated from the institutional church no longer attend church every Sunday, but go only now and then. These alienated yet practicing Catholics have chosen to practice in their own way.

Another way of "defecting in place" is to continue to participate fully in the life of the institution, bringing those feminist perspectives that are at the heart of one's alienation into the midst of parish life. More than two-thirds of the women who feel alienated are still active members of a parish and attend church every Sunday. Some are drawn to the liturgy or by a spiritual bond with the Eucharist, while others are actively engaged in various programs of the parish. The Notre Dame Study of Catholic Parish Life found "a female face to participation" in Sunday liturgy and in parish activities. Women participate in parish life and in ministerial leadership in far greater numbers than men.[211]

Some of the church-going women of our study are the ones fulfilling those parish functions, and our data suggest that these women, who are at the heart of parish life, have come to see things differently. Since they are highly educated and articulate, it stands to reason that many are telling others about their concerns, about the need for inclusive language. No doubt they are sharing their images of God, the ones that are decidedly female, and are pushing for an even greater degree of women's participation in liturgical and decision-making roles. Women who are defecting in a parish place are helping to raise feminist consciousness, an essential step before the tradition can consider systemic change. Such women are potential change-agents within local congregations, something that a number of women in our study are choosing to be. One writes: "I feel called to remain within the church and be a voice crying for change." This is echoed by another: "I still struggle to bring about change in the structure." And another: "If we all work together, we may be able to change matters in the long run." There are many who would agree with the woman who says, "God is doing great things, and it is my strong desire to be a part of it." And probably just as many who would say with this respondent, "I don't want leaving to be the only solution."

While many women are working from within to make the future present, *there are others for whom the congregational route is no longer a viable option.* By the time this report is completed, more women will have left the church and still more will consider leaving. This woman speaks for others when she says, "I belong on a day-by-day basis." Another admits, "I have one foot in and one foot out." And still another woman reveals: "About every three days I want to leave the institution." The needs of many women are not being met, and the depth of their alienation compels them to leave the church.

On the other hand, the courage to question and confront oppression has spawned a tradition within the Tradition that has the power to transform and heal. "A transformation has begun," writes one of the women in our sample. "Women are the agents of a major shift in the church," writes another. And again: "I believe women are transforming the church." And: "It is women who can and will lead the church toward its true mission." Feminist Catholics, laywomen and Sisters, are deeply concerned about the mission of the church and justice for all peoples. And they want to live responsibly for the sake of the next generation.

In a moving personal testimony, Bishop Murphy speaks this word on behalf of feminist women:

I want to affirm the influence and enrichment brought to my own learning and to my growth as a person and as a bishop by feminist scholars and many deeply committed and gifted women. I also express profound sorrow for my own failures in communication, language, and relationships with women co-workers and friends.[212]

With the stroke of a pen a bishop takes a giant step toward mutuality, hinting that within the patriarchal Catholic Church, it may be possible to begin again.

Chapter 4

Feminist Spirituality Groups for Support and Alternative Liturgy

Women share with us what their female support groups and feminist ritual experiences mean to them.

~ ~ ~

"In my community, meeting with women at least twice a month to talk about our place in the church, as well as celebrate faith, has been one of the most joyful, rewarding, stimulating experiences of my life. Our women's group is essential to me. It has given me freedom to see God in many ways, to see myself in many ways. Our group makes me strong."[1]

~

"It seems that 'women's guilds' are fine, as long as they aren't feminist, but feminist spirituality groups meet much resistance — both fear on the inside and hostility from without. And I'm not talking about militant groups."[2]

~

"I am a Lutheran pastor and a radical feminist. In the past I have belonged to a number of women's spirituality groups. Currently the groups with which I am involved are in transition and are not as helpful as they could be, but I have no doubt that soon I will find or help create such a group. At present there is a definite split between my public and private practice of religion. I believe that over time my private voice and public voice will grow closer together. This will make me healthier and make my life more harmonious."[3]

~

"More and more I am finding more spiritual compatibility from women who are not highly religious or who have 'graduated' from local congregations. I find getting together with other women who don't necessarily follow orthodox theology or paternalistic hierarchy stimulating and liberating."[4]

~

"I am tired of trying to educate others to feminist issues in my church. I am tired of being the only one who thinks 'differently.' Being a part-time seminary student and a member of a feminist Christian group has helped preserve my sanity and faith. I struggle with wanting to leave my church to be with people who think more like I do, but feel a call to stay in my church and press for change."[5]

~

"I'm shocked and saddened by the sexism I have encountered during my first year in an Episcopal seminary. We have formed a women's support group at the seminary, and I am also connected with local women who have formed the Appalachian Women's Guild. These have given me tremendous support and encouragement."[6]

~

"The group of which I am a member is very intentional and some-what threatening to the perceptions of women who have not decided to become involved, but who belong to or organize the activities of a longer standing women's organization traditionally known as a women's service group. Presently our dilemma is that the average group of twenty-five or so realizes its need to continue to take risks politically and to become strategic on certain issues of power and sex-ual abuse (in families, church, and counseling relationships), while at the same time we are realizing that we are deepening the inner struggles and want to become a safe circle for our own pain/rage and that of others. We see that we must move through the rage even as we want to exercise carefully the power that we seem to have, to be conscience in our conference."[7]

~

"I love and respect my sisters in Women-Church, WOC [Women's Or-dination Conference], and other such groups. I applaud their guts to hang in there and continue their presence, visibility, and strug-gle. I'd like to think there is a huge number of women like me who have moved to a more peaceful existence of taking their own power and creating the reality they seek, not waiting for church fathers to recognize or approve."[8]

~

"I want to learn, and changes to occur, for the sake of my three daugh-ters! I look forward to having a women's group of Christian and non-Christian friends meeting in my home."[9]

~

"I began studying theology in a women's support group. I can only say that it wasn't until I stopped trying to fit my former ideas about theology into what I perceived as women's reality in the church that things began to make sense to me. I have gradually loosened my ties to the church, although they are not severed completely."[10]

~

"Having lived many years on the East Coast and more in the Midwest, in large cities and small communities, I find it interesting that women in various settings continually find a need to gather for discussion, support, worship. Though the groups to which I have belonged over the years have varied considerably in age, career orientation, but especially in the degree to which they would claim a 'feminist' approach to religion, *all* have articulated a need for something other than what traditional church structures/worship allow. Relationships among women at a level of intimacy not always available to our mothers are seen as not only necessary, but also as a means of understanding God more readily. I think any woman who has a feminist consciousness and remains in the traditional church today must be at least bicultural and bilingual. There seems to be a large network of women's religious groups centered in women's culture, but in my experience, this culture is still on the margins of the more visible church."[11]

~

"The power of women-church was very real during my seminary days. Women made up about one-third of my class, and we began meeting weekly for prayer and support. We pledged that if one of us spoke up about sexism in a classroom, another of us would join her voice — to combat the 'it's one person's issue' misconception. And I remember well during my senior year that our class's core course instructor said it was the first time he'd ever really experienced the presence of women in his classes. We were accused of holding secret feminist rituals during community chapel times and of plotting sedition when we asked to meet with only the women on the seminary's board. We wove ribbons into belts and attached prayer beads for each woman in our class and wore our ribbons instead of rope cinctures at graduation. We had lobbied for — and been granted — the first (to the best of our knowledge) female commencement speaker in our seminary's history. I grieved terribly when I had to leave this women-church. I survived in splendid isolation as a clergywoman for almost two years before others were placed/called here. It took no time for us to organize our calendars to make time for our women's group."[12]

~

"I have many disagreements with my church about how they treat women, about positions available to women within the church, and especially about the lack of ritual involvement for women and coming of age ceremonies for girls. I am not sure, however, that just giving women the same priesthood as men is the answer to these problems. I think women need their own priesthood which recognizes their 'unique' attributes (their bodies and cycles, the earth, etc.) Within my own group of friends, we are attempting (not within our church but on our own) to give some ritual participation to our daughters, such as recognizing their menarche, etc. We are definitely making it up as we go along."[13]

~

"The institutional church is becoming a less important part of my life; at the same time I find myself in a period of great spiritual ferment/ growth. My women's spirituality group started at my church and moved as we began to explore nontraditional forms of spirituality and wanted privacy with a closed group. We've studied/explored witchcraft and other forms of goddess worship. We're not all in the same place. I may be more skeptical than a few of my sisters, but I have found our shared study to be powerful and a jumping-off point for my own spiritual journey. Although our group isn't involved in community/social justice work, all of our individual members are."[14]

~

"Years ago I was very involved in women's issues within the Catholic Church. I and a few other women gave retreats, worked for change. It seems that women cannot make a commitment to continue or hold together. It has not been ongoing. I have become somewhat dissatisfied and frustrated in establishing connections. Sitting around talking does not work for me, and I did the social route for years and burned out on that. A group of women is still very important to me, but I do not want to rehash old stories of church."[15]

~

"I find it stimulating to be with groups of women which have a common bond of justice seeking, but frustrating to be with women threatened by such activity. Particularly with regard to feminist issues, I have found much stronger support from men committed to egalitarian relationships than from tradition-bound women."[16]

~

"There is an increasing need for me to become actively involved with a group of women for ritual, prayer, discussion, support, and social action. We are in the early stages of forming such a group and the prospect is exciting. It's time for women to develop their own rituals using language and symbols that are meaningful to us, while drawing on the rich depths of our spirituality. I find myself seeing things so radically different in a relatively short time and am very thankful for two new women friends who bring me their experiences and understandings. My own two daughters, ages twenty-one and sixteen, have been fantastic models for me, helping me to let go and stop aiding in my own oppression. I'm not convinced that women should spend much time and energy on seeking leadership in our present Catholic Church structure, and not any in saving it. I'd much rather see it simply crumble. A new order is called for, and that's where our work lies."[17]

~

"The lack of a feminist women's group within or related to my local church is a big part of my inactivity in the church at present. Without such a group, the consciousness of the congregation is not changing much with respect to women's issues and sensitivity in worship."[18]

~

"I presently do not attend a church. My church is the women's group I attend. I really don't know how I would function without it. I just bought a copy of Sandra Schneiders's *Beyond Patching* and was startled to learn that by her definition I am a radical feminist. Since I've been described by friends as everything from reactionary to conservative to liberal, this was a shocker! I'm happy to see women entering ministry, but I'm not sure they should buy into the present system. I know I could not. And that was before I read *Beyond Patching*."[19]

~

"Moving to five different cities in the last nine years has been difficult because I've hated to leave my groups of women friends. I am frustrated in my present location because I haven't found those 'kindred spirits' with whom to celebrate feminist liturgies."[20]

~

"I am not happy/challenged/satisfied in my denomination, but my husband is a clergyman in it and his position would be affected if I left. So I *need* my feminist friends and group in order to survive. It's where I experience support, acceptance, and stimulation. It's what 'church' needs to be — at least for me."[21]

~

"My women band together as much to ease their pain and bolster self-respect and self-esteem in the context of a new understanding of Mother/Father God as for any other reason."[22]

~

"I belong to a circle of women who meet about twice a month for ritual and sharing. All of us come out of the Christian tradition, both Protestant and Roman Catholic, and we are in contact with other circles in our area. I am amazed at the numbers of women (and in some cases, men) involved and at the rapid growth I perceive. I believe we are part of an amazing revolution in spirituality."[23]

~

"I am now convinced 'organized religion' is not adequately assisting women's *spiritual* growth and more than 90 percent are finding growth outlets outside the church. Organized church groups don't seem to be seriously addressing injustices women have suffered, and indeed, the patriarchal roots may not be able to allow that to happen. Spiritual growth in the 1990s will take place via small groups, via Jungian thought, via reclaiming the Goddess and justice to the planet. The church might begin to acknowledge what is happening in inner-growth workshops, meditation, etc. outside the church today. 'Secular' literature over the past eight to ten years of publishing has become more 'spiritual' than 'religious' publishing. Unless the 'top religious structure' begins to wake up, be less myopic and self-serving, the church will be an antiquated structure."[24]

~

"I feel like my spiritual activity with the godsisters is on the edge, outside the circle, not condoned as a valid way to express myself spiritually in a community. Although what we do in our rituals is beyond our denomination and is based in earth spirituality, I shy away from groups that are too blatantly 'New Age,' even though some of the tools may be the same. I know there must be many other such groups. It would be nice to have a loose newsletter linking us together."[25]

~

"Through my work in leading seminars and retreats, I have brief experiences with a number of women's religious groups. I find women very important to each other and very willing both to reveal themselves and to support each other in the matter of spiritual, emotional, and relational growth. The women I meet also generally find nurturance in the church, but they draw together out of more intense spiritual need than can be met in routine congregational life. My concern about this is that it seems primarily focused on the subjective individual. It may be, though, that many of the same women in these support groups or networks are involved in significant outreach elsewhere. I don't know. I also don't know how much effect we are having on 'church power structures.' There seems to be little immediate result, yet I see enormous change over the past thirty years."[26]

~

"In April, 1988, about thirty women met for the first time for the purpose of forming a Womenchurch. Today, three years and one month later, we still meet once a month in each other's homes. The group averages between fifteen and twenty at a meeting. Several denominations are represented. There are ministers, psychologists, an author, nuns, social workers, media librarian, chaplain, and me, the token crone. On this past Mother's Day I sat in a Roman Catholic Church (not my own congregation) and listened to the pastor tell me that Eve and I introduced sin into the world and the Blessed Virgin Mary redeemed us. Ah, but women have their ways. My ninety-year-old mother turned off both her hearing aids and I composed a poem."[27]

~

"How little women truly participate in the whole church. We have had to make special groups for ourselves to feel like we are fully participating. What a shame."[28]

Feminist Groups

A number of the women in this study belong to feminist women's groups. Many of the groups have names; others are referred to by phrases descriptive of the group.

The names of groups that surfaced in this study give some indication of the wide range of feminist collectives that exist for support, study, spirituality, creative expression, ministry to women, political action, and ritual innovation.

Among the groups named are: Women-church, WomanChurch, Women of Fire, Women Empowered, WomanSpirit, WomanGift, Women of Vision, Women of Wisdom, Women's Way, Woman Spirit Rising, Braided Streams, Searchers, Moonwomen, Birth and Beyond, Woman Stories, Dawn Women's Group, Mary's Pence, Lilith, God Sisters, Hidden Castles, The Critical Mass, Little Ladies of the Light, Sarah's Circle, Feminists of Faith, Sophia's Circle, Circle of Stones, Via Vita, Matrix, Limina, Rapport, Mary's Place, Sisters Against Sexism, Friends of Creation Spirituality Group, Wise Women, Hannah's House, Spiritual Sisters, Sacred Space, Twelve Apostates, Sisters of Sophia, Sophia Group, Earth Cycle Group, Underbelly, Martha's Vineyard, Bonding Group, Sprouts, Celebrating Menopause, Cakes for the Queen of Heaven, Women in Theology, FBW (Five Beautiful Women), Grow (Gathering Rituals of Women), "Burp" ("because the church brought us up"), Rahab (because of feeling like an outcast group), Arachnae (from the Greek, symbol of the spider in the web), Chrysalis, Lesbian Catholics Together, Dream Support Group, Spiritual Direction Group, Emmaus Women's Group, Black Women Professional Clergy, Black Women Seminarians, Ecumenical Women Ministers Support Group, Asian Women Theologians, Women of Color Theological Anthology Group, Christian Women's Ministry, Feminist Sunday School Class, Monday Morning Support Group, Monday Night Women's Group, The Women's Wednesday Worship,

First Friday Group, SLUTS (Seminary Lesbians under Theological Stress), Women in Religion Discussion Group, Women Reshaping Theology, Working Women with Small Children, Women's Center, Women's Energy Bank (WEB), Women's Covenant Group, Women's Liturgy Group, Women's Theology Group, Women's Koinonia Group, Women in Spiritual Progress (WISP), Weavings, and Women, Word and Song.

Among those groups without a formal name but known by a descriptive or generic phrase are: Women Artists, Breakfast Group, Feminist Seder, Book Study Group, Dreams Group, Women's Reading Group, Indian Liturgy Group, Peace and Justice Group, A.A. Women's Group, Support Group for Professional Women, Reflection/Action Group on Homelessness, Ad Hoc Group on Racism, Sexism, and Classism, Women in Their Spiritual Journeys, Prayer/Share Group, Sisters Ministering in Small Rural Parishes, Unitarian Women's Group, Clergy-women's Support Group, Women's Writing Collective, Women's Journal-Therapy Group, Moon Ritual Gathering Group, Dianic Moon Worship Group, Roman Catholic Women's Support Group, Women's Concern Committee, Women's Support Group, Women's Group, and Women-church.

Mixed-gender feminist groups also surfaced, such as house churches, political action collectives, groups for a specific ministry, and a federation for ministry and mission. While we recognize the value and importance of these initiatives, because of the limitations of this study, they will not be featured here.[29]

Profiles of Feminist Groups

The following are among those feminist groups of spiritual support and ritual innovation that are the subject of this study. They model the variety and scope of feminist collectives springing up around the United States. In each case, a group convener or representative responded to our initial questionnaire and then participated in an in-depth telephone interview of approximately forty-five to sixty minutes. Group profiles were drawn from surveys and interviews. We have omitted the names of individuals and groups, specific geographical locations, and any other identifying information in order to guarantee anonymity. While this might not have been necessary in every case, for some individuals and groups it is absolutely essential that they not be identified.

~

Coming Together for Support

1/ Eight years ago, an ad in the church bulletin of a Catholic parish in the Northeast invited women to come together to talk about what it meant to be women in the church. Fourteen women responded, but the group was soon down to half that size. It was not meant to be a feminist group or even a religious one. Today the group is both feminist and religious. Through the process of sharing their lives with one another, seven women came to the realization that they are feminist indeed.

The group meets for approximately three hours every Sunday evening to support one another and to examine feminist issues. There is no set agenda and conversations are confidential, creating a climate of security and trust. Participants are white and middle class, married and single, and are theologians, teachers, a librarian, and a school principal in their forties and fifties. Theirs is a closed group because of the bonds and shared history over the years. All seven are or have been Catholic, although several go either to a Presbyterian church or don't go to church at all because they can't stand the clericalism and the sexism, particularly the church's attitudes toward women, sex, and sexuality. All agree that they do not get much from going to church, even though two still go with "great devotion." They find no nourishment in the liturgy.

Their meetings center on sharing their experiences as women and what is happening in their lives. Several times a year they celebrate Eucharist together, with bread and wine and occasionally the words of the Roman Catholic Mass. They pray for one another and for others whom they know, for women, for the poor, and for the world. Sometimes they use readings, sometimes they use a poem, and at times they create their own prayers. Individuals have been changed by being in the group. Coming together strengthens and encourages them to go out and be different as a result. Ordinarily they meet only as a group, although three of the women get together socially once in a while.

The group is definitely feminist, but without a group definition. To the one being interviewed, feminism means action and thought that critique the culture and the cultural approach to women, with emphasis on supporting the full human life of women. When asked whether she herself is Catholic, she replied, Of course I'm Catholic. I get my life sustenance from Catholicism. I disagree with it, argue with it, but I have always loved it. I learned spirituality and contemplation from it and love the power of scripture and good liturgy. I appreciate its ethos that the world is sacrament and in every place you find God.

I am a catholic with a small "c" because it is not the rules and regulations and magisterium but the living communion of solidarity with the world that I embrace.

~

2/ As a joke, the seven women in the Southwest who come together regularly sometimes call themselves the Bitch and Stitch group because they have made many quilts. They have come a long way since they first began meeting fourteen years ago as a mixed-gender group under the leadership of a male minister with a study plan. When the group was studying its third book, a woman who was reading aloud to the others tossed the book to the ceiling and said, "This is too sexist for me." That ended the study plan — and the mixed group. The minister insisted the women could not use the group's formal name unless they followed the study plan, but they did use the name and still do.

Although originally UCC, the group today includes other Protestants and a Catholic. All are white, and among them are married, single, widowed, and divorced women between forty and eighty years of age. The group is open and would welcome other women. There are no leaders. Each one gives a little and they get things done, like the quilts.

The women meet weekly in homes from 9:30 a.m. to 12 noon and sometimes end with lunch. Everyone brings fruit or something to share. Meetings begin informally. It is a time for sharing problems and giving support, and there are lots of hugs and tears. Prayer happens spontaneously in response to expressed need. They consider themselves feminist — their founder threw a book in the air — and would define this to mean that women have a right to be who they are. They would admit, however, that even those who say they are feminist still acquiesce to female stereotypes. They themselves continue to contribute their services to the church through banner-making and cleaning the sanctuary when it needs it. They are aware that their giving is not reciprocated, that for the most part they operate outside of church structures, but they are delighted in simply having survived.

~

3/ This group is called "Cakes for the Queen of Heaven." It is not the only one. Named after a Unitarian Universalist curriculum that deals with women in religion and with the Goddess myth, this group of twenty women who meet in the deep South have all taken the twelve-week course. It is prerequisite to group membership. When they finished the course over four years ago, they wanted to keep on meeting for continued growth and support. So they did. At first the group was closed to new members because of the closeness that had been achieved, but now it is open to any "course graduates" who care to join.

Usually ten or twelve women meet every other Saturday from 10:00 a.m. until noon and many go to lunch together afterward. Although the group is mostly Unitarian, it includes unaffiliated Protestants, a former Catholic, and a Jewish atheist. They begin their meetings by sitting in a circle and passing a candle from one to the other as each says aloud: "I am the daughter of ... who is the daughter of ... who is the daughter of...." Then they share what has happened since the last time they met. If the Deity is addressed, it is usually as Goddess. What is emphasized is woman's value and heritage, the power of women going back to ancient times. Most meetings end with hands joined and sometimes held high in praise as all chant "ohm."

The group holds a weekend retreat once a year with a planned program of a spiritual nature, usually focusing on some aspect of women's sexuality. They might dance around a bonfire, or do some pagan ritual, like dancing the circle-eight dance. The group member whom we interviewed goes for the fun of it. She is not into religion, so these are the only rituals she can remember. She thinks some of the rituals and superstitions are silly, but she has some really close friends in the group, so she can manage with the rest. Every summer they participate in a "Cake Mix" with other support groups that have spun off from the course. It's a pot-luck social and a chance to mingle. Once a year the groups lead a service in church. Some men think males should be allowed into the group. The woman we interviewed understands their point. However, she still wants an all-female group because "there are some things you just can't talk about with men present." The group is definitely feminist and many are active on behalf of civil rights, particularly with regard to abortion and a woman's right to choose. They belong to the League of Women Voters and many are members of NOW.

Our source thinks the "Cakes" course will continue to grow and will have more and more impact. You have to approach it with an open mind, she says, and you see things differently when you're through.

Coming Together for Support and Action

4 / Fifteen years ago in the South, two women set out to build community among the women in an area where the population was transient. They were newcomers themselves and early efforts "fizzled out," but with persistence their initiatives grew into a nonprofit

organization that raises funds for the needs of women within the broader community.

Although the group is a recognized corporation, it has no formal organization and no set membership. About a hundred people regularly attend social events. A number of activities and subgroups exist under the auspices of this group, such as a newsletter with a national circulation, an ethics subgroup where women discuss and take action on ethical issues, and an ecological subgroup. It is essentially a support group for women where support is expressed in a variety of ways, through a sense of community, awareness raising, providing a "safe space," helping to meet psychological and financial needs, and exercising a strong social justice commitment through social services and action.

At the heart of the larger network is a core decision-making subgroup of between five and twenty women who meet once a month in a Quaker meeting house, the usual venue for group activities. The core group ranges in age from twenty to sixty and includes Hispanics, African Americans, Asian Americans, and Caucasians, who are in the majority. Many of the women are lesbians. Some of the women are married. Some of the women are professionals; others are technically skilled or unskilled workers. The woman we interviewed is an ordained minister in the United Church of Christ. Within the group there are "recovering" Catholics, UCC, Jews, and adherents of Goddess spirituality. They don't talk religious affiliation, however, because "these borders are not so defined by women." Decisions are made in the Quaker mode, by consensus and explicit facilitation. Their agenda includes the boycotting of certain products, issues of handicap access and lesbian rights, and political action relating to racism and aging. The group provides emergency funds for loans and grants. They have a child care facility for working women. They have an extensive lending library that functions out of the home of one of the women. A "salon," which exists for gathering and socializing, has become a model that now extends to other cities in the state.

Sometimes the group has interfaith rituals, usually focused on the healing of persons and the planet. They celebrate in circles, using the moon, earth, and pine branches as symbols and sea water for a cleansing ritual. They often share a meal within the ritual to celebrate a change of season. When they call upon God, which is not very often, they say God or Goddess or Spirit. The group identifies itself as feminist, defining feminism to mean equality, community, nonpatriarchal, nonhierarchical, and united with all living things. Our source has been a member of this group for five years. As a part-time adjunct professor and a clergywoman, she spreads the word more widely through teaching, preaching, and community building among other groups.

~

5/ Four years ago an entire congregation of Catholic Sisters made a decision to focus on homelessness and encouraged its membership to respond to this need both individually and corporately. Initially twenty-five Sisters committed themselves to meet every six weeks to share experiences, reflect theologically, and to plan for action. They also educated themselves on the issue, inviting resource persons and community groups to come and share with them.

Today approximately twenty members of the original group continue to come together every two months. Nearly all are actively involved in some form of ministry with the homeless. Ranging in age from forty to seventy-three, all are professionals working in health care, social service, education, and pastoral care. All are Caucasian.

Their meeting lasts for two hours and always begins with a meal and time for personal sharing. Then up to an hour is spent in prayer, which includes a shared reflection based on shared experiences. There is an effort to be inclusive regarding the imaging and naming of God. This is followed by a time of information-sharing related to their projects and organizations. There is also time allocated for planning and for making necessary decisions. Two members serve as conveners, coordinators, and facilitators of the group, and these functions are shared on a rotational basis. Decisions are made in a consensual mode. A major decision has been to encourage their congregation to utilize some of their corporate resources for a center for the homeless and to help plan how to do it.

The group itself has done some collective action related to the homeless and to homelessness, namely, advocacy through the legislative process and alerting the laity to possibilities for volunteer work, such as rehabilitation of affordable housing. They have been effective in creating partnerships for action, in some cases bringing together the religious congregation and the parish. It is felt that there has been some impact on the local diocese with regard to the issue of homelessness.

Nearly all the members individually link into other women's groups, but is the group itself feminist? "Well, some would say yes, and others would say no." One member's understanding of feminism is: some effort toward inclusivity; a sense of equality and mutuality; a sense of women's voice, worth, and power to shape the world; a respect for differences; and the avoiding of polarization.

~

6 / Four years ago several women in the West, inspired by their denomination's annual women's event, began a women's group in their congregation. Initial meetings were shaped by guided meditations from the book *Circle of Stones*. They constructed a ritual altar, and for the first year participants would bring their own small stone to put on the altar.

A core group of twelve continues to meet two evenings a month for an hour and a half in a cozy room at the church. Among those who come quite regularly, there are eight UCC from the host congregation, two Catholics, a Lutheran, and a Methodist. Occasionally a Jewish woman participates. Ages range from thirty to eighty in the total group and from thirty-five to forty-five among the twelve. The group is open to all women, and now and then a woman from the host congregation will attend, but she usually doesn't return.

On meeting nights members leave their shoes at the door and enter a room arranged in a circle around a ritual altar. Whoever is leading the worship that evening will light the candles and place some ritual objects on the altar. After fifteen minutes or so of silent meditation during which "centering" or "gathering" music is played, all join hands and there is verbal prayer. Then the group is led in a ritual incorporating the objects on the altar, and there is sharing among those present. Once a woman brought her collection of dolls, which illustrated different times in her life and different images of women. Another brought a lot of candles—some twisted, some stumpy, some thick, and some tapers that were long and thin — in order to illustrate how different types of people make lovely lights. Once the ritual was a dance as a way of celebrating their bodies, because so many women have negative feelings about their bodies. In their sharing, the women talked about how body images affect other parts of our lives. The female image of God used most is the Gaia image, an earth mother, warm and comforting. A guided meditation may follow the ritual, or group study of a book, or a discussion of women's issues, which is often related to battered women because that is the group's special action focus. The session closes with women holding hands and encircling the altar as they lift up special needs in prayer.

In addition to the regular meetings, there are other group activities, such as a visit to a Native American sweat lodge for women, and there are also retreats. A key component of one retreat was just having fun. Some realized they had forgotten how to have fun, and they wondered where the creative, joyous child they once were had gone. An important group activity is preparing careboxes for the local shelter for abused and battered women. They are given lists to guide them in providing individual women and their children with what they need for setting up their own apartments.

The woman we interviewed feels that the group is feminist, although not all would agree, mainly because they have problems with the term. In her opinion the group's purpose is to "affirm women *in a safe place* as total human beings," helping each other "and all women by listening to their pain." She and the others still attend church services, and even though her skill in liturgy is known in wider denominational circles, she does not try to change congregational worship. For her it is the group that gives her the freedom to trust, to risk, to try new things, and to break the bonds of patriarchy. She feels that the women have come a long way. They are always exploring new ways to grow and to understand themselves as women. They have also learned how to have fun together, to rejoice and celebrate.

Coming Together as Church for Ritual, Liturgy, Worship

7/ After Sister Theresa Kane publicly challenged the pope with regard to women's ordination during his visit to the United States in 1979, approximately twenty women in the Mid-Atlantic region decided to assemble on a regular basis for Eucharist, liturgy, ritual. They wanted a context for sharing their pain with the Roman Catholic liturgy, a place to celebrate real life and to share faith as women of faith. The majority were Catholic Sisters.

The group is still in existence and its purpose is the same, but its membership today includes women who are neither Sisters nor Catholic; some of the women are Jewish. There are business and professional women in the group, quite a few women religious, a number of married women, and several lesbian couples. There may be as many as fifty, but usually between twenty-five and thirty attend regularly. Little girls accompany their mothers and are part of the liturgy. The majority of the women are somewhere between thirty and fifty years of age. The group is open to other women who learn of it by word of mouth. While there is some mobility as women move away, most have been members for about five years, and there is a surprising number who have been with the group ever since the beginning.

The community convenes twice a month on a Sunday evening for about three hours, meeting on a rotating basis in one another's homes. The hostess of the home in which they meet usually plans the liturgy. There is also a pot-luck supper and time to socialize. The community is loosely organized with an informal, nonhierarchical leadership.

There are no offices, no decisions made, and, strictly speaking, no members. The women are participants. One of the founding participants cannot recall a single conflict in the community's history. When asked what motivates her and others to continue, she responded: It is our feminist community. We want to experiment with liturgical creativity, to express our faith in a place that is safe. The group empowers them to speak out to church leadership about sexist attitudes and actions.

Indeed, the group identifies itself as feminist, defining feminism to mean claiming woman power to define who we are and what we're about; being able to define theology, scriptural interpretation, faith, and liturgy in a way that is meaningful to women; being aware of women's issues. Feminine and female God images and names are used almost exclusively. They call upon both Goddess and God, avoiding, at all costs, calling God Father or Lord. Among their God images are "birthing," "creative suffering," "dancer." Among their liturgical symbols are the egg, blood, water, wind, fire. Individually participants have linkages with a variety of other women's groups, for example, WOC, WATER, Women-church Convergence, Quixote Center's women's activities, and the Conference of Catholic Lesbians. Some still attend worship in their church or synagogue.

These women are politically progressive on both domestic and international issues. Most are activists in groups and organizations in which corporate stances are taken on a diversity of issues. We interviewed a woman religious with a Ph.D. who is a peace and justice activist. She has no desire to be ordained within the present system of the Roman Catholic Church.

~

8/ In a large metropolitan city in the Midwest, a group of women meet regularly to bring the feminine aspect to conscious affirmation and reverence. Seven years ago three women prepared an alternative worship event and sixty women came. Today about sixty women still attend various events throughout the year. Their ages range from five to eighty-five and they include approximately seven African Americans, several Hispanics, several Asian Americans, and a large number of Caucasians. Except for the group's leadership, who are for the most part members of various churches, the majority are either Roman Catholic or religiously unaffiliated. They are artists, therapists, business women, professors, and women who are otherwise employed. The group is open to all women, and its events are advertised to women through a newsletter that has a circulation of about twelve hundred. Approximately 10 percent who attend are new this year.

Women come "to be part of a community of women engaged in personal quest and development."

The group's purpose is to provide a context in which the experience of the world can be affirmed and celebrated. Ritual is central to the group's assembling, and there is a strong psychosocial orientation to what they do together. Celebrations include a psychic and spiritual quest shared with one another and facilitated through artistic media. In celebrating life cycles and passages of earth and/or women's bodies and psyches, women experience and affirm their own inner authority and the power that comes through life's turning points.

The group comes together six times a year for a period of approximately five hours. It has been described as "a traveling road show" because it meets in different churches and community centers throughout the metropolitan area as one way of achieving visibility. A typical meeting consists of many elements that are woven together in ritual. Registration is followed by browsing in the book and jewelry "stores" that travel with the group, and women socialize during this leisurely preritual gathering. The ritual itself begins with harp music, a bard, and storytelling. Poetry, reflection, guided imagery, and story help participants to focus on the theme. Ritual elements include singing, personal sharing, group discussion, and ritual action. Goddesses are named, claimed, and honored — classical Greek goddesses, the Japanese Amateratsu, the Dark Mother — and Native American imagery is used. Symbols include corn, fire, candles, mirrors, fruit, leaves, textiles, banners, painting, animal images. Usually the ritual ends with a circle dance and is followed by food and more socializing.

In addition to ritual celebration, which is central, the group's activities now include an educational forum with resource persons who address such matters as mothering and menstruation. The group also has a newsletter and is preparing a video on goddesses of color to share with other women's groups. They have received a grant to work with women prisoners, a commitment that forms an important social action dimension of the community. The women are active politically as individuals, but not collectively as a group.

At the heart of the community is a decision-making council of approximately sixteen self-selected women who initially served as an advisory group to the founders. From the beginning the founders saw their initiative as a movement and their own role as a vocation. They began to share creativity and participation in making things happen. Eventually the decision-making extended to others and took the form of the present council. Making this fully functional has taken a lot of time and energy on the part of many women, and the community is now in a period of transition as this new style of leadership forms.

The group self-identifies as feminist. To these women feminism "gives power and authority to women's interpretation of the world as it comes out of the center of their being." They are definitely having an impact on area churches as they move from place to place. Since many of the participants are leaders in their parishes and congregations, the church has to deal with empowered women in many aspects of its life. The woman we interviewed, a Caucasian in her thirties and mother of two, is an ordained pastor and a pastoral counselor in a church-based counseling center.

~

9/ For eleven years some women in the Pacific Northwest have come together for mutual support and to explore women's spirituality and alternative forms of worship.

The group began when fifteen young adults, all of them in ministry in the Catholic Church, felt a need for a separate female group to offset the male domination they were experiencing, particularly in campus ministry meetings. They decided to have a women's "slumber party," and they have been together ever since.

They were a group of ten for a time, and now they number seven. All are Caucasian and middle class with a Roman Catholic background. They range in age from thirty-eight to fifty, and all have master's degrees. They work in education, consultation, and the social services, and they are married, divorced, single, and celibate. For the first two years of the group's existence, all were in ministry in the Roman Catholic Church, and inevitably their time together was taken up with the venting of a lot of anger and frustration. Then some left the ministry and even the Catholic Church, and the energy of the group turned toward a consideration of women's spirituality.

They meet quarterly at the change of seasons and are together for about six hours. The theme and its facilitator are set at the previous meeting. They begin by checking in with one another, each sharing what is in her heart. They do this creatively, through a story, art, a weather report. Then they discuss the theme, which is usually of an experiential nature. Some of their themes have been sexuality, menstruation, death. Their discussion is brought to a close with a ritualization of the theme. Through ritual they celebrate women's passages, bless homes, deal with the loss of loved ones, etc. They have used the "talking stick" from Native American tradition. They have anointed one another. They have created their own altars. In their sharing and prayer they have named God as Mother, Creator, Loving Presence, One Who Speaks the Truth, One Who Dances in the Light. The drawing in of the ritual is accomplished through silence and prayer, sometimes using visualization or guided imagery.

The discussion and ritual lasts two hours and is followed by dinner together. The gathering is brought to closure with a song sung in a circle.

The group's dual purpose — to provide mutual support for personal growth and to experience new ways of exploring women's spirituality, worship, and ritual—has been integrated through experience, and both needs are being met. Decisions are made by consensus. There is no formal leadership but rather a self-selected rotation of responsibility from one gathering to the next. They also meet annually for two or three days and have hosted other women for a weekend event to encourage them to initiate women's groups. They have marched together as a group, but on the whole, such activity as a group is minimal.

Yes, the group identifies as feminist. In their understanding, feminism means reclaiming the importance of female energy in the world and in the culture, which is both a personal and a political act. It means learning to use creative and intuitive dimensions to bring the forces of the world into balance. One woman said: "My husband is also a feminist, but he probably wouldn't say so."

Coming Together to Effect Change

10/ Four years ago, eleven Roman Catholic Sisters who are members of the same religious congregation were on the verge of asking permission to transfer to another province of the Order. There were relatively few among them who were actively supporting change. They wanted more freedom to explore the possibilities inherent in Vatican II and perhaps new forms of religious life.

The group decided to maintain a loose contact with the congregation and to do some serious discernment, both individually and as a group. They met with a professional facilitator, but their future remained unclear. Later that year the congregation's leadership encouraged all of the members to form regional clusters for the purpose of sharing vision and accountability. The group of eleven formed a project cluster and went "public" as a group, stating their desire to become "a separate group" so as to live out their call more freely and authentically and to model a new form of religious life. They encountered a lot of anger. It was expressed in words like, "What are they going to do that they couldn't already do?" and "What will happen to us if our most highly educated women in the congregation abandon ship?"

They are now a group of six ranging in age from forty-five to fifty-one. They meet monthly to share with one another and to think and rethink what they are about. They take turns facilitating ritual and prayer, they bless and share bread and wine, they reflect on life events, and they theologize together. They have an annual retreat with a woman director and have come up with a plan for the future.

The group has proposed that they be a parallel track for pastoral planning while retaining a loose contact with their congregation and that they be accountable directly to their General Council. This proposal has been accepted. They are not yet inviting others into formal membership in the group, although several other members of their congregation are considering joining them. Their corporate vision includes:

- the fostering of membership in small base communities in ministerial contexts

- a pro-feminist stance within the Roman Catholic tradition

- an orientation to service

- porous boundaries between "lay" and "religious"

- the modeling of feminist leadership

- advocacy for the powerless

- working to change systemic injustice

- growth in interdependence

- creative networking rather than common life

- alternative prayer forms

They have entered the second phase of their development, which includes a long-range plan. They are considering whether they will integrate with the total congregation, and if they decide to do so, then how. They intend to focus future deliberations on governance, new members, and finance.

The woman we interviewed finds herself energized in this time of ambiguity. She says: "Something new is trying to be born. We are trying to help shape the religious life of the future. We are searching for new ways to express and live it. We're not going to leave, but we're not going to continue to sustain irrelevant structures and theologies." She says they are tired of arguing against conservative theology. They see theology as basically relational and transformational. She feels that many women religious have not moved from victimization to survival and therefore have a low energy level for handling the future. Their personal agenda is too absorbing. Those who feel differently have to more forward. Basically, she says, we have to ask ourselves: "Are you comfortable putting an airplane together while it is in flight?"

~

Because of the public nature of the next two groups, we sought and received permission to reveal their identity.

11/ A group whose membership is nationwide began as a support group for mutual encouragement among Korean women clergy and Korean women aspiring to ordination within the United Methodist tradition in the United States. It was established eight years ago as a denominational response to the expressed need of several Korean clergywomen who wanted a gathering space for themselves. These pastors who felt a need for mutual encouragement and support called a national meeting. There were fifteen participants, the majority of whom were seminarians or those about to be. Only three or four of the women present were actually ordained. They shared their experiences of sexual discrimination and helped the woman we interviewed, who was a seminarian at the time, see her gifts for priesthood.

The annual gathering has continued as a three-day meeting to "rekindle lights and to share inspiration." Usually about twenty clergy participate together with some other women in related ministries. They worship together twice daily. Evening services follow Methodist rubrics while morning prayer is more informal, consisting of song, silence, scripture, personal testimony, and a concluding benediction. They sit in a circle for morning prayer and sometimes use feminine images for God. They struggle with the English language because in Korean discourse God is called God — there is no "he" or "she."

This annual meeting consists of electing officers and planning projects. Decision-making is consensual. One of their group projects was to meet with Korean clergywomen both from and in Korea. Three years ago, twenty-three Korean women came to the United States. The following year, eighteen members of the group traveled to Korea.

Our source provided some background on the issue of women's ordination in the Korean tradition. Methodist women have been ordained in Korea only since 1989. Married women are denied ordination. How can a married woman be ordained as a pastor? In the congregation she would be over her husband! It is difficult for women to get pastoral experience in Korea, but even more difficult is the cultural reality that "woman is under man's authority." Nevertheless, there are now a hundred ordained women in Korea.

The group challenged the National Forum for Korean Clergy because ordained women had no status in the organization. The forum is in the process of changing its by-laws so that clergywomen might be included on the executive committee.

A majority of the group identify as feminist although there is difficulty with the term. Some feel it has negative connotations or that the term itself has been handed down by the male tradition to discredit the struggle for women's issues. Others feel it implies aggressiveness or something disruptive of the harmony that is a core element of Asian culture. Our source defines feminism to mean helping women be women in the way God intends; working for sexual equality for all; liberating women from wrong perceptions of women caused by culture and theology. A married woman in her thirties and mother of two children, she is an author with a doctoral degree who ministers to an English-speaking congregation of second-generation Korean Americans.

~

12/ Mary's Pence is a feminist Catholic initiative that dates back to 1986. The impetus came from a group of women who worked as volunteers visiting female prisoners in Chicago. Many programs were developed, namely, crafts, dance, etc., but what the women in prison wanted most was spiritual direction. Financial resources were needed for this, so the volunteers wrote a project request to Catholic Charities in Chicago, asking for $5,000 for this purpose. The response in the form of a letter from the archbishop told them to keep up the good work, but he didn't have any money. Two weeks later a headline in the Chicago newspapers read: "Church grants $250,000 . . ." for a gang-related project. The women were devastated. Couldn't $245,000 have been given to the priest for his ministry and $5,000 been allocated for women? So that women's ministries would not have to be subject to male hierarchical control, the women turned to people and to the church in general for help. They decided to set up a fund that would be parallel to Peter's Pence, the international Catholic collection whose funds are controlled and disbursed by the Vatican, naming it, symbolically, Mary's Pence. It would be designated for the needs of women in the church, and it would be run by women.

Women from justice groups in the Chicago area came together to reflect on what to do and how to do it. They met for nearly a year, brainstorming, setting goals, devising strategies. An initial board of thirteen women with diverse backgrounds and from diverse contexts agreed to be the governing body. The first direct mail appeal was sent in April of 1987. One year later $20,000 was dispersed as support for Catholic women in ministry.

Mary's Pence is a Catholic women's organization that collects and distributes funds for the self-empowerment of women. It responds to the needs of economically deprived women by providing an opportunity for women and men to direct resources to the least powerful in our church and in society, and to Catholic women working in their interests. Its mission statement says that it links donors and grantees in the work of social transformation. Maureen Gallagher, O.P., the group's national coordinator, who graciously agreed to this interview, says that because Mary's Pence came into existence when the bishops' pastoral on women was just getting off the ground, she thought that the bishops would be delighted. Here was this women's initiative, a positive movement of women taking responsibility for their own growth and for development in the church. She expected their enthusiastic support. As she admits, she was somewhat naive. A letter was sent to every bishop asking for financial support, asking that they give in honor of Mary the mother of Jesus and in honor of their own mothers. Four bishops sent donations.

Today the project has a mailing list of four thousand donors. Funding for administration comes primarily from grants and gifts given by religious congregations, mainly women's congregations. Forty-nine parishes throughout the United States have allowed special collections or tithing by parishioners. As of October 1992, Mary's Pence has disbursed $181,000 to 159 women or groups in thirty-five states and six Latin American countries.

Central to the project are the principles of diversity and inclusion. Every conceivable effort was made to ensure that board members were women who reflect the racial, cultural, economic, and professional diversity characteristic of the U.S. Catholic Church. The board consists of two Native Americans, three Hispanics, two African Americans, and four Caucasians. They are wife, mother, single, religious, divorced, lesbian, convert, a woman who has known and still knows what it means to live in poverty. All board members are Catholic, which is a rule of the foundation because of the focus on women's oppression within the Roman Catholic Church. The governing board meets three times a year: once to review and make grant requests, a second time for the workplan and budget, and finally for evaluation. All decisions are consensual. Meetings begin with prayer prepared and facilitated by one of the members, often incorporating ritual pertaining to nature or to the elements of the earth. There is time for personal sharing related to their experience as women and particularly as women in the church. Meetings are concluded with ritual, which usually connects to the content of what has gone before.

Needless to say, the group considers itself feminist. Maureen understands feminism to mean "love and respect for women and recognition that their gifts are needed in today's world." Board members have a phenomenal number of linkages with other women's groups at the local, regional, and national levels. Does Mary's Pence have any impact on the institutional church? Probably very little. "The institutional church probably sees us as a dandelion in a garden of roses." But women's power is growing. Mary's Pence is intentionally directing money away from the institution. It has created a structure within the church that gives the people in the pews the authority and responsibility to decide where and how their church donation will be used. It is women claiming their power together in a process that empowers women.

More Feminist Groups: A Sampling

Two years ago, three women in the **Seventh-day Adventist** tradition came together to create feminist worship services to meet women's needs following their denomination's decision not to ordain women. There were ten services the first year, but only two the second because the women, working in full-time jobs, ran short of energy and time. The services, which do not compete with official worship, have been well received by the many women who come from all over town. This initiative in the Mid-Atlantic region has become a model for a similar venture on the West Coast. Both are a constant reminder to the tradition that women are actively involved in worship leadership, whether or not they are ordained.

~

Female faculty and staff of a denominational college in the Pacific Northwest began to meet together secretly eight years ago for stress release and to learn how to laugh at difficult work situations. Their purpose — not to take life too seriously — and the group itself are no longer a campus secret. Now any woman can join, but she must have a sense of humor. This **ecumenical** group of professionals, professors, administrators, and secretaries, who are Catholic, Quaker, Mennonite, Presbyterian, and Southern Baptist, give one another support to question what is not right in the churches.

~

Originally an ecumenical support group of clergywomen irregularly ordained in the Episcopal, Reformed, and Presbyterian traditions back in the 1970s, the group is now a place of integration and exchange for **Presbyterian clergywomen.** They meet once a week for lunch to share what's happening in their personal lives and to do political planning on how best to impact the presbytery on issues of significant concern. Occasionally they may have a ritual, but for the most part the group is an anchor for them, where they can talk about whatever they like and know it is not they who are crazy.

~

A number of women who feel called to ordination within the Roman Catholic tradition are coming together annually from all around the nation to pray and worship as a community and to model a renewed church. Following a WOC conference in 1986, twenty-five women decided to continue meeting as a group and to pursue the ordination of women as a justice issue of immediate concern and not something for the distant future. Eighteen women who now meet for four or five days twice a year see themselves as **a covenant community.** They say: "We are redefining church and what it means to be a Catholic."

~

A group of **Mennonite** faculty women from various academic institutions in the Mid-Atlantic region decided to form a peer group six years ago. There were seven founding members. They meet twice a month to share whatever surfaces in their personal and professional lives, to deal with issues of male power and control, and to be both affirmed and challenged.

~

A group began seven years ago in a liberal West Coast **United Methodist** church in order to create a new vision of spirituality. Six women planned feminist liturgies for morning worship around imagining a feminine God. Now twelve, sometimes twenty women gather every Saturday morning to tell their stories and celebrate alternative rituals with drum or chant or however the spirit moves.

~

Seven years ago five feminists in the North Central region met to talk about spirituality. A strong focus on social justice and community action during the last two years has developed into a larger nonprofit organization that acts as a catalyst for change in the community and has its own governing board. The five who are at the heart of this enterprise continue to meet separately as **a spirituality group** approximately every three weeks. They share, have fun, and celebrate rituals with female images of God.

~

Two Roman Catholic Sisters founded a shelter for homeless women in the Southwest region seven years ago. They wanted to create a space where the needs and concerns of economically poor women could meet with some response. The seven women who share responsibility for the shelter see themselves as "women reaching out to women" and have formed **a community oriented to service** and to political advocacy for women. It is a multiethnic community of Hispanics and Anglos and has its share of stress. Even though most see each other every day and four meet daily for common prayer, they gather once a month to discuss issues related to the project and the community and for ritual celebration.

~

A dozen years ago, a woman in the Northeast who was interested in dreams invited some women to join her in sharing **dream interpretation.** While membership has changed over the years, eight women continue to meet to reflect on their dreams together. The group includes post-Christian, Native American, Catholic, and "spiritual" and "eclectic" women who are nurse, artist, clergy, therapist, and salesperson. They meet in the morning, twice a month, in the office of one of the therapists to discuss the imagery and its interpretation in the dreams of two group members. There is also an annual overnight retreat, which focuses on spiritual journey and how it relates to all of life. The personal growth and spirituality of each member affects other arenas of their life, including their participation in church.

~

Three women began an **A.A. Women's Group** in New England two years ago to give women who might not speak up in a mixed group a facilitating context. Based on the twelve-step program, which focuses on recovery, it provides a rootedness in spirituality for at least one of the founding members. The group meets weekly in a local church and is very trusting, open, and supportive. All of the steps have been recast in inclusive language. As the women try to relate to a "higher power," many struggle to overcome images of a punishing, negative, judgmental God, to relate to a loving and accepting God, and, if possible, to use feminine images. An intimate group with lots of laughter, participants share from the gut at a level they could never do in their churches.

~

A **Church of the Brethren** women's group began in the 1970s because of a dissatisfaction with the status of women within the denomination. A group of women on the West Coast formed to advocate women's ordination, to present worship materials with inclusive God-language, and to support reproductive rights. As issues such as the ordination of women get resolved, the eight members reassess where they are and what they are about. An advocacy issue at present centers on the exclusivity of "brethren" in the denomination's name.

~

Two years ago in the Southwest, two **Episcopalian** women's groups, one of them a clergy group, merged to form a larger group for support and information sharing. About thirty-five women meet quarterly for worship, sharing, and resourcing on issues relating to women.

~

About thirty-five **Catholic lesbian women** meet monthly as a church and celebrate liturgy. They have been denied both support and recognition by the institutional church, and they are often put down by other lesbians for remaining Catholic. However, they value the rituals, sharing, and personal support of this Catholic community.

~

Four years ago in the Midwest, five women in a bar decided to continue meeting regularly as a group. All were from the same **Lutheran** congregation. Professional women, all in their forties, they meet for mutual support and because they enjoy one another's company. Although active in their congregation, they are definitely a feminist group that continues to learn from reading books and discussing what has been read.

~

A **clergywomen's group** in the Mid-Atlantic region was begun by an African American pastor for sharing and support. Just a year old, its members are from a variety of traditions — Presbyterian, Southern Baptist, Church of God in Christ, Christian Methodist Episcopal, Lutheran, Episcopalian, Catholic, and a "New Age" sister. All women clergy are welcome. The group meets once a month for lunch. When there is an outside speaker, forty or more clergywomen attend.

~

About five years ago, in the Pacific Northwest, a woman called together a group out of a need to feel connected with the universe and to be deeply grounded in spirituality. Theirs is not a support or therapy group, but intentionally a ritual group and **nondenominational.** The founder is post-Christian. The group of five meet every two weeks to plan and then celebrate a ritual, keeping a clear distinction between ritual space and social space. Because of their experiences together, group members are less frustrated in their relationship to the church.

~

Women's groups for support and service are a tradition in the church.
    Women have come together with other women ever since the churches in this nation were established. Women still come together for personal and spiritual support and to accomplish a task or meet

a need within or beyond the community. *Two out of every three women participating in this project are presently members of a women's group that has a spiritual or religious orientation* (see Tables 5 and 6, pp. 265, p. 266).

In the Protestant churches, women's groups and organizations have been a nucleus of denominational loyalty and a source of companionship for dedicated members.[30] Mission boards, ladies aid societies, altar guilds, women's circles, and similar associations have contributed substantially to the finances and ministry programs of the church, providing tangible assistance to those in need in both local and global missions. The Mormon women's Relief Society fulfills a similar mission within the Church of the Latter-day Saints. While the overall programs of Protestant women's organizations reflect a spiritual dimension, more specific spiritual needs are addressed in less formal groups of women meeting for Bible study, sharing, or prayer within local congregations. Deaconesses and orders of nuns have their own unique opportunities for spiritual growth and support.

In the Catholic Church, women's sodalities, altar and rosary societies, and mothers clubs have met the needs of generations of women through prayer, support, and service. The National Council of Catholic Women, with a network, of local chapters has organized women on a larger scale. Religious congregations and orders of Sisters and cloistered nuns have long been a rich resource of women's spirituality and dedicated service, as have other associations of women for women like the Grail and centers for spirituality and retreat.

Women's World Day of Prayer, Young Women's Christian Association (YWCA), and Church Women United extend beyond denominational boundaries to strengthen solidarity among women. Organizations such as these have resources, visibility, and continuity. On the opposite end of the spectrum are the informal, invisible, ad hoc groups meeting primarily for spiritual support within or beyond congregations.

Only 14 percent of the women surveyed have never been a member of a women's spiritual support group. Reasons for not participating vary. Most prefer mixed-gender groups. Others say they are not joiners of groups, or they are simply too busy, or they would like to join a group if they could only locate one that is congenial.

While 66 percent of the women surveyed are currently members of women's spiritual support groups, an additional 20 percent once were but are not now. The major reason women give for not continuing with a group is that their group has disbanded, usually because key members have moved away. They are unable to find another congenial group and have not had time or the inclination to form a group themselves. In many instances their "dropping out" is seen as temporary.

One-third of the women surveyed belong to traditional women's groups, one-third belong to no group at all, and one-third are in feminist spirituality groups.

~

Feminist spirituality groups — a new type of women's group — are spreading throughout the United States.

Feminist spirituality groups are a newly emerging phenomenon focusing on women's spiritual growth through the sharing of women's stories as they nurture a vision of a just society within and beyond the church.[31] Such groups pay particular attention to the spiritual journeys of participating members and to the raising of feminist consciousness. They often include alternative ritual rooted in feminist theology and women's experience.

The size of feminist spirituality groups ranges from five and fewer to well over one hundred for specified events, with an average attendance somewhere between eight and twelve women. Some groups meet weekly or twice a month, some no more than a few times a year, but most meet approximately monthly. Women share responsibility for setting the agenda, providing a space and refreshments, and facilitating the meeting. Decisions are made by consensus, or at least democratically, in nearly all of the groups. Gatherings are usually informal and quite often in someone's home. Nearly every group at nearly every meeting designates quality time for some kind of personal sharing, whether a quick catching up on how things are or what has happened in between meetings, or an individual in-depth exchange related to one's personal or spiritual journey. Even in groups where the focus is primarily on the study of books or theology, invariably part of the time together will involve personal integration that is supportive and affirming.

Groups differ not only in size. They vary in purpose or in focus, in how and why they were started, and in the nature of their membership.

Groups formed to provide support show a variety of emphases. Some focus on developing self-esteem or the content of a twelve-step program, others on personal spiritual growth, still others on providing a safe space for women in the public arena. There are groups composed of women who are in the same profession, such as clergywomen from a single denomination or from a geographical location; theologians; seminary students; business women; teams of service-providers; artists; and Sisters in the same religious order. Many other groups exist because the members share something in common. It may be ethnic or denominational identity, an orientation, or a circumstance. For example, there are support groups for lesbian women, women who are victims of sexual abuse, pregnant women, nursing mothers, and mothers with small children.

Groups also form for the purpose of raising and deepening feminist awareness. This may be done through a study focus or perhaps through group discussion or as a follow-up to a course. Groups also convene to accomplish a specific task that is often service-oriented, others to embark on a new venture or to inaugurate a new mission, still others to support a political cause or to engage in advocacy. Specialized caucuses for specific reasons, such as promoting women's ordination in a given denomination, usually go out of existence with the accomplishment of their goal. Then there are groups that focus primarily on liturgy or ritual or worship, celebrated most often within the group but at times designed and implemented in a public event for women.

In addition to purpose and focus, support groups often have an ethos related to the reason for their founding. For example, some groups form for "survival" because of a religious or spiritual crisis usually related to patriarchy. Such groups spend significant time and energy venting frustration and anger as they deal with the source of their pain. Groups intent on consciousness-raising usually raise group energy as members break through to new levels of feminist awareness and understanding. Groups sensitive to the environment are ordinarily oriented to earth and planet and the rhythms of the seasons. Alternative, innovative ritual groups express a lot of creativity.

Feminist spirituality groups attract middle-aged women, those older than thirty-five and younger than sixty-five. There are, however, groups with younger members and some with women who are older. Taking action on behalf of a political cause is difficult if the group is varied. There may be conflicting interests, and more often than not, the group does not have the financial resources needed. But feminist groups do get involved in good works in the community, for example, working with homeless women, supporting a battered women's shelter, reaching out to women in prison, raising funds for a particular cause.

Feminist spirituality groups are more likely to be outside of denominational and congregational structures. In this study, only one-third of all the women's groups associated with a local congregation are feminist spirituality groups. One may wonder why there are any at all since, by their very nature, such groups are not typically accepting of traditional theology. Interviews suggest that women's groups may begin within congregations when women decide to study a book or experiment with styles of prayer. Then as members share experiences and get in touch with their feelings, they begin to grow in self-confidence and become feminist in orientation. Whether these groups remain congregationally based depends to a large extent on how the congregation reacts to their presence, especially the clergy, and what return they get from continuing to be associated with the congregation. *Among feminist spirituality groups, only 14 percent of all the groups surveyed are located within one congregation.*

Denominational feminist spirituality groups consist of women from several or many parishes or congregations within a particular denomination. Such groups usually start out as a legitimate diocesan, judicatory, or national group concerned with women's issues or a specific justice agenda. Like those feminist spirituality groups within Catholic parishes that are disbanded with a change of pastors, a diocesan coalition or a committee concerned with justice for women or liturgical reforms often comes to an official end with a change of bishops. Such action so angers the feminists involved that they often continue to meet as a self-organized group independent of diocesan control and become even more feminist in orientation. Protestant groups consisting of women who come from different churches or areas of the same denomination are more likely to meet less often. They usually have a denominationally sponsored action agenda with the necessary funding. A regional or national group representing women of the denomination may be outside of official church structures. *Among feminist spirituality groups, 41 percent of all the groups surveyed are within one denomination or religious order.*

The most prevalent form of feminist spirituality groups are those with members from diverse denominational and religious backgrounds. Feminist women concerned with spirituality find they have more in common with other women who share some of the same convictions about women and God, church and society, patriarchy and theology than women of their own denomination. *Feminist spirituality contributes to the blurring of denominational identities*, at least among liberal mainline Protestant denominations. Interviews indicate that women who begin a feminist spirituality group find that news spreads through word of mouth, that friends bring friends, and that women from a variety of religious and denominational affiliations or none have been searching for such a group and want to join it. *Among feminist spirituality groups, a plurality of the groups in the sample (45 percent) consist of women from a variety of religious traditions or none.*

~

Interviews support the generalization that *women who become members of feminist spirituality groups are likely to have experienced disenchant-*

ment with the patriarchal church before *they form or join such a group.*
When asked why she joined a feminist spirituality group, one woman
replied: "Because our experiences of church were not very satisfying
or fulfilling. I had been looking for a church with social action and
inclusive theology and had not been able to find one."

Feminist spirituality groups within our study that are composed
of women of similar racial/ethnic minority background are seldom
within local churches. Cheryl Gilkes has shown that there is less impetus for women in African American "sanctified" churches to seek
more esteem and status, since they do enjoy a higher status and receive greater appreciation in their churches than white/Anglo women
do in theirs.[32] However, the research of Delores Carpenter points
out that black clergywomen who are trained in mainline ecumenical
seminaries are much more aware of sexism within the black church.
Perhaps not surprisingly then, the few African American feminist
spirituality groups found in this study tend to be either ecumenical groups of clergywomen of color (mostly African American and
Caribbean) or theological study or book writing groups.

Those feminist spirituality groups in our study that consist only of
Asian women are almost always made up of women with advanced
theological degrees. They meet outside local churches, although they
may be denominationally sponsored within Protestant circles. Some
Asian women who are Catholic and feminist do attend large women-
church regional and national gatherings. Asian women, however, are
likely to have their own version of feminist spirituality, a finding
confirmed by other research.[33] They may prefer to meet with Asian
women of similar national origin and language, but do meet with
those who are Asian Americans of varying backgrounds as well.

An important source of Hispanic American women who espouse
feminist spirituality is the organization Las Hermanas, a national
Catholic network of women very involved in social justice for Hispanic women in society. Not all members of this organization would
support or even accept feminist spirituality. Nevertheless, even the
more theologically traditional tend to value women's leadership role
in church and society, envision God more as a creative force than
a male figure, and put a heavy emphasis on outreach to minority
women and others who are in need.[34] Certain local chapters of Las
Hermanas may be quite feminist in theology as well as in social
outlook. Narratives in the previous chapter indicate that individual
Hispanic Catholic women are among the more radical feminists in
this study.

Catholic Sisters have taken the lead in many dioceses in establishing feminist spirituality groups intentionally involving Catholic

laywomen. Sisters bring a sustained professional leadership and the resources available to religious orders, particularly with regard to space. Participants in these groups believe they are having a subtle but certain impact on Catholic parishes and even on the diocese,[35] although from the data in this study, that would be hard to verify. While Catholic Sisters may not be as consistently feminist on issues regarding church and society as feminist women in other denominations, they are often involved in social action activities whatever their feminist viewpoints. For this and other reasons, many prefer not to compromise their position in the diocese by becoming visibly affiliated with a feminist spirituality group. Interviews indicate that Catholic laywomen convene groups that draw women from a number of parishes in the diocese, as well as women who have dropped out of parish life.

Certain characteristics can be said to be common to feminist spirituality groups. For most groups in this study, the group:

- arose out of a felt need
- is fairly small and relatively stable
- meets regularly, ordinarily in homes
- compensates for what is lacking in institutional religion
- contributes to the raising of feminist awareness
- liberates individual women
- deepens spiritual connections
- results in group loyalty and bondedness
- is feminist with or without the label
- continues only for as long as it is meaningful

The following characteristics of feminist spirituality group meetings are representative of most groups in this study. Meetings reflect:

- flexible design and agenda
- shared leadership
- full participation
- freedom of expression
- decision by consensus
- personal sharing and integration

- acceptance and affirmation
- nurture and empowerment
- creativity and inventiveness
- alternative worship experiences

The following observations point out additional characteristics reflective of most feminist spirituality groups:

- Group members are usually dissatisfied with and often alienated from the institutional church.

- In some groups members have been together a long time, in others the membership changes either periodically or constantly.

- Groups with a history of deep personal sharing are characteristically closed; its members exhibit strong bonds and a commitment to the group.

- The focus of group concern is the well-being of its members, not group expansion or self-preservation.

- Groups are remarkably free of status issues and hierarchical framework.

- Groups and individual group members seek some aspect of change in religious and social institutions.

- Groups are usually located on the margins or outside of the institutional church and almost always lack the resources available to traditional groups, such as finances and a formally designated space.

- Unlike traditional women's groups, feminist spirituality groups do not exist to support or foster institutional goals or to promote institutional loyalty, but to offer critique and challenge.

- Group members are often individually involved in outreach service and in social and political action and are likely to be networked to other feminist agencies and organizations.

- Groups empower and embolden women to be and do what they previously had not dared.

Feminist spirituality groups are the primary religious affiliation for some of the women surveyed. Groups support and enable denominational affiliation and congregational participation for most of the women in this study. They function as an exit community for those leaving institutional religion for a very small number surveyed. Data suggest that some women with a church affiliation are supported and energized to work for change constructively from within, other women are more deeply committed to overthrowing the institution, and still others are moved to conclude it is not worth the hassle and consequently leave the church.

~

Feminist spirituality groups are modeling new ways of being church.

To envision and model new ways of being church are goals of women-church, a global ecumenical movement of local feminist base communities of justice-seeking friends who engage in sacrament and solidarity.[36] While these groups reflect some common patterns, there is also a lot of diversity. The future church may reflect this pluriform pattern. One of the women interviewed is a member of women-church. She said:

"We are redefining church and what it means to be a Catholic, and we feel it's all right not to fit into a patriarchal structure. We are validating our own experience as women in prayer, ritual, and relationship. We are modeling church and we are calling all to conversion."

Women-church is a movement. In this study, women-church is also a type of group with certain characteristics. The women-church movement consists of women-church type groups, and in fact exists only in such groups, whether or not the groups know that they are women-church and whether or not they are affiliated with the movement.

Women-church type groups have innovative liturgy as the central activity of the group, typically with personal sharing integrated into the liturgy itself, or sometimes subsequent to it. Similar to traditional church services, groups are open to anyone and membership is fluid. A core group takes responsibility for the meetings and for hospitality toward others who drift in and out, some of whom become core members. Women-church groups are very often started by Roman Catholic women and have a high proportion of Catholics in attendance at rituals, primarily because women are so angry at the exclusion of women from liturgical leadership and at liturgical language that offends. Catholic women also have a greater love of liturgy than is ordinarily typical of women in other denominations.

Through innovative ritual and both personal and spiritual sharing among members, women-church groups model how worship and church can be. This experience, which women value and which is often so very different from what is encountered in parishes and congregations, may drive some women further away from the institutional church. But interviews indicate that these groups also enable women to remain in congregations because, as one woman put it, "women ask less of their church because they are fed in this group." For many the opportunity to share with women from diverse denominational and religious backgrounds provides a support and a sounding board for strategizing about how to approach things in their churches.

Because liturgy is so central and so visible in the Catholic Church and so constitutive of the tradition, the central role of ritual in women-church gatherings leads to a juxtaposition of institutional church and spirit-church by women-church adherents and by others. At the heart of this claim to being church is Vatican II ecclesiology, which says that the people are the church. Again and again the women in this study, Catholics and Protestants alike, say: We are the church! Many would agree with the respondent who says:

"I believe the women have become church by creating community and serving the needs of each other and those of society."

One of the women wrote on her questionnaire: "We are learning to find our own way to salvation." This statement was not made lightly. As the narratives of the women themselves state clearly, a deep soul-struggle for spiritual survival lies behind a feminist woman's ability to make such a claim. "Let us create new models of church while being faithful to what we hear from God." This statement echoes the convictions of a number of women in this study who are part of feminist spirituality groups. They believe in the Spirit within them and the wisdom of God speaking through them, and they claim, completely and unequivocally, the gift of being female. Feminist women want things to be different, not only for themselves, but especially for their children. They recognize women's role as keeper of the heart's traditions. In the words of one of the women in this study:

"Women pass on religion through the generations. We are the church."

Chapter 5

Feminist Spirituality

Women are learning a new language of the spirit as they share with one another their experiences of the sacred.

~ ~ ~

Language That Includes

"I am continually amazed at how few women are conscious of language as not only expressing concepts and faith, but also as shaping concepts and faith. We have a long way to go in conscienticizing ourselves."[1]

~

"My daughters are another generation. Male language excludes and 'puts off' my youngest from the church. My other daughter rejects the church, but not spirituality. My daughters have been the most significant influence in raising my consciousness."[2]

~

"My congregation doesn't know what 'inclusive language' is, but they've been hearing it for four years. No one seems to miss 'God the Father' either, although some have become less involved in the congregation. The tremendous growth here has come in the twenty-to-forty-five age group, both men and women. When I arrived I was the only one under the age of thirty-five (not including children). Now there are over fifty. I think it has to do with a place whose language, theology, and emphasis meet people where it matters, and where people are valued, men and women, adults and children."[3]

~

"Language, its power and limitation, seem particularly important as we seek to participate, to heal, to reconcile, to reach."[4]

~

"My use of inclusive language from scripture is so threatening to some that they label me, humiliate me, even hate me. I see and teach the Bible as good news, liberating news, but many in the church use it to ring out bad news."[5]

~

"The exclusive language of the liturgy, which I do love, always presents a challenge. Perhaps Episcopalians will one day begin to worship inclusively. Until then, I'll translate the language of the liturgy for myself, not unlike I once did when worshiping in Chinese while living in Taiwan. How sad that many women in worship feel like strangers in a strange land."[6]

~

"On the one hand, I believe that changing our language will change the power structures. On the other hand, issues of the environment, liberation, etc. are ultimately more important...I think!"[7]

~

"Never thought much about inclusive language until joking around in choirs in the early 1980s. Then we came to this diocese and this bishop and suddenly the position of women in the church was an issue I was willing to fight for."[8]

~

"One very painful experience is to be at a congregational gathering with feminist rituals, inclusive language, and then return back to my ministry area and see sexist liturgies that are awful. The disparity between the inclusive celebration and the 'regular' church makes it harder to attend 'regular' church."[9]

~

"I have recently been quite distressed with several young male clergy who have commented to me that all the 'language stuff' they learned in seminary seemed irrelevant to them in the parish. I think this is the result of the issue of language having been framed in an ideological context rather than in prayer and worship. Therefore, it has been interpreted as expendable, or one ideology among many, when it could be seen as the stuff of our spiritual life."[10]

~

"I find myself being much more aware of language and how it is used in regard to all kinds of prejudice — sex, color, ethnic background, religion, etc., in or out of the church setting. When I think of 'inclusive language' or lifestyle, I think of a way of life that includes *all* people."[11]

~

"I think men would benefit a great deal from an inclusive, *person*-affirming faith, just as much as women would."[12]

~

"Women must *hear* that the love and grace extends to them, not just tell themselves that it extends to them through the he's and him's in their lives."[13]

~

"As a few women of our church attained more awareness about inclusive language for God and God's people, we tried to institute it. The congregation mocked us. As more of us find that the male language is an obstacle to our presence in worship, we have started attending a Unitarian church."[14]

~

"There's still a long way to go regarding inclusive language. Many say it is not an issue. Very few are aware and the rest act negatively to the topic of inclusiveness regarding humans and God language."[15]

~

"I think inclusive language is critical. It sounded awkward to me at first, but now when I attend a traditional church the traditional patriarchal language stands out and interferes with my experience of the scripture."[16]

~

"Since I have no support from family or friends regarding my commitment to inclusive language in liturgy, nor respect for my need to pray using feminine images of God, I just keep going on alone. I read about similarly committed Catholics all the time. I just can't seem to find them in the flesh."[17]

~

"I feel efforts on my part to encourage use of inclusive language are resented by other church members, so I have not been as outspoken as I really feel I should be."[18]

~

"During a two- or three-year attempt to make the language and music of worship more inclusive, some members left and some organized opposition toward the minister, who was perceived to be the source of the change. A new hymn book was introduced and was and is rejected by some. A more inclusive doxology was introduced and is still resisted by some who continue to sing the 'familiar' words. Following a survey which the minister sent to members of the church last summer inviting input about worship, the language and music of worship is no longer consistently inclusive, as it had been. This is particularly painful to me. The differences co-exist. Some use inclusive language; some do not. Some see justice concerns as legitimate concerns of the church; some do not."[19]

~

"Inclusive language in hymns has not even started in the Lutheran Church, at least at my church. It would be greatly appreciated."[20]

~

"My pastor supports my use of inclusive language when I lector, but I'm the only one who does it, and there have been complaints from the congregation and from other lectors. If there are those who support it, none have come up to me and said so. It feels as though feminist spirituality, in a place like this, is an *underground* thing—like being a secret dissident or something. Maybe if I lived somewhere where heterogeneity was accepted (or was the norm!), it would be easier to 'come out' as a religious feminist. As it is, it's pretty lonely most of the time."[21]

~

"I wish I could at least find a church using inclusive language/ imagery so that my daughter wouldn't have to grow up with negative male imagery and feel the alienation and ambivalence that I feel."[22]

~

"I have just lost my job, primarily because of my use of inclusive language. One man accused me of sexual harassment in writing, in a statement attached to the session's minutes, because of my refusal to use 'men' and 'mankind' generically. Another man said that unless he heard the word 'man' or 'men,' he did not feel included. The session said they might consider letting me stay *if* I would promise never to use inclusive language again in worship. I said that I couldn't do that without betraying my faith or compromising my personal integrity. The pastors preceding me for the past twelve to fourteen years had used inclusive language. However, I made the mistake of naming what I was doing, explaining in a sermon why I was looking forward to the new RSV [inclusive language Bible] and the new Presbyterian Hymnal. From that point on, people became critical and negative and began to talk openly about the 'radical' woman preacher who changed the language of scripture. This issue was the primary issue that led to my being asked to leave, after only eighteen months."[23]

~

"The women in my congregation are more reluctant to use inclusive language than the men!"[24]

~

"The noninclusive language of our liturgies offends so that I use my own inclusive terms. It's the only way I can handle community worship."[25]

~

"Inclusive language is not a focus in our worship. I've learned to be patient. A retired minister, and my dear friend and mentor, often sits behind me during worship and, in his lovely tenor voice, changes the brotherhoods to the sisterhoods, just for my sake!"[26]

~

"I have been a clergy spouse for over six years now. I grow increasingly frustrated with the hierarchical structure and the exclusive language. My husband makes a great effort to bring the congregation along in its thinking to a new place. He struggles though, because the structure as it is is all he has known for thirty-two years. I believe the key to effective change in the world, both in church and society, is language."[27]

~

"I consider myself to be feminist. In the courses I help teach, I encourage inclusive language use. I try to begin with treating it as a learning experience to help the student see how much gendering does play a role. I noticed that when students felt threatened, I had little success. When it was presented as an exercise in gender awareness, they were much more receptive. Perhaps it will aid in the future as they are participants in various churches. I've also had fun raising such issues in junior high and high school Sunday school classes."[28]

~

"What I hope to do is to encourage the men and women around me to open their eyes and raise their awareness. Instead of always being the strident voice or the one who clears her throat when 'man' is used generically, I want men sitting on either side of me to make the necessary connections."[29]

~

"By about 1984 I was beginning to be offended by the use of exclusive language and had begun to work for change as diplomatically as possible, especially in music, since I was a choir member. My efforts, my needs were not only 'unappreciated,' they were received as hostile and malicious. By 1986 I was no longer able to attend worship in 'my own' church without spending the rest of the day being angry. Within a few months I stopped attending worship in the congregation of which I was a member. During that time, I 'identified' a congregation which had a stated commitment to the use of inclusive language and I began to worship there occasionally. In 1988 I moved my membership to that congregation, which was a different denomination. My decision to move my membership was based on the characteristics of worship in that place, rather than on the denominational label."[30]

~

"I get depressed at how much consciousness-raising is yet to be done with the people I work with on a day-to-day basis. Women say to me, 'But *I* know 'men' includes 'women,' as if I have a problem — and men are just totally 'out to lunch' on the issue."[31]

~

"We are currently the only church in a fifty-mile radius that I know of which uses nonsexist language in our liturgy. People have commented on it favorably and unfavorably, but it has not affected our attendance or membership in any case."[32]

~

"Inclusive language is harder in our local church than in the conference or denomination. People want to cling to the old familiar images even when they are restrictive and painful for some in the congregation. Our hymnal was picked by some people who had *no* sensitivity to theology or inclusive language. I guess most of our folks sing without listening to what they are saying, but some Sundays I just can't sing — and when I have to pick hymns myself, there are few in the hymnal I can tolerate."[33]

Experiencing, Imaging, Naming God

"Language is so powerful that to refer to my creator as Mother, Grandmother of all, Goddess, has changed how I will live forever."[34]

~

"Though we use feminine terms for God in our home, the children hear the traditional God the Father much too often."[35]

~

"I experience God as a presence in my life, more as a spirit, with images and symbols being important to that experience."[36]

~

"I am much influenced by the Quaker concept of God Within to whom we should constantly turn for guidance, and I try to live in the presence of God, asking God's light to illuminate our lives and choices. I often make contact with God/Goddess during therapy sessions (and before and after) and attribute much of the positive changes I see in my patients to God/Goddess using me as a channel to heal them."[37]

~

"I have real problems describing the nature of God. I considered it a grandiose endeavor all throughout seminary. That still is the case. My sense of God's attributes is that they are veiled and revealed and veiled again, that as spiritual people our experience reflects some of the Divine, but when we name the nature of God we get caught up in a discussion whose underlying effort is really to capture our idealizations about humanity. However, exploring images (versus attributes) of an intransigent Being is helpful to me as I pursue finding an image of God where the femaleness of my life is affirmed. 'Nature of God' seems a ridiculous category to me, where talking about images does not."[38]

~

"Because of an experience with sexual molestation at age fourteen, my concept of God became very muddied and polluted. That God was very male, judgmental, vindictive, and blaming. While dealing with that rape experience, I rejected God completely. Only recently have I been able to experience God as female, positive, and nurturing."[39]

~

"Our minister has changed the doxology to Creator, Savior, Holy Ghost and gotten lots of complaints. He is now using the NRSV [New Revised Standard Version of the Bible]. And a few women in the church yearn for a feminist interpretation of scripture, a feminist hermeneutic."[40]

~

"It is only within the last three years I have begun to realize woman God within by experiencing worship which is purposeful in its inclusion of female images and language. Without the female, God is not only misrepresented but misunderstood, and missing something."[41]

~

"I do sometimes attend churches, but I usually get so offended by the exclusion of women and the references to a male God that I do not enjoy my visits, so I go as seldom as possible."[42]

~

"While my image of God is definitely expanding to include the feminine, I can't say that I'm totally comfortable with it yet. It's difficult to let go of what has been culturally engrained for so many years."[43]

~

"Within there is a terrible tension between my hunger for a Woman-god, a God that I image, and the fear that this search will cause me to have to choose between the God within and the sacraments of the church, especially Eucharist."[44]

~

"We need to promote a more mothering image of God or else take out all the gender orientation from our references to our Creatress."[45]

~

"The most spiritually gratifying church I have ever attended was Unity Church of Christianity while living in Oklahoma. The pastorship was a man-and-wife team and the dual nature of God was continuously acknowledged throughout the worship service."[46]

~

"I am very concerned over the idea of Christians being the only way to God or 'salvation.' I do not believe that. I feel I am all alone in trying to relate to a universal God."[47]

~

"I am a Christian whose images of God have not been Christ-centered and for whom the image of Christ as sacrifice is very destructive. How do other women experience God? Am I the only one who has trouble with Christ? As someone ordained who has functionally been out of the church institution for several years, I have so many feelings I have not yet worked out. There is a lot of pain there."[48]

~

"I am not comfortable with imaging God in masculine terms, but at the same time I haven't passed over entirely to feminine images. 'Friend' speaks to me most. 'Mother' is not all that benign an image either! A lot of women are trying to heal their relationships with their mothers and a lot of self-hatred is involved. The Goddess images fit better because they help me realize that there are several ways of being woman, not just what my mother taught me. Yet 'Goddess' sounds pagan and the word sticks in my throat. Maybe the 'divine feminine' is more palatable."[49]

~

"God 'the father' still dominates my image of God, although I try very much to change that to a more female image. I regret that my gut feeling image of God is male. Intellectually, I reject a completely male God, but twenty years of indoctrination is hard to overcome."[50]

~

"This was not very effective for me, that Christ is a concept and a condition beyond the historical Jesus and that the force in the universe which loves me is very female. I can't entirely rub out the male/flesh image of my youth and of my parents' teaching, and I can't talk in the other, more mystical terms to most Mormons who would be confused at my departure from orthodoxy. So I retain the 'Heavenly Father' image at church functions, and in private prayer and with select friends, I feel free to range, to explore the nature of truth in more satisfactory metaphors — as female, as consciousness, as light, as duality."[51]

~

"Mormonism has a long-standing concept of a Mother in Heaven, which Mormon feminists find compelling. However, in true patriarchal fashion, her role traditionally has been defined as that of an eternal homemaker, the perfect wife and mother, a sort of divine Donna Reed with God the Father as the presiding authority. Obviously Mormon feminists reject this construct while exploring the possibility, for many the reality, of a female deity. Most remain relatively literal in describing the gender and personal attributes of God the Father and Mother. This is partly because Mormons are materialists. Spirit is seen as 'more refined matter.' Interestingly, the traditional dualism which has associated the female with the material, and therefore the corrupt, is not the problem in Mormon thought that it has been in traditional Christianity. Of course, one of the problems with such literal-mindedness is that it has to this point reinforced traditional, patriarchal patterns by giving them eternal significance. Thus the prospect for a radical shift away from patriarchy among the male church hierarchy is dim."[52]

~

"Growing into and owning feminine images of God seems to require a being present to the expressed pain of women who have suffered discrimination and slavery to the patriarchal powers of the church. I mourn the slowness of the clergy to help us bring to birth this enlarged experience of God which we have been deprived of all these centuries. Receiving no help with this in the worship of my church, I often feel isolated and alone in this interior evolution. It is a struggle to grow beyond one's secure understanding of the Divine into something unknown, unconfirmed, untaught, and for which one may become the target of ridicule or criticism. Yet it is a Way, once taken, one cannot return to that old comfortable place. The comfort of knowing a 'good Mother God' and all the attending rich symbols and metaphors fills me with joy some days, and confusion other days when I do not know what to do with that old and familiar Father, and God becomes once again mystery-unity-source-creator-love. It is a struggle worth taking, but gives me pause before initiating another to join me on the Way."[53]

~

"I cannot relate to God as Father or as male. My experience of my own father, along with traditional church images of God as Father, had a negative effect on my ability to trust God. My father was domineering, intrusive, controlling, abusive, and belittling to my mother in my presence, always right, could always tell better than myself when I was telling the truth. I lived in fear of him and could do little but withdraw emotionally to survive. Even after I was 'born again' in college (out of fear of going to hell), I felt that my faith was just a head trip. My experience in the 'traditional church' — even my current parish — has little to offer me. It is through feminist theology, twelve-step spirituality, and Goddess and other non-Christian approaches to God that I have found what I need to try to transcend my 'programmed expectations' of God."[54]

~

"I believe issues of female influence (symbolically, spiritually, psychologically, and in body) are central to the salvation of our limping world. I am a feminist, not an anti-maleist. As within each of us (individually), male and female need to be united under one rubric within our planet and our total concept of reality. God encompasses all, and we are foolish to try to say this is of God (male) and this is not of God (female). This is true for all existence. Spirit is an active guide where allowed in. Without the guide of Spirit, human whim reigns supreme, but not always wise."[55]

~

"I believe God is male, but I also personally believe we have an as-yet unknown Heavenly Mother, for if we were created in 'His' image, and we are earthly children of Heavenly Parents, then there must be a mother/female up there somewhere. It is not important for me to know more about 'her' at this stage."[56]

~

"As recently as 1984, I was resistant to a women's group at our church that was exploring goddess worship and pagan ritual. The primary participants were a little intimidating to me. Besides, I didn't believe in or worship a male God; why should I evoke the Goddess? Today I am much more interested in feminine imagery for God, and I have preached on feminist theology. I am increasingly irritated by exclusive people-language and God-language. My prayers are generally addressed to a gender-neutral Being—Creator God, Holy One, etc."[57]

~

"The congregation has accepted use of inclusive language for the human family, but most members are threatened by varied images of God. My husband is the pastor of the church. While he favors more use of female imagery and names for God, he does not have the same sense of urgency or feelings of anger that I have."[58]

~

After moving to a rural area from the big city and a feminist Presbyterian church, I started to attend a Methodist church, since the choices were Methodist or Roman Catholic. The male-oriented symbols of God and the 'our heavenly Father' invocations drove me crazy after six years of inclusive terms and a feminist perspective. I find a certain comfort in the Goddess writings as well as Zen Buddhist writings. When I find a void I cannot completely fill by reading, I'll probably reach out and find a group, even if I have to drive back to the city."[59]

~

"I struggle and still hold on to, in some ways, my childhood sense of a punishing, judgmental, authoritative God and work on an ongoing basis to change that image."[60]

~

"Until the institution pays attention to female deity, it will hold little meaning for me. Historically, women have had to translate whatever the male norm is. It is a tiresome, enervating activity that makes no sense. It is important to talk about *women and femaleness and Goddess* while we make the transition from a patriarchal church centered on *men and maleness and God.* If we talk of androgyny only, we deny the validity of our sexuality and also bypass the store of past mistakes and the resulting emotions accumulated around the centrality of maleness. Organized religion tends to validate as well as reflect society. We must explore all the corners and certainly also discuss the church as validator of patriarchy. A good dose of goddess talk might shock us into recognition."[61]

~

"I personally feel very comfortable with the father image. I was abandoned by my father and was raised in the 'company of women,' so I see women as competent, autonomous, etc. and God was, from an early age, a projection of what I thought 'father' should be. I counsel many women who see God as the father who abandoned, punished, etc. How much does one projection or the other prevent the accessibility of God?"[62]

~

"Mary has an important place in Catholic worship, my worship. I feel close to her 'womanness' and call on her often to intercede on occasions which necessitate compassion and understanding. Because of Mary's place in Catholic worship and the many women saints and lives which populate the Bible, I am not frustrated by a He-God, although I don't believe that God is either a He or She."[63]

~

"It is of critical importance for us to use female imagery and language in our God-talk, especially since we have made such exclusive use of male imagery and language until very recently. But I would also like to put in a plea for gender-neutral language as well. No, gender-neutral language is *not* good enough to satisfy me, not all the time anyway. But I do not want to imply in word or deed that God our Mother is not great enough to include references to God our Father, or to imply that women are more fully in God's image than men. I realize we are far from that extreme in the church right now. It is, nevertheless, an extreme which I believe we must not allow to happen."[64]

~

"There needs to be much more emphasis on the important role that women play in the world and in the spiritual life of all human beings. I don't believe in an anthropomorphic Goddess/God, but do feel more comfortable with female values and images."[65]

~

"I have a very strong father image of God. This image nurtured me during the years of my earthly father's alcoholism. Now that my earthly father has quit drinking and seems to be experiencing some healing within himself, I wonder if I will start to explore more the feminine side of God."[66]

~

"I find the most resistance to feminist theology coming from women themselves. Most of the women in my congregation hit the roof if I mess with God language to make it inclusive. God as Mother is not well accepted. Jesus called God 'Father' and that's good enough for them."[67]

~

"I believe all language about human beings should be inclusive. I do *not* think God-language should be. This is not because I think of God as exclusively male. I am a strong believer in the androgyny of God. Most 'inclusive' God-language is impersonal, and I find this contributing further to the (primarily male) overemphasis on transcendence at the expense of immanence in God. I am powerfully convinced that all theologies, all other 'religions,' *must* be addressing the same Unknown. The different religions, and their subdivisions into varying theologies, correspond to different languages. All of us have a 'mother tongue' (our religion/theology either of birth or choice), but that in no way invalidates other 'tongues.' God is polylingual. They are all 'mother-tongue' for God."[68]

~

"I remember reading in a Quaker journal once that 'we may not all worship the same God; but there is only one God for us all to worship.' I believe that women have a very important role to play in the common bonding of spiritually committed people across faith and denominational lines. We should work to forward the concept of universal spiritual bonding."[69]

~

"I have some antipathy, which I don't understand, to the idea of *my* personal image of God being goddess. Since I think feminine as well as masculine images of God are valid, and that the feminine images have been ignored and suppressed, I don't know why I resist the goddess stuff so. Maybe because, as far as I know, it's outside Hebrew, Christian, and Islamic scriptures. I'm a monotheist, and maybe I see goddess theology as polytheistic. Or maybe goddesses are too sexy for me! I really think of God as sexless — that's essential to my theology — *genderless*, I mean, encompassing all sex, complete. My definition of 'God' is both male and female. My definition of 'goddess' is only female. I am a poet and do not accept being called poetess. Same applies to my God. Because (perhaps) of a conflicted relationship with my mother, and because I saw third-grade girls turning on one another, I learned not to trust women in general, though fortunately, I have trusted some in particular. Now I have more understanding of my antipathy to goddess. I've just explained it to myself. Thanks!"[70]

~

"I am personally in a very lonely place spiritually. I see the need to develop my own unique image and understanding of God in relationship to me and others. I find little or no help within my faith community. I attend a parish church with my family. The parish is noted for its alive, healthy, committed nature, but I do not feel a part of it because of the total disregard of a need for inclusive language in the liturgy. I'm hanging in there, but there's not much joy or celebration in my heart."[71]

~

"It is vital for me to try to understand a relation to the transcendent that has never had to bow to patriarchy."[72]

~

"I now happily call myself a post-Christian and am exploring other forms of worship that focus on a female image of the divine. It's not that I reject male images of God. However, I currently feel a need to emphasize female aspects as a corrective to the almost totally male images I have lived with most of my life. I feel very much in transition, on a voyage of discovery. I know that I image the goddess as _within_ rather than outside or over, but some of the implications of this image are not yet clear to me."[73]

~

"In public worship I use the traditional Father/Son/Holy Spirit formula — but privately I invoke God as female. I love scripture and regularly find, beneath the patriarchal imprint, the substance which is the Wisdom of God."[74]

~

"When I get really stressed out about these issues, I stop reading, I stop listening, I stop paying attention, and instead I float along in some fetal mental place where God and I are connected in some primal, effortless way. I have learned to trust God to keep connected to me too."[75]

~

"I believe in Goddess — a transcendent, loving energy/spirit linking all life together, a Goddess of justice and equality. She may be glimpsed in churches and speaks to all human beings."[76]

~

"I have found God in the well deep within me, but it is not clear to me where I stop and where God begins. Not two. Not one. God is *someone* I love, in whom I exist."[77]

~

"My own faith development is in constant change, but with it my belief in women's equality both in and before the Divine is growing daily. My dream is for an understanding that we are all created in God's image and likeness that is lived out in reality. As a result of this, every created being is given due respect and loving care. And God is recognized as being beyond male or female, but the fullness and more of both. The absolute fullness of creative love, community of love."[78]

~

"I must admit that as I get older, I pray and sing less in images than in presence."[79]

Spirit, the Spiritual, Spirituality

"I see many good spirits sucked dry by trying to make changes in an institution that neither respects them nor wants their involvement in the fullness of who we are. When women wait until their spirit has been wiped out before stepping out of the male-run church, we often have trouble resuscitating our spiritual lives and need to celebrate them in community."[80]

~

"The new consciousness and convictions that have grown in me about women in the church have broken up my old patterns of relatedness with the institutional church. This has left me with much pain and some anxiety about being disconnected from what used to be a source of spiritual strength. But I experience a deeper fidelity and sense of peace in enduring the pain and anxiety than in denying the reality of my new consciousness and beliefs. I am finding hope and comfort as I discover more and more women and some men who are undergoing the same eruption/disruption in their spiritual evolution."[81]

~

"Before attending seminary, I was very involved in a co-ed group focusing on spiritual growth. I found this exciting and liberating. At the first seminary I attended, I was part of a community which also was supportive of spiritual growth. Then I transferred to my denomination's seminary. Spiritual growth was discouraged. There I learned to theologize with my head instead of my gut and experiences. Ten years later, I am still trying to undo the damage this has done to me."[82]

~

"My church (religious) upbringing rooted me in relating and meaning and shifting and sorting and connecting in ways that have both hindered and helped me in journeying ever deeper and wider as a 'spiritual' person. I've been redefining for a long time. I'm comfortable with God-talk, with non-God-talk, and lots of places in between. I love *talk* which connects and probes and illuminates, and confronts sometimes. It's one wonderful way of being spiritual for me. *Talk!*"[83]

~

"Artificial barriers which limit persons from exploring, choosing, and becoming that which God designed them to do and be must be brought into focus, weakened, and removed, until only those limits which God placed so perfectly to guide us into growth remain."[84]

~

"Women's spirituality and their belief in themselves as valued human beings needs to be encouraged, supported, and celebrated!"[85]

~

"I hope we can move spirituality from a feminist/womanist perspective from the pockets off the main garment (women's groups, prayer groups, etc.) to center-bodice. The key to that still seems to be in women valuing *themselves* enough to trust their beliefs and feel they (person and beliefs) are worthwhile and of value. And that requires a spirituality and theology that is feminist. It's a slow-moving circle, but I believe the Divine Good is spinning it. We are moving, we are moving...."[86]

~

"How deeply I have experienced my connection with God/Universe/Goddess through the small spirituality group in which I participate. In weaving together the interpersonal associations within the group that have enabled us to worship together, we have created a beautiful fabric of selves and spirit. I had given up on this ever being possible. And yet — here it is!"[87]

~

"I talk regularly on the phone with a woman who is deeply spiritual. She is a lay person, was very active in the church, became disillusioned and tired of meetings, so attends sporadically but finds many ways to nurture herself spiritually. We share in depth about our relationship to God. She is my spiritual mentor. I also see a woman therapist every other week. She is an ordained Episcopalian priest and is very helpful in all areas of my life. This is important to my spiritual growth."[88]

~

"I have undergone a major shift in the nature of my beliefs this past year. Part of the process of questioning traditional views of God, the Divine, and the nature of faith has been a profound psychological/ spiritual crisis in my life during the past year or two from which I am beginning to emerge. This has involved a journey stemming from something I agreed to do as a 'good Christian' that had a devastating impact on my life but got me in rather direct contact with the child within me who had been sexually and emotionally abused as a child. So, for the past year, I've been going through the painful process of reconnecting with this child and trying to put back the pieces of my life."[89]

~

"Women have been alienated from spiritual endeavors by men for eons. It is time we acknowledged this and the importance of spirituality in our lives. If we are not included in the 'traditional' faiths, then it's time we create our own religion(s)."[90]

~

"I am married to a clergyperson. I was very involved in leadership within the church through college. After marriage and becoming a minister's wife, I completely lost my sense of identity as a person and within the church. Spirituality has remained important, but denominational Christianity seems very limited and permeated by a subtle rigidity. I am by far more comfortable with an expanded belief system that incorporates the unconscious, the superconscious, feminism, Indian spirituality, metaphysics, new age concepts, reincarnation, etc. I have taught many spirituality workshops — inner healing workshops. My friends say I'm a 'cutting-edge' person that helps lead the way. I am within the organized church, but this is not where I find spiritual nourishment."[91]

~

"I've struggled to find a church which could be a spiritual home. I have not found it in the Presbyterian Church. I have a physical disability. During the severe time of my injury, surgery, and recovery, I found my church at the time to be helpful. However, my condition is now chronic, and in some ways invisible, and I have found neither comfort nor help as a woman, nor as a person with a disability. For lack of anything else, I have created a personal spiritual center (altar) in a space in my home and, with the use of books (feminist spirituality) and tapes, I create spiritual times. I long for soul mates but don't know where to look."[92]

~

"I am a member of Dignity and find a good deal of my spiritual needs as an individual and a woman met there."[93]

~

"I believe we can learn a lot from children, and that we must pay careful attention to our use of images and attitudes in their overall, as well as spiritual, development."[94]

~

"My recent interest in Native Americans is, I believe, a spiritual search, a quest for a unity of life that connects me to the past, to nature, to others, and to myself. But I can change denominations more easily than I can change ethnicity. Because I am middle-aged, I am interested in how the place in the life-cycle influences our spirituality. I have always been spiritual but have only recently discovered that I am not religious (in the church's definition). I believe that the institutional church cannot minister to my spiritual needs, even though I am a member of a congregation that has two outstanding female pastors on its staff."[95]

~

"My experience with religion has always been somewhat obscure, but my spiritual experiences have been extremely profound! The religions that have made an impression on me are of Eastern origin — Tao, Tibetan, Hindu, and also the ancient matrilinear cultures. The writings have clear messages on balancing the male/female energies within an individual, regardless of gender differences. And when this occurs, it allows the balanced energy to merge and move into a higher vibrational level, which is what the Buddha, Christ, Nirvana, etc. state is all about. Yes, it is a state of grace. This process is different for everyone. I've experienced this briefly and profoundly. We, especially women, have been shut off from the true knowledge of what and who we are and what we can become: beings of Light manifested on the physical plane to experience the feeling world without guilt, fear, shame; to experience our incredible lightness of being; to sound forth our individual note and merge it with the universal song. And what we need is very simple: clean air, clean water, clean food, movement and touching laced with feelings and love, to grow up and transform back into the light above."[96]

~

"I think we need to step back from our religions and focus more on our spirituality and personal relationship with God."[97]

~

"I think the power of women's spirituality lies in the opportunities it creates for helping us make meaning in our lives. This world has a long way to go before all that happens in women's spirituality groups can be incorporated into the traditional life of the church. Every woman should have the opportunity to be a part of a women-only group for at least ten years."[98]

~

"I believe that women's spirituality is a challenge to institutional religion. We speak a lot about 'subverting the dominant paradigms' in education, psychology, ethics, politics, and spirituality. My hunch is that women are instinctively ecumenical. They are much more comfortable with ambiguity and uncertainty, so do not have to have religious doctrines clearly defined. I'm thinking more and more about different denominations and religions simply being an expression of diversity. Why are we so intent or anxious about convincing people that one denomination or faith tradition has more access to God?"[99]

~

"In general, I feel very frustrated with organized religions, largely because of their lack of concern regarding women's issues. The last couple of years I have let myself drift away from 'religious' activities and have become more interested in my own spiritual quest or my efforts to understand God, my place in the universe, etc. My goal for the next five years is to find a cohesive, stable community in which to further explore these issues. Whether this community manifests itself as a church, a group of friends, or something else remains to be seen."[100]

~

"I've found it very difficult to find a spiritual peace today. I enjoy Quaker practice but have not been interested in joining an organized religion. I feel I'd be more interested in a spirituality-based group. I'd like to learn how women find a place for themselves in a male-based religious philosophy which has historically been oppressive, whether intentionally or not."[101]

~

"I am currently — and have for some time — been investigating my own spiritual inclinations, which are very vague at this point. I was not raised with any religious faith whatsoever, nor do I have one now. I did look into Christian denominations, but was alienated *very* quickly by many of the tenets, inherent value judgments, and what I felt to be twisted or skewed belief systems. I also felt a very strong anti-female bias, which was quite off-putting. At this point my inclinations are moving toward a symbolic, immanent-transcendent God/dess belief system on a personal, individual level, but they are only inclinations at this point in time."[102]

~

"Although historically Protestant, I am not affiliated with any congregation, nor have I been for some time. I would not say I am even Christian. Yet spiritual concerns are deeply important to me and to many others like me who, for various reasons, are not starting from within existing congregations, nor are we likely to ever be part of one again. Affiliated with 'open' groups of spiritually oriented persons, yes, but!"[103]

~

"I am pulled between the idea that the parish should be the center of my worshiping life and the fact that the most spiritually enriching experiences that I have had have not occurred in the parish."[104]

~

"Too many churches are simply into maintaining the institution rather than focusing upon spiritual growth. Spirituality, becoming whole and bringing wholeness to the universe, is so often lost in the midst of church politics — a tragic commentary! Raising our consciousness makes a great difference in perceptions and in our actions."[105]

~

"The church, both clergy and laity, have not yet taken seriously — at grassroots — the theological or ecclesial implications of the feminine dimension in all creation and in God, and implications for spiritual growth. In my work in the church I have found the most response, energy, and hunger in the area of spirituality. I believe this hunger will eventually change the structure and mission of the church."[106]

~

"My own spiritual growth has suffered since I've been ordained and worked full-time in the church, and I am beginning to reclaim that. I am concerned that clergy seem to provide *religiosity* for the (passive) congregation, rather than challenge them to develop their own spirituality. I find myself juggling several roles/goals, striving to be a senior pastor of a large church, a spiritually grounded person, wife, mother, and wholistically healthy and healed. I find that I *must* have time away with women to nurture and empower myself."[107]

~

"Until last year, women's spirituality was an extremely important issue for me, and I felt a strong desire to be part of a group focused on that issue. This summer my church had a week at the beach together which included daily a women's spirituality group, and also a spirituality group for the men. The women's group decided to continue meeting monthly. I elected to be part of that group, but I find that some of my passion for and need for a women's group has dissipated. My spiritual focus has extended to all of creation over the past year. As I became less self-conscious, I began to notice all the natural parts of God's creation and was filled with a desire to know their names. Human relationships continue to be important, but the hours I spend alone in the woods seem equally important."[108]

~

"This survey made me realize how little time I have devoted in the past year to my spiritual growth. But that is because I have a ten-month-old daughter, and I tend to believe that God the Mother regards the care of babies as an act of worship in itself."[109]

~

"I am an incest survivor and my former therapist often prayed with me at the end of a session. It was a wonderful learning experience for both of us. I have survived and will continue to grow as my faith grows."[110]

~

"While my sense of God in my life is a powerful one, I receive little nourishment from the worship services provided by the institutional church. I find that the RC Church is an expression of almost total male spirituality. Perhaps that is why I have chosen women to direct my retreats for the past fifteen years."[111]

~

"Women, in my perspective, are not united enough to create change in the church. We need to undo the 'tapes' we've received and re-think and re-create new images, symbols, pathways to reflect our spirituality."[112]

~

"I do not consider religion to be a positive aspect of my life but prefer to identify more with spirituality, which is the most important aspect of my life. My thought is that dogma removes from spirituality the very essence of its power, which is direct knowing of spirit."[113]

~

"I think healing the inner child in all of us is the most exciting spiritual movement in this country. Churches frustrate me. Co-dependency flourishes."[114]

~

"I believe women's role in religion is in a state of transition and will change much over the next decade. Women in my age group are re-discovering their spirituality and this trend will change religion in America."[115]

~

"Two years ago I chose to leave the yoked (two church) parish I was serving. Doing so felt an important step to reclaim authenticity. I had done everything 'right,' i.e., followed the male model for ministry, but it didn't feel right. As an older woman who had raised four children before getting a college education, I experienced myself as not having had adequate opportunity to explore the world physically or intellec-tually. As a result the dogma/doctrines/theology of the patriarchy, with my belated exposure, became increasingly untenable as I was faced with the weekly task of preaching. I needed to find my own voice. For the past one and a half years I've been engaged in a program of study which has provided the setting where I can follow the movement of the Spirit. That Spirit has led me into some pretty interesting stuff — the role of the feminine in history, especially studies of the Goddess in the pre-Christian world; why the patriarchy has had such a vested interest in monotheism, accompanied by attempts to expunge the influence of the feminine from religion, both divine and human; the need for goddess archetypes in the psychological well-being of females; the ways in which masculine (linear) thinking has led to the exploitation of people and the earth's resources; the need for reclaiming of the feminine (intuitive, nonrational, communal, all-encompassing perspective) in order to restore feeling, creativity, joy, sensuality, *juiciness* to life. I'm quite excited about what is happening in my life right now, but of course it leaves my relationship to the institutional church up for grabs."[116]

~

"I have been practicing the Transcendental Meditation technique for many years and, while not a religious practice, it has provided me with a way to regularly experience an inner silence that, to me, is the basis of spirituality."[117]

~

"I see emerging today, in groups of people and groups of women, a quest for spirituality, a hunger for God and for meaning, for religion with power, and they are not finding it in traditional churches. Some leave, some remain connected but are walking a spiritual path that departs from the tradition they were raised in. Women in particular, in my experience, are on this quest for God. They may name it by different names, but ultimately, it is a seeking for nurturance for their souls, and for some, for the finding of their own souls. And they are discovering God in the poor, in the earth, with other women in small groups, doing liturgy and worshiping God, and for me, this is church in its truest and deepest meaning."[118]

~

"I have been struck recently by a realization, rather a connection, between the old feminist saying, 'the personal is political,' and discussions in my faith community over what is spiritual and what is political. Many women of Christian heritage seek a spiritual center of some sort and, for women, spirituality often is a *very* personal aspect of themselves. I wish, however, to have spirituality examined in an amplified way, to draw connections between what I very *privately* say and feel toward God and how I interact, behave, cope, make decisions in my faith community and in the larger world. The personal *is* political, and for me, it has only been recently that I have been able to articulate to my friends in faith/women-church that my political work *is* my spirituality. Too often, other women bypass or avoid hard issues, ethical questions, and try to focus the group more 'spiritually,' as if turning our eyes heavenward would help us more than frankly facing and engaging with each other. 'Political' has been a tough word for Christian women, yet we cannot evade it. We are spiritual, we have private lives, and there is a personal aspect to each one of us. The *spiritual* must straddle both what is *personal* and what is *political*. It will also inform what is private, but what is private should remain so. Work — much work and hard work — must be done to articulate and define this, and apply it to our lived experiences as Christians, and as women."[119]

~

"Most women I know are deeply interested in spiritual matters. We long for new challenges in our spiritual growth that take us and our experiences seriously. We long to learn to do an authentic theology that is *ours* — not imposed upon us. We long to share and celebrate our stories and the wisdom gained. We long to be free to sing our songs!"[120]

~ ~ ~

For a growing number of women in the church, a new spirituality is emerging.

As women struggle to integrate the God of religion with the God of their experience, the life of the spirit within them deepens and their perspective changes. In exploring new names and new images for God, women are encountering "She Who Is" in biblical and goddess traditions,[121] reaching for female role models in scripture and in society,[122] and giving birth to liturgies and rituals that seek to redefine religion and reshape their spiritual life.[123] Women are preaching from their changed perspective[124] in a language they comprehend.[125] Like yeast, they are there in the communities of believers, desiring transformation, and like bread, their voices are rising.[126] This feminist spirituality, rooted in women's reality, earth-centered and embodied, is oriented toward global justice, sensitive to sisterhood, and seeking a connection to all living things.[127] While it may seem that the focus is on the externals, such as language and leadership, such issues are the strategies for approaching and effecting change.

~

The women in this study want inclusive language to be used in all church worship.

A large majority of the women in this ecumenical sample want inclusive language. They want this inclusiveness to extend not only to relational language but also to images and names for God. Of those surveyed, 84 percent feel inclusive language should be integral to all church worship. Only 6 percent disagree. At the same time, 79 percent feel there should be more hymns and prayers using female imagery and names for God. Only 10 percent disagree. Women who are in feminist spirituality groups score 93 percent affirmative for inclusive language and 92 percent regarding female images and names for God.

Because this is a feminist sample, these results may well be expected. What is surprising, however, is the high percentage of affirmation from women in more theologically traditional groups. Three-fourths of these women (76 percent) also want inclusive language in *all* church worship, while two-thirds (67 percent) want their hymns and prayers to include female images and names for God. This report focused on feminist spirituality groups for the more feminist aspects of our sample, yet here is indisputable evidence that feminists, or women with feminist tendencies, are not only in feminist contexts but in traditional settings as well. Since women share with other women and feminists invariably influence others, it seems reasonable to suspect that women in theologically traditional contexts who support inclusive language and image God in female terms are important agents for effecting change in parishes and congregations.

~

The women in this study are likely to have a number of images of God.

In April of 1992 a headline on the front page of the *Wall Street Journal* read: "Image of God as 'He' Loses Its Sovereignty in America's Churches." A subhead of this article by R. Gustav Niebuhr announced: "More Worshipers Challenge Language That Describes Supreme Being as Male." Sweeping social shifts "have crashed against the ancient Christian picture of the cosmos." These changes, which Niebuhr attributes primarily to the influence of feminism, are deeply troubling to some who are committed to a male image of God and to others who are more concerned that the loss of a shared image of God will lead to "confusion" among Christians and dissension in the churches.

For the past twenty years feminists have been publicly challenging exclusively masculine images of God. Mary Daly led the way in 1973 with the publication of *Beyond God the Father* and her blunt assessment: "If God is male, then the male is God." Since then feminist scholars have continued to show the feminine aspect of God in the Bible and its incarnational presence in history. Social psychologists and others have pointed out that the picture one holds of God and the kind of relationship one feels is possible with God are extremely important to an individual's personal adjustment and self-esteem and for the transformation of society. Women writers within the last decade have stressed how vital it is to women's self-esteem to see God as in part female.[128]

Opportunities for women to see God as more than just male are emerging in popular culture and consciousness. Jean Shinoda Bolen's *Goddesses in Everywoman* is teaching women the value of seeing the goddess in themselves. Gloria Steinem, sounding like feminist theologians, explains in her autobiography that "any religion in which God looks suspiciously like the ruling class is very different from spirituality that honors the godliness in each of us."[129] Steinem is popularizing something that researchers doing image of God studies have known for some time: there is a relationship between concepts of God and concepts of self. She asks: "If men had grown up seeing God portrayed only as Mother and She, would they feel an equal godliness within themselves?"[130] In her own imaging of God, Steinem experiences a return of self-esteem and spiritual connectedness that she never knew was missing or even possible. Yet no matter how valuable it may be for women to see God as in part female, most churches remain staunchly patriarchal in official language, leadership, and liturgy. Images of God reflect and legitimate a male-dominated culture and, as such, will not easily change.

A question fundamental to this study is: *How do women who are typically well-educated feminists and at least nominally Christian envision God?* A second question accompanies the first. *What particular "cultural milieus" appear to influence their perception of the Divine?*

Our data show that the great majority of women respondents are inclined to have shifting, changing images of God and not one or two clear, definite images (see Tables 7, 8A, and 8B, pp. 267, 268, 269). They do see God as Father or as Mother at least to *some* extent, but only one-fifth (21 percent) say they envision God as Father or as Mother to a *great* extent. Half the sample see Jesus as a major figure in their image of God. But if women were to choose *one* image that is most important or pivotal in their conception of God, it would be "Encompassing Presence."

For the women in our sample, images such as "Encompassing Presence," "Wisdom," "Liberator," and "Help" are considerably more a part of their overall conception of God than images of God as "Father," "Mother," "Jesus," "Goddess," or even "Father-Mother" or the

Trinity (Father, Son, Spirit).[131] These findings are in accord with Rosemary Ruether's recent observations that Catholic feminists affirm God as "beyond gender, literally neither male nor female."[132] Research shows that African American clergywomen envision God more as a creative force than as a male figure, and that this is also true for Hispanic women.[133]

Although the dominant images of God are not personified as male or female for the majority of the women in our sample, when God does take a gendered form, is it as female or as male? Most people do not worship God as "it," but rather as "he" and, to a much lesser extent, as "she."[134] While God may be seen primarily as genderless in this sample, God-imagery tends to become gendered in church services as God the Father, God the Son, or "Mother God." Furthermore, many women who stay within the Christian churches, as well as those who have left, do espouse "goddess" imagery for the divine, although seldom exclusively. Therefore, whether God is envisioned mainly as genderless or whether God is depicted as more male than female is a question that assumes importance for reasons already stated: a female rather than a male image of God is important for women's self-esteem and growth, and a *strong* female image of God can be revolutionary for Christian churches.

Among the gendered identities for God, Jesus is clearly preferred by all groups, with the exception of the more conservative Protestant laywomen, who prefer "Father." As some feminist scholars speculate, Jesus may not be seen by some Christian feminists as personifying a male image but rather a concept.[135] Jesus is given the greatest emphasis among the African American and Hispanic American women. This may in part be due to a more traditional theology, but it is also because the male identity of Jesus is of minor importance compared to other aspects, namely, Jesus as liberator and help to the suffering and downtrodden.[136]

An androgynous Mother-Father is more acceptable to this sample than either Mother or Father, again with the exception of women in the more conservative Protestant denominations, who prefer the Father image. The Mother image of God is lowest among Catholic and liberal Protestant laywomen. It is highest among racial-ethnic minority women, particularly African Americans, and among women in the more conservative denominations, but for different reasons. In historic black religion, women's experience was not only incorporated into prayer, song, and testimony, but it was formative. Even in preaching, traditionally a male preserve, women's experience and female images of God were lifted up.[137] A national study done in 1991 found that African Americans, as well as Asian Americans, are more likely to endorse a Mother image of God than those of Anglo-European origins, in part because in these cultural groups "mothers" are respected as powerful figures.[138] Conservative Protestant and Mormon women endorse a mother image probably less as a strong, independent female deity and more as a supportive mother-wife for the Father. This is particularly the case for this sample, since the majority of the conservatives here are Mormons, for whom a distinct Mother God fulfills this role.

At first glance Catholic and liberal Protestant laywomen indicate surprisingly less enthusiasm for Mother as an image for God. The reason is that they prefer "Goddess" for a female God-image instead of a parental image. The Goddess image is seen as a major aspect of the Divine by between 20 and 25 percent of most subgroupings in this sample. This suggests that some may equate Goddess with Mother God, while others may see Goddess as outside of or challenging the patriarchal Christian images. For Catholic feminists the Goddess image is a strong Sophia or other goddess image quite distinct from Mary as Theotokos (Mother of God) or Mediatrix or Queen of Heaven and Earth.

Seeing God as either Goddess or Mother is apt to be a "feminist" perspective in this sample as a whole. Envisioning God as a female, rather than without gender, or especially rather than male, is significantly associated with women's holding what are usually deemed "feminist" values regarding women's role in church and society. For example, women who endorse affirmative action are significantly more likely to see God as "Goddess," but definitely not as "Father" or "Master." Not surprisingly, inclusive language is supported more by women who image God as Goddess or Mother, or even as Father-Mother, rather than as mainly Father or Master. Seeing God as Jesus has little impact on whether or not women want inclusive language. Still, Jesus is somewhat more likely to be associated with the nonfeminist positions than with feminist ones, while Father is more consistently related to nonfeminist positions as Goddess is related to feminist ones.

Generally, those who put great emphasis on male images of God, and this includes the Jesus image, are happier in the institutional church than those who endorse distinctly female images. Envisioning God as primarily genderless or androgynous is usually unrelated to alienation from the institutional church. The fact that two-thirds of this sample often feel alienated from the institutional church may well be because of the male imagery for God supporting and supported by the predominantly male church leadership.

~

Jesus and Goddess are compatible God-images in the God-language of many women in this study.

A major concern of many Catholic bishops and of Protestant leaders as well is: To what extent will women speaking of God as "Goddess" totally reject the Christian church because Jesus was a male? Bishop John Sheets wants the Catholic bishops to condemn the women's movement for this reason. Rosemary Ruether counters with the observation that the bishop has completely misunderstood the nature of Catholic feminism. Believing in the divinity of Jesus and also seeing the Divine as in part Goddess are not necessarily in theological opposition. According to Ruether, Catholic feminists see God as mainly beyond gender, but also include Jesus in their total imagery of the Divine.[139] This study supports Ruether's contention, not only for Catholics, but for Christian feminists in many denominations.

When we examine the God-images selected by women in this study, the major cluster of images reveals an overall conception of the Divine as One who is healing, creative, helpful, friendly, wise, genderless — *and* the image of Jesus. The more conservative women and those who are of racial-ethnic minority backgrounds also include the Father–Son–Holy Spirit Trinity in this major cluster. Goddess is part of the second major cluster and is generally envisioned as both within women as they interact with others and as a force in opposition to the paternal and male power figures of God. Although neither Jesus nor Goddess is among the top ten God-images of women in this study, they warrant some comparative analysis.

Do women in all social contexts see the same gendered images of God as having the same characteristics? They do not. This is apparent when the images of "Jesus" and "Goddess" are grouped with other images. Jesus appears to be seen in two different ways: as part of the power Trinity headed by the Father, or as a supportive, loving protector and advisor. Catholic Sisters to some extent combine these categories. They see Jesus as part of the Trinity, but also as loving, helpful protector and friend. Protestant clergywomen see Jesus mainly as a helpful friend, but not necessarily as part of any Holy Family. Laywomen — Catholic and Protestant, both liberal and conservative — see Jesus more as part of the power Trinity of Father–Son–Spirit, with the role of Master and Judge.

Asian Americans see Jesus as part of the Trinity headed by the Father, and little else. In contrast African Americans and Hispanic Americans perceive Jesus as their liberator as well as a divine friend. African American women have the most inclusive conception of Jesus of all of the subgroupings in this sample. They see Jesus as part of the

Trinity, but also as embodying strong, protective, wise, helpful aspects that make him their champion.

Catholic Sisters see the Goddess differently than Catholic lay-women. Sisters tend to see the Goddess as present in women through an emerging connection with others and as an elemental force that will challenge patriarchy. Catholic laywomen in this sample, however, are more inclined to see the Goddess as a warmer Mother Goddess or as part of a dual Mother-Father divinity. This distinction may well be due to the lived realities of these subgroups. When women begin to see themselves as truly created in God's image, it is natural for them to image God as a reflection of themselves. For those women who may be mothers and wives or whose primary concern is the fam-ily, the Goddess of their experience is the maternal one who gives birth, nurtures her young, has concern and compassion for all living things, and may be in partnership with another. Showing some sim-ilarity to Catholic Sisters, Protestant clergywomen see the Goddess as a strong elemental force, but one that can destroy as well as cre-ate and one that is everywhere, not only within but between persons. The Goddess conception of liberal Protestant laywomen is like that of liberal Protestant clergywomen. The conservative laywomen's concep-tion, however, is nearly identical to that held by Catholic laywomen, that is, Goddess is a Mother God serving with the Father and the Son.

If women in the denominational or racial-ethnic groupings here see Jesus as part of the power Trinity, they are likely to see the God-dess also in more parental terms, as providing the more maternal aspect. This is true for Catholic laywomen in the sample and for con-servative Protestants and Mormons, and also for Asian Americans. On the other hand, if women in the sample see Jesus as more of a friend, protector, and help, they are likely to view the Goddess as a powerful figure and force within and beyond humankind, but not part of any Divine Family grouping. Jesus as friend and Goddess as a potent Spirit within women is more the orientation of Catholic Sisters, Protestant clergywomen, and African American women.

Laywomen in liberal Protestant denominations depart from these patterns. While they see Jesus as part of the power Trinity, they do *not* envision the Goddess as a warm mother figure, but as a mighty female divinity, another power, a separate force.

For most women in this sample, Jesus is associated with the gen-tlest images of God and is humanly helpful and accessible. Even though Jesus is also part of the power Trinity headed by the Father, it is the supportive qualities that prevail. Goddess, for the most part, is a force or a power within and between and among humankind but also in all of creation.

Reflecting on these findings, one may conclude that those who accept both Jesus and Goddess as legitimate manifestations of divinity tend to balance both human factors and elemental forces in a harmonization of contrasting images. If one is friend, the other is a force to be reckoned with. If one is accessible and approachable, the other is much less so. If one is a familial figure, the other is elemental spirit. Liberal Protestant laywomen, for whom Jesus and the Goddess are in potential conflict, show a departure from this pattern. For some women Jesus is liberator from racial or social oppression. For others Goddess is the liberating force who will challenge and dismantle patriarchy to set her people free. While women in the study tend to image God in different ways, analysis suggests that God-image patterns relating to religious and social contexts yield image clusters that tend to group according to denomination and culture.

From these findings it would seem that Jesus and the Goddess are not necessarily at odds with one another. In fact it seems more often the case that they are complementary for Christian women.

~

The gendered God-images of Jesus and the Goddess are potentially in conflict for the more alienated women in feminist spirituality groups.

The social-cultural context that does put Jesus and the Goddess at odds with one another is most likely to be found in feminist spirituality groups.

By definition in this study, feminist spirituality groups are those that use *female* images for the Divine at least "to a great extent," but seldom exclusively. Women in feminist spirituality groups are more likely than those not in such groups to see Jesus as part of the power Trinity headed by the Father and therefore not a helpful image to incorporate into the ritual and prayer of those who feel abused by patriarchy. These same women often see the Goddess as a dynamic female *very distinct* from Jesus and from the Father and the Trinity. Many of the women who participate in feminist spirituality groups tend to be alienated from the church. Many have indicated through questionnaire responses and telephone interviews that they have been able to remain in their local churches and denominations only because of their women's groups that nourish them spiritually in ways that their churches do not. Alternative rituals that are at the heart of most group experiences explore and celebrate God-images that are liberating to women who have long been treated as second-class citizens. Women crave such alternative experiences of God/dess in order to be healed and whole. In group rituals, Jesus is "invited in occasionally," as one group leader put it, whereas female and feminine images are a regular part of group expression. In "women-church" groups where most of the meeting time is spent in ritual and the image of God is pivotal to the group, more often than not Jesus is simply ignored.

Many of the highly educated women in this study, particularly those who have joined or formed feminist spirituality groups, have difficulty with the patriarchal images of God. They may prefer androgynous images, but the image of Goddess is liberating in ways that Jesus cannot be for them, at least for now. For many, it may well be their religious tradition or particular congregational services and programs that implicitly or directly associate Jesus with patriarchal images of God. These findings suggest that if churches want more active participation of women with feminist values, they would do well to stress the Jesus who is liberator, friend, and helpful protector, rather than image Jesus as the loyal Son of the Father who is Master and Judge of all.

~

Alternative liturgies and innovative ritual are an important component of feminist spirituality.

Three-fourths of all women's groups in this study have some spiritual component in the form of worship or prayer whenever the group meets. *For one-fourth of the total sample, liturgy or worship or ritual is the major focus of the group.* Most of the groups for whom some form of liturgy or ritual is central are feminist spirituality groups. *Liturgy or ritual is the primary focus for one-half (56 percent) of the feminist spirituality groups in this sample.* These feminist spirituality groups with a liturgical or ritual focus are ecumenical women-church type groups.

The rituals and ritual components of women-church type groups illustrate what is meant by feminist spirituality. In these groups, language, God-images, symbols, context, ritual elements and orientation, the role of women, and essential attitudes toward women differ starkly from what happens in traditional patriarchal liturgy and worship. These decidedly feminist celebrations are the locus of what radical feminism is about. In fact, the alternative liturgies and innovative rituals of Christian feminists are at the heart of women's ambivalence about remaining in the institutional church. More often than not they reflect the integration of those alternative biblical, theological, ecclesiological, social, psychological, and cultural perspectives foundational to the feminist movement in the church. These liturgical and ritual experiences are not only informative in the sense of raising and deepening feminist consciousness among participants. They are essentially formative and transformative, changing women and their perspectives in ways that push them beyond the limitations of patriarchal ecclesiology. Feminist ritual reflects the paradigm shift already present within feminist women and, through them, within the institutional church.

In a women-church group in the Midwest, feminine images of God are shared and occasionally "Jesus might be spoken of." For the most part, physical objects such as sand, water, rocks, wood, feathers are incorporated as symbols of women's connectedness to earth. One night the women baked bread together. While it was rising they shared their feelings and their prayers with one another to symbolize the nourishing, creative Woman Spirit of God rising within women. Then they punched the dough down, punched it hard when remembering painful moments of the past, punched harder when they recalled their experiences with the patriarchal church. Then the women put the dough into plastic bags and went home and baked bread for their households.

In another women-church type group, the ground rule is that God is never to be referred to as masculine and only female pronouns may be used. One time the members blessed and shared milk as they remembered significant women who had nourished those women who were present. At another time participants brought wildflowers. These were admired and blessed as representative of the women present and then formed into a lovely bouquet, which was placed on the celebration table. Sometimes a reading reflecting women's spirituality is central to the liturgy. Discussion and integration help connect the learnings to women's lives.

In a Catholic feminist spirituality group that grew out of a disbanded diocesan office for women's issues, monthly meetings have been devoted to a variety of ritual and related activities: art therapy, guided imagery, sociodramas on biblical women, dream analysis of how God speaks to us, sacred dance, and exploration of the goddesses. Parent, mother, woman, wisdom, creator, and goddess are some of their images for God. One of the members explains, "Jesus is not ignored but kept in perspective."

A number of women in a liberal Protestant congregation felt their pastor had ignored women's contributions in every one of his sermons. When on Easter Sunday he failed to mention that women were present at the tomb, they gathered women from the congregation and from around town and formed a group that meets monthly. Ritual is a part of every meeting. They use feminist rituals and symbols from Starhawk and Barbara Walker and the songs and ritual books of Miriam Therese Winter.

A ritual used by an ecumenical clergywomen's support group in the West focused on the theme "in our mother's gardens." Breaking into small groups, they shared what they had received from their mothers and then summarized this for the full group. At another time they pasted cut flowers all around the room to represent those things they would like to see come to flower in the church. A third ritual involved sharing different kinds of beads and what these symbolized.

At a clergywomen's support group in the South, members held a croning ceremony when one of their members turned fifty. They talked about what it meant to be fifty, about how it felt for those who had already turned fifty, and about moving on to the next stage of life. Each woman held a lighted candle as she expressed a wish or a blessing for the woman who had come of age.

In a ritual group in the Northwest, Goddess is the generatrix of life force. Once the women used a very large cinnamon roll to represent the universe and fed each other as they shared from the heart. They blessed a cup of apple juice, in honor of Eve. One time they brought items symbolic of the women in their lives, such as a grandmother's apron, a photograph, a locket, a scarf. The centerpiece of their ritual table, which is adorned with symbols, is a Goddess figurine, a porcelain female face with eyes and mouth cut out and a candle in the middle. When lit she becomes everywoman. Four candles are arranged around her, and she is often decorated with different colors for different rituals.

In a Unitarian group in the East, the meeting is always opened by closing the circle. There is an invocation that is often a prayer to the four directions to prepare and protect the space. The women bring their feelings and their needs to the circle. Sometimes the women create works of art. Or there may be massage, or prayer, or chanting, and there is often singing and dancing. They always close by opening the circle. "May the peace of the goddess go with you. Merry meet, merry part, merry meet. Blessed be."

At one of the rituals of a spiritual support group in the Midwest, the theme was "coming home to God." Women were asked to bring any object that expressed this theme for them. One of the women took out her journal and proceeded to share that she was an incest survivor and that her journal represented the ways she was angry. She passed her journal around, and each of the women blessed it and reflected on what it meant to her. It was a powerful moment for the group. At another gathering, one of the women took a peony from a vase that was there in memory of her mother, who had died just two weeks earlier, and each one blessed her mother. It was a very meaningful and healing ritual for the woman, for the funeral had been offensive to her because the priest had allowed only readings from his old ritual book and it was all so male and exclusive. She had felt so invisible then. In the group she could connect with her mother.

At one of the rituals of a Catholic women's group in the South Central region, each woman was given a strip of cloth. After telling her story the first woman tied her cloth to the cloth of the woman next to her who proceeded to tell her story. At the conclusion of the storytelling, the women were joined by one long "rope" of knotted cloth. The leader cut the strip between the knots so that each woman had a knot to take home with her as a reminder of how all women are joined in their stories. At another ritual the women lit one hundred votive candles for the victims of sexual abuse and spent a lot of time "naming" women who had been exploited or abused. One woman shared for the very first time that she had been raped while in college. On Ash Wednesday the ritual took place around a centerpiece of a ceramic bird surrounded by ashes, which symbolized a phoenix rising. At first the women had referred to these rituals as "para-liturgies" because they were not the "real" Catholic liturgy. Eventually they realized that what they were doing *is* real liturgy, and that is what they call it now.

On Pentecost at a women-church gathering in the Northeast, the women all brought their favorite bread. Twelve different kinds of bread were placed next to a platter of fruit on the coffee table of the host. The ritual opened with dancing to the joyous "Salve Regina." The leader combined different fruits in a cup, and all partook of the fruits and the breads to celebrate their differences and their unity. At the end of the evening they collected cash donations, soap, and other necessities and packaged these for the local women's shelter, which was their outreach project for that meeting.

From these few examples it is clear that feminist rituals are constitutive, not only of certain feminist spirituality groups, but of feminist spirituality. Feminist women are not only redefining church; they are redefining their own spirituality, and in the process they are finding themselves.

~

On the strength of an inner authority, women are claiming responsibility for their own spiritual and religious lives.

Feminist spirituality is a very serious challenge to the institutional church, and to the Catholic Church in particular. According to Sandra Schneiders in her book *Beyond Patching*, it directs women to go beyond attempting to make church structures inclusive of women. It encourages and empowers women to question the whole tradition. Schneiders defines feminist spirituality as "a reclaiming of female power, beginning with the likeness of women to the divine, the rehabilitation of the bodily as the very locus of the divine likeness, and the right of women to participate in the shaping of religion and culture."[140]

Most feminist writers would agree on the core characteristics of feminist spirituality, that it is rooted in women's experience; embodied; profoundly concerned about earth and all creation; seeks an interconnectedness with all living things; and places an emphasis on ritual that is "participative, circular, aesthetic, incarnate, communicative, life-enhancing, and joyful" as "a deliberate rejection of the rigidly unemotional, overly verbal, hierarchical, and dominative liturgical practice of the mainline churches."[141]

This development of a feminist women's spirituality is surely among the major paradigm shifts within the institutional church of this century. Many women are beginning to make a distinction between their religion and their spirituality and to admit what they have long known, that the rites of institutional religion do not touch that innate hunger for God crying out from deep within them, nor do these nurture their spiritual lives. Surprisingly, as this study shows, many feminist women intend to hang in with the religious tradition to which, however tentatively, they belong, for as long as this is possible. But they also intend to pay closer attention to those spiritual longings within them and to continue to nurture and develop their spirits in ways that satisfy. And they will gather with other women to experience church, to be church in the freedom of the Spirit.

Proponents of feminist spirituality are not easily classified. Practices and emphases differ from woman to woman and from group to group. Although diversity is characteristic of feminist spirituality, it is possible to speak of some shared themes that shape a common spirit. For example, in a complete reorientation of theology, women are choosing to ritualize what is of significance to them as individual women and collectively as female. Rites of passage, seasons of earth and seasons of the heart, significant events and ordinary occasions are the stuff of their liturgies. The liberation and empowerment that comes to women from listening to their own inner wisdom and responding to the movements of the Spirit through creating meaningfully symbolic liturgy has provided the impetus to defect in place as a strategy of transformation for some, and the freedom to walk an unaffiliated path for others in the patriarchal system. While the source of alienation for women in the church is patriarchy expressed in practices that continue to exclude and offend, there is far more to the issue than might be evident at first. Deep down in the female psyche is an orientation to the rhythms of life embedded in both humanity and planet, an intuitive and integral connection between the life forces of earth and people. Religion as something set apart and at times against what is natural, normal, and sacred is yet another violation to the planet's female species, however and wherever incarnate. Women want to weave together what has been torn asunder by designated rites and discriminatory canons. They are doing this through rituals that rehearse a hope for a new age and that promised new creation.

Once women experience the fullness and freedom of celebrating the Holy within and beyond, the business-as-usual of organized religion makes less and less sense. To exercise one's own authority for one's own spiritual life is to say to those in authority in the church, you have no power over me. At the same time women are also saying that there is the power of belonging that is associated with a tradition, and there is the pull of relationship felt in the communities of our churches. This study confirms that this is a reality many women do not want to lose. What women are saying is, We are different, our spiritual needs are different, our experiences and our theology are different, our view of the world and our place in it and our understanding of what God expects of us are so very different. Work with us. Listen to us. Share an experience of God with us, but allow us to remain true to the Spirit and to the integrity of grace within us. This is not an easy agenda, but it is the only possible agenda for the church of the new millennium if it hopes to have feminist women from its past participating in its future.

~

Most feminists in this study who embrace a feminist spirituality are involved in social justice action and are either undertaking or supporting initiatives aimed at transformation.

Sandra Schneiders proposes a final characteristic of feminist spirituality. She says: "Perhaps the most important characteristic of feminist spirituality is that from the very beginning it has involved commitment to the intimate and intrinsic relationship between personal growth and transformation and a politics of social justice."[142] The principal investigators and consultants to this project wholeheartedly agree. Many of the women participating in this study have said they share the feminist conviction that "the personal is political."[143] Whether rationally or intuitively, most project participants are coming to realize that "the problems [they] have experienced as their personal and private concerns are actually systemically caused and can only be rectified through structural reform." Women are coming to understand through a feminist spirituality and participation in feminist spirituality groups that "societal transformation is only possible through and on the basis of personal transformation."[144]

A major question this study addresses is: What is the relationship between women having a personal feminist spirituality and the degree to which they are involved in social justice action? One of the main feminist critiques of feminist spirituality in general is that women's energies are drained off or diverted from the transformative political agenda through feminist spirituality groups focused on individual support and ritual celebration. Drawn apart into secure and satisfying subgroups, will women have any interest in changing church structures? Will they give even less time and resources toward working for justice for women and other oppressed groups in society?[145] Some would exempt from the debate Catholic feminist spirituality.

To test the hypothesis that feminists who belong to feminist spirituality groups are not ignoring a social justice agenda but are more acutely open to justice issues and do participate in justice actions, a social justice action scale was formed from survey items asking respondents how much time they spent in various activities such as supporting political candidates; changing laws or public policies to benefit the needy; participating in peace or anti-war efforts; obtaining rights for racial and ethnic minorities and for gays and lesbians; advocating better job opportunities and working conditions for women; and taking action to benefit the environment.

Although there is certainly a range in how much time individual women put into such activities, the results showed that Catholic Sisters are more likely to put a lot more time into social justice action than any other subgroup in our sample. There are also direct correlations between commitment to feminist spirituality and performing justice actions. Women who most want inclusive language in all church services and women who are in feminist spirituality groups that use female imagery and names for God, or who themselves image God to some extent as "Goddess," give *more* time, not less time, to social justice causes. Personal health and free time are important factors in how much energy can be volunteered for social justice crusades. A number of women wrote in the margins of their surveys — I wish I could do more but I am at home with several small children; I was involved for years in action and advocacy but now I am too old...or too tired!

Catholic Sisters are likely to be in feminist spirituality groups that, if made up primarily of Sisters or led by Sisters, often undertake some *group* action to promote social justice, such as a specific ministry to abused women or advocacy for a cause. Sisters in this study score highest on our social justice index, a fact that supports the research done by Marie Augusta Neal among congregations of women religious.[146] Protestant clergywomen are next highest. Catholic laywomen and laywomen in the liberal mainline Protestant denominations have a somewhat lower but identical score, and laywomen in conservative denominations have the lowest score on social justice activities.

What then is the relative impact of goddess spirituality and feminist spirituality groups on women's participation in activities promoting social justice? Catholic Sisters are apt to be involved in social justice activities no matter what their images of God or the kind of women's group they participate in. But they are more likely to be *very* active in social justice causes if they have a strong feminist spirituality, regardless of whether they are in a feminist or a nonfeminist women's spirituality group. A support group of other women seems to be an important reinforcement for Sisters to remain active in social justice causes. Catholic laywomen are also more involved in social justice activities if they have a strong personal, feminist spirituality. Unlike the Sisters, however, their motivation to be involved in social justice activities appears to diminish if they are *not* proponents of feminist spirituality and not in a feminist spirituality group.

Protestant clergywomen are more apt to be active in social justice causes than Protestant laywomen. A personal feminist spirituality and membership in a feminist spirituality group have a clear additive effect on the amount of time clergywomen spend in social justice causes. For Protestant laywomen, belonging to a feminist spirituality group is more important than a personal feminist spirituality and is especially important for laywomen from conservative traditions. Unless women in conservative denominations are members of a feminist spirituality group, they are unlikely to be involved in social justice activities no matter how strong their own feminist spirituality.

This study demonstrates that feminist spirituality, especially when reinforced by group participation, helps women to be more involved in social justice actions and leads to political actions. The more a woman is committed to a feminist spirituality, the more likely it is that she will be involved in social justice causes. Women who image God as female are advocates of social justice and support political actions for systemic transformation.

~

Women who are committed to a feminist spirituality hold an image of the just church that differs from their experience of the churches of institutional Christianity.

In well over one hundred lengthy, in-depth telephone interviews with women who had responded to our initial questionnaire, the question was posed: What would the just church look like? Put another way, the question was repeated: What is your vision of the just church?

The question itself raised a potpourri of feelings. "You want me to tell you what heaven's like!" And, "I wish more women could be asked this question. It makes me weep just to be asked." And, "This question brings sadness and tears just to be asked to dream about this again." Many women responded with tears. After listening to one woman dream of a just church, the interviewer asked if there was anything she would like to add. She started to cry, actually to sob. "It is so good to know," she said, "that there are other people who care about these things." "This is a great question," said another, then announced that she was going to go and write in her journal. Before hanging up she added, "This question leads me from disenchantment into a mode of re-creation!"

Many spoke of a just church in terms of images, reaching for metaphors to describe the indescribable. "It would be that of the loaves and fishes." An Asian woman gave the image of water. Like water, there would be no distinctions, no walls or boundaries, all flowing together and equal, with power to effect change. Another woman used the image of a "fully developed orchestra with different musicians and instruments reflecting independence and interdependence." Then there was the image of a tree, deep roots with lots of branches reaching out, connected and connecting. "A circle instead of a pyramid," said one. Many used the image of circle or spoke of a circular model or of concentric circles of base communities. The images were imaginative. "I have the image of Tahiti. There would be many South Sea islands that you would journey to in canoes and at each island there would be different things...you go collecting what you need" — collecting, connecting, independent, interdependent, in a climate of harmony and peace. One woman saw a structure "with very few walls, round, nothing to stop the breath." Symbols, changing constantly, would be open to interpretation. There would be colors of orange and purple and red, and communion would be central. The just church would be "inviting, warm...it would embrace people who are afraid...it would be full of music and every instrument and people would be dancing." Not everyone could fantasize so easily. One woman, struggling for creative images, said, "The present model paralyzes my imagination." When asked about models of a just church, several mentioned the Quaker model, and one woman made reference to the mission statements of the Unitarian church, where she was experiencing a just church at present. Another woman described a church in the Southwest that had been involved in the sanctuary movement and had been a haven for political refugees. The just church, she said, "is a sanctuary where everyone can come in and not be suspicious or afraid." Many spoke of smaller communities, small base communities that would be people-centered and not afraid to take risks.

Women came up with a long list of qualities and characteristics when asked to describe the just church. Nonhierarchical and nonpatriarchal. Inclusive, open, embracing everyone. You would be accepted and loved as you are. There would be gender equality, with women in every facet of decision-making and ministry, shared power and shared leadership. Differences, diversity would be celebrated.

The just church would look at theology to see if it frees or oppresses and would honor and celebrate all gifts. There would be social outreach and social justice because it would care about the community and would actually do what it says. In the just church there would be solidarity and harmony, a genuine sense of community, and power to facilitate change. People would nourish one another and be a prophetic presence. They would speak out on issues concerning the world, be responsive to the needs of people, be in solidarity with those suffering racial discrimination, be involved with those who are oppressed.

The church would face issues of sexual orientation and abuse, dismantle the celibate icon, affirm human sexuality, recognize human limitations, speak no threat of damnation, be a place that rings with laughter, a place where women and little girls are encouraged to voice their dreams. Sharing would be based on the principles of economic justice, and the life experiences of people would feed into the development of doctrine and dogma. It would be a collaborative effort, not a structure but a gathering where people listen to one another, where power comes from the bottom up, and it would include the poor. There would be a lot more support and space for the Spirit and a lot of different rituals, with movement in the ritual, a place where we pray with our bodies and worship with all of our senses, where we use many images and names for God, where God's feminine face is visible. We would celebrate Earth, live in harmony with Earth, honor the cycles of Earth, body, psyche, and be involved in ecology.

The just church would be participatory and would foster relationships, be a place to express doubt and struggle, a place to test beliefs, a place to deal with problems, where there is acknowledgment of conflicts and the will to work things out, where there is openness to multiple interpretations of the spiritual life, where there is commitment on the part of all to go out and help God transform the world. It would be a microcosm of the just world, not only countercultural but transcultural. The just church would be a global church, an international democratic institution, and it would make a difference. It would use its power for good.

"Is it possible this side of the river?" This was an African American response to the query of how we might bring this about. For the most part, energy faltered here. Many wondered "if that will ever be possible." Can we incarnate the impossible dream? "If such a thing *were* possible," one woman responded, "insecure men would not be in charge." Another said, "We can try; we will continue to try."

The investigative team felt it was important to touch into the feminist vision and to give that vision flesh. To envision something is to take a tangible step toward bringing it about. To give birth to the just church is the goal of radical feminism. Sister Theresa Kane tried to explain this to the pope back in 1979. She says it again, quite simply, in an effort to explain to the American church, frightened to death of feminism, what it is and what it seeks to accomplish.

> "I understand feminism as a movement to express in our structures and in our attitudes the equality that was intended by God for women and men."[147]

Conclusions

Christian women who espouse a feminist spirituality and Christian women in feminist spirituality groups have been the subject of this study.[1]

The preceding chapters have examined the phenomenon of feminist women within Christianity, their relationship to the institutional church and to membership in parishes and congregations, and the effects of feminist spirituality groups on their members and on the churches.

We list here the major conclusions that emerge from the foregoing chapters.

~ ~ ~

- **Feminist women are distinguishing between religion and spirituality.**

Through a long process of coming to awareness, individually and more recently in groups, feminist women are experiencing a unique spiritual awakening. They are discovering that the very lives they live are the locus of God-with-us and are beginning to shape a spirituality on the strength of an inner spirit that they associate with God's own indwelling Spirit as guardian and guide. Accustomed to seeking God from the outside in through religion and tradition, feminist women are questioning the role of religion that often fails to put them in touch with the God encountered through their own experience, denying their right to theological independence and ritual spontaneity.

- **On the basis of an inner authority, women are claiming responsibility for their own spiritual lives.**

In the area of spirituality it can be said that feminist women are truly "marching off their maps."[2] In unprecedented numbers, in a variety of ways, they are embracing a journey of the spirit along uncharted paths, convinced it is God who draws them forward into the unknown. The doubt, the fear, the loneliness that surface from time to time are no longer sufficient to restore confidence in the word of a

194

traditional religion that once held their unquestioning trust. In claiming responsibility for their own spiritual lives, feminist women are not putting ultimate trust in themselves over against an institutional wisdom. On the contrary. In learning to trust and value themselves and to honor their own intuitive wisdom, they are putting their unconditional trust in God/Goddess, however they know or name the One who is Ultimate Authority.

- **Feminist women are seeking out and joining with other feminist women to explore and nurture spirituality.**

Feeling very much alone in the midst of their denominational theology and congregational religious practice, feminist women are embracing some additional or alternative spiritual group experience that supports and celebrates the feminist perspective as God-given and normative. Through sharing their stories and testing their new assumptions in a context of mutual affirmation and support, women deepen their feminist consciousness, strengthen their feminist convictions, and celebrate their newly emerging spirituality in wholistic and enriching ways.

- **Feminist spirituality is different from other more traditional forms of Christian spirituality.**

Christian feminist spirituality differs in style and substance from all other officially recognized expressions of the spiritual life. At the heart of this spirituality is an individual's understanding of God based on the right to image and name the God of one's own experience. It is intentionally inclusive in a variety of ways, most notably in group participation and in ritual leadership, language, symbols, and forms. It moves beyond the sacred/secular dichotomies of our religious methodologies, resisting those barriers and structural divisions that separate people from one another, because it embraces a vision of the household of God that is open and welcoming to all. Christian feminist spirituality is rooted in the biblical concept of justice and proclaims a commitment to the liberation of all who are oppressed. It is wholistic and spontaneous, innovative and egalitarian, and is comfortable with ambiguity. It accepts a woman's right to design and implement alternative liturgical celebrations, because women are created in the image of a God who is understood to be maternal and female. This God of all people, women and men, of all races, cultures, and religions, is the God/Goddess who is acknowledged in feminist spirituality.

- **Feminist spirituality often leads to a new understanding of "church."**

Free of patriarchal restrictions and the expectations of polity and canons, many feminist spirituality groups are experiencing a genuine *koinonia*, and on that basis are redefining "church." They are doing so within the Tradition, for many Christian traditions now teach and preach an ecclesiology based, not on hierarchical structures, but on the *laos*, the people of God. Christian feminists are rejoicing in their discovery of what it means to be church and are exploring the potential inherent in the realization, "We are the church!"

- **Women who espouse feminist spirituality say they often feel alienated from the institutional church.**

From all that has been said so far, it should come as no surprise that a growing number of feminist women are finding it difficult to survive within the institutional church. Faithfulness to the tradition implies suppressing one's individuality in those areas of deepest concern, thereby risking the loss of a newly emerging life of the spirit within. Religion does not tolerate alternatives when it comes to creeds and external codes, but demands obedience to even those precepts one may no longer believe in. One can remain if one keeps silent, but more and more women are finding it impossible to live with a divided heart. When the environment is socially and ritually inclusive and sensitive to women's concerns, it is possible to remain and be somewhat nurtured despite feelings that are suppressed. Many Christian feminist women feel they are caught in a time of transition, when a paradigm shift in principle has yet to be incarnate in everyday life. Meanwhile, women emphasize relationships to offset the damage that structures impose and are far more accepting of the institution than the institution is of them.

- **The majority of feminist women in this study are remaining in the church, but they are remaining on their own terms.**

This brings us to what we think is our most remarkable finding. Many feminists of faith, however alienated or angry, are not pulling out of the churches, but instead are "defecting in place." While women in our study hold fast to the truth of their own experience, either alone or with other women, and insist upon honoring their own inner voice, they remain committed to their faith communities, to congregations and denominations. The need for continuity, for community and connection, the desire to remain a part of a tradition in which one has one's roots is significant for many women. So they choose to remain in a way that will not violate their integrity. At the same time, deep within is the hope that the values they profess will one day be accepted and that the institution will change.

Concluding Reflections

"Defecting in place" is a metaphor that tries to capture the paradox of the Christian feminist position in relationship to the church. "To defect" usually means to abandon, but the women who are "defecting in place" are not, strictly speaking, "defectors," because they haven't gone anywhere, at least not yet. They are rebels, yes, protesting once again the limits of institutional religion. This time, however, Catholics and Protestants support the same shared values, although they may choose different strategies. Theirs is not a struggle for a new religious expression but a movement *within* the institution in which they pledge allegiance to a whole new paradigm. The movement may be seen by outsiders as rooted in dissent, but proponents believe just the opposite. Their stance is positive, not negative, for their dissent flows from a prior assent to the initiatives of the Spirit. Their "yes" to the Spirit is the basis for their staying within congregations or denominations to work to bring about change. As Toinette Eugene would put it, with a touch of whimsy, there is "no defect here."[3] *The women who are "defecting in place" are the modal group of women in our sample.* Although they may share similar feelings of alienation, the women in our sample are "defecting" in different ways. For example, nearly half of the women in this study who often feel alienated from the institutional church are still active members of local congregations. A recent study on church attendance designated certain congregational members "critics" and therefore "marginal members," marginal in part because they "are largely negative about the institutional church," have unconventional religious views, find the church services unfulfilling and the church itself less involved in social justice than they would wish.[4] This is an accurate description of the alienated women who we say are "defecting in place," only they are *not* marginal members. All but 4 percent attend church at least monthly, and 73 percent attend *every week*. Moreover, they are very involved within the congregation, often in leadership roles. This is a very important point. *Alienated women are remaining active in congregations with the hope of changing the church.*

Perhaps because weekly Mass attendance is mandated for Roman Catholics, and definitely because Catholics understand their membership in the Church universal to exist beyond a parish affiliation, a growing number of Catholic feminists are "defecting in place" by not attending Mass on Sunday. While women stay away for a variety of reasons, many see this as a viable strategy for effecting systemic change. It is fairly easily accomplished because, unlike Protestant congregations, Catholic parishes are often large and impersonal and one's presence is seldom missed. Also, there are so many reasons today why a woman might fail to be a Catholic in "good standing" that no one is too surprised if she should stop attending church. *A number of women in this study who claim to be fully Catholic are not "going to church" regularly, or at all.* This is, in the very least, a form of protest against the church's canon that legislates religious practice. The church insists that the penalty for noncompliance is that one commits a sin. Feminist women "defecting in place" believe that God sees things differently, and that Jesus, who existed before the church, would not have set it up that way. The hierarchy may have made liturgy an obligation, but women have made it a way of life. Whatever their specific strategies, the majority of alienated Catholic women in this study are electing to "defect in place."[5]

The term "defecting in place" is not really accurate for African American women in this sample, even though reasons for feeling alienated are often the same. Toinette Eugene speaks of a "spirituality of survival" among those women struggling with and within the church.[6] African American women typically enjoy respect and a certain deference in their churches, especially in the "sanctified churches," far more so than most white women experience in theirs. Although their authority is seldom exercised from the pulpit or through church governance committees, black women have a strong, visible, informal influence within their congregations and denominations. Other issues, such as racism and poverty, that directly impact African American communities are far more important to them than the sexism they encounter. There are, of course, exceptions, and in our small sample there are some highly educated professionals, clergywomen, and business executives who feel more than equal to any man and are fed up with the sexism they experience, not only in their jobs, but also within their churches.[7]

Feminist spirituality groups are a support to alienated women staying in churches and denominations. Our study shows that two-fifths of those who are "defecting in place" belong to feminist spirituality groups. While membership in such a group will not ensure that those "defecting" will stay "in place," on the other hand, neither is it true that membership in feminist spirituality groups is the cause of feminist women leaving the church. Women who remain "churched" and women who leave the church are in feminist spirituality groups in about the same proportion. Other characteristics of the women, their groups, or their churches play an important part in whether alienated feminist women remain in the church.

It is also important to remember that *there are more feminist women and women who support feminist values who are active in local congregations than would self-identify as feminist.* Many of these women are in leadership roles and are influential in congregational life. They too must be considered when attempting to assess the impact of feminism on the life of the congregation and on the shape of the church of the future.

Some would say that the claim to direct one's religious and spiritual life as exercised by Christian feminists parallels, in some respects, the general religious consumerism present in our society. People shop for churches that fit their personal beliefs and needs. At the same time, the "unchurched," with no institutional affiliation, often describe themselves as deeply spiritual people. Robert Bellah and his colleagues in their much-acclaimed study *Habits of the Heart* write about a woman named Sheila who refers to her faith as "Sheilaism." Faith, to her, means "try to love yourself and be gentle with yourself...take care of each other," because God "would want us to take care of each other." Commenting on Sheila's religious perspective, which integrates a firm belief in herself, the writer states that this woman "has actually named her religion (she calls it her 'faith') after herself. This suggests the logical possibility of over 220 million American religions, one for each of us."[8] Indeed, "Sheilaism" has become synonymous with fiercely individualistic faith, and although individualism is characteristic of American life, the independence of Sheila, which reflects that of so many of the women in this study, is viewed negatively by many today. Some worry that religious individualism in general is undermining community and eroding commitment and threatening the very foundations of the church. They look with nostalgia to an earlier time. Others would condemn the religious individualism of feminist women in particular. Bellah himself asks, "How did we get from the point where Anne Hutchinson, a seventeenth-century precursor of Sheila Larson, could be run out of the Massachusetts Bay Colony to a situation where Anne Hutchinson is close to the norm?"[9]

Sheila Larson continues to represent to many the opposite of "keeping faith" with tradition. The same might be said of feminism by those who share this point of view. "Faith" has traditionally come under the auspices of religion. Feminist women, however, tend to associate faith with spirituality. Many women in this study struggle to "keep faith" with the God of their experience through the urgings of an inner Spirit, even when this choice threatens to isolate them spiritually within traditional religion.

Perhaps it is not just coincidence that two women — Anne Hutchinson then, Sheila Larson now — bear the onus of representing that which is taken to be destructive of community: a personal inner authority. And this in an age when many churches honor the primacy of individual conscience. Women are once again caught in the confluence of change, on the cutting edge of a new understanding and experience of church.

In articulating a theory of change, Janet Chafetz notes that women, in specific times and places, organize to accomplish systemic change by rejecting those gender ideologies, stereotypes, and norms whereby men reinforce their power over women to maintain the status quo. Such change-oriented, grassroots movements grow as gender consciousness increases, and often accomplish intermediate gains as they work to achieve their goals. Her analysis shows that it is vitally important for women's movements "to articulate specific proposed changes and a rhetoric or ideology that legitimates such changes" so that "the bulk of potential supporters who are not themselves activists" can identify with them. On the basis of her theory, feminists should strive to "affect public opinion," for "it is the pressure of changed public opinion that is primarily responsible" for specific change. In other words, Chafetz argues, women's movements do not directly cause change, but in fact emerge "because a change process is already under way."[10] Feminist women "defecting in place" in Protestant and Catholic churches are there because a movement for change is already well under way. What remains now, as the next step, is to give visibility to the movement, so that individual feminists in separate congregations are not seen as isolated examples and dismissed, one by one.

Feminists know, as Gerda Lerner states in *The Creation of Patriarchy*, that "patriarchy as a system is historical," and because "it has a beginning in history...it can be ended by historical process."[11] It is this conviction that fuels the feminist fire, both in society and in the church. While society struggles to prevent spiritual influence from entering the public domain and the church often lives apart from the world as if it were not really in it, feminists work to weave it all together, for feminism knows no separation between the personal and the political, or in the case of many within the church, between the spiritual and the political. Although often a cause of controversy, it is feminism's special strength.

We agree with Gerda Lerner that we live at an unprecedented time in history. Whereas in the past women's voices were lost and

the wheel had to be reinvented generation after generation, the socio-
cultural context today is a powerful, pervasive women's movement
supported by many men who identify as feminists. Because women
who accomplished something in the past were forgotten by succeeding generations and the women coming after them had to start all
over again,[12] it is important to remember, to recall the silenced voices
of the past and to hear them again into speech. One can trace a
feminist presence in the church back to the very foundations of our
nation, a tough, tenacious, resilient spirit embedded in the bones and
surviving despite all attempts to dispel or destroy it.

There is no doubt that patriarchy in the church is sustained and
perpetuated by "the systemic silencing of other voices" or through
actions by which the dissenter is simply "marginalized out of existence."[13] Yet, as our study shows, this is becoming more and more
difficult to do. Women who are speaking up and speaking out are refusing to be silenced. They are reinterpreting tradition's sacred texts
and initiating a new tradition, indeed, "a new creation" in which
they are making "all things new." Feminists in the church are moving from the margins to the center even as they remain marginalized
and powerless in the system. In this sense there is movement, genuine
feminist movement, within the Christian church.

Feminists now know there is no going back, for they have come
too far and their numbers are too many. They have found their voice,
they are connecting with one another, and they are learning to survive in the grip of patriarchy by creating "women's space" as an
alternative cultural reality wherein women can explore, experience,
and embrace their own way of being and behaving as a "basis for a
feminist future" they fully intend to bring about. By participating in
these "women-defined enterprises," feminists "create a new culture
which is radically subversive within the dominant culture."[14] This is
precisely why radical feminism frightens both the hierarchy and the
people in the pews, because it is not really about adjusting things to
make the situation bearable. It is all about transformation, which calls
for radical change.

Changing the way things have always been is inconceivable to
most people. To lose the secure and familiar, to lose control of ideology and an exclusive "power over" in a radical redistribution of
power is an awful lot to lose. Some radical feminists, tired of waiting, have moved away from the patriarchal church and have turned
to alternative models. Others stay, hard as it is, and hope for radical change. It remains to be seen just how feminism will affect the
institutional church.

Upon hearing our description of the feminist vision, a puzzled male colleague asked us, "What's the difference between the goals of feminism and the goals of the gospel?" The good news — the really good news — is that there really isn't any difference. If anyone else should ask us, that's exactly what we would say.

Reflections by
Project Consultants

Elizabeth Bettenhausen
Katie Geneva Cannon
Toinette M. Eugene
Elisabeth Schüssler Fiorenza
Beverly W. Harrison
Ada Maria Isasi-Diaz
Marie Augusta Neal
Diann L. Neu
Rosemary Radford Ruether
Letty M. Russell

The following reflections by our project consultants locate this study within a wider context, providing a multifaceted framework for addressing the issue of feminism in the church.

Elizabeth Bettenhausen speaks of the "burdens of faithfulness" borne by feminist women who, in seeking to change both the academy and the church, struggle to remain faithful to the system and to their beliefs, noting that any kind of systemic institutional reform is difficult and "dangerous" work.

Katie Cannon documents the significance of women's contributions to the black church in America and emphasizes the "in but still out" position of African American womanists in their struggle to survive.

Toinette Eugene focuses on Catholic womanists as she reflects on their "spirituality of survival."

Elisabeth Schüssler Fiorenza reminds us of the distinction between women's spiritual support groups and "feminist" groups, both of which are included in this study, and stresses the importance of recognizing that Western systems are not only male-centered but master-centered, making it necessary to analyze women's situation not only in terms of gender, but also of race, class, and ethnicity.

Beverly Harrison describes how "oldline" Christianity has been influenced by feminism, has even internalized some values that are significant to women, and contrasts this changed church with newly emerging white feminist spiritualities.

Ada Maria Isasi-Diaz reports on the ways Hispanic women are also "defecting in place" and offers some concrete strategies whereby *mujerista* and other feminist religious groups might become feminist religious *action* groups oriented toward systemic change.

Marie Augusta Neal, in a sociohistorical overview of feminism in America, highlights those feminist issues of particular concern to church and society today.

Diann Neu describes the development of the women-church movement and its justice-based spirituality.

Rosemary Ruether reflects on the phenomenon of women-church and the "both-and option" of "defecting in place" for those alternative communities claiming to be church.

Letty Russell offers her "church in the round" as an ecclesiological model for feminist communities searching for a "spirituality of connection" and for all who envision a more just church and seek to live that vision now.

Feminist Movement

Elizabeth Bettenhausen

When economic conditions are desperate for more and more women and growing tighter for the middle class, what have feminist theology and ethics to say? When violence against elderly women, against lesbians, against children, against wives is epidemic, what have feminist theology and ethics to say? When difference is met with xenophobia and concern for the other is discounted as "politically correct," do feminist theology and ethics have anything to say?

The question about saying is a question from the academy. What do we think, how do we reflect, what are our words on these matters? The production of words in feminist theology and ethics is fairly ample (although more in theology). The new generation of feminist scholars is reason for confidence in the future of feminism. I think of Ruth Duck's work (at Garrett-Evangelical in Illinois) connecting domestic violence and language about God, of Elizabeth Bounds's analysis of communitarian social theory (at Virginia Polytechnic), and Joan Martin's work with African American women and comprehensive health questions, which she will be bringing to the Episcopal Divinity School. They and many other women are bringing new vigor and imagination to these disciplines. Fortunately, they are often also in a community base from which they do their reflecting and saying.

I think the future of feminist theology and ethics will be in large part a function of their connection with women outside the academy. While feminist faculty and students tend to pay more attention to everyday experience than do other scholars, the pressures in these highly competitive institutions and professions can leave little time for direct contact with persons outside the academy. Reflecting on "women's experience" tends to become reflecting on academic experience directly and on others indirectly and at a distance, if at all. Academic disciplines and discourse tend to become self-referential, looping around word-interactions that grow increasingly abstract and removed from concrete moral and spiritual matters.

Since the academy and the church reflect key characteristics of the society as a whole, other restrictions of access to women's experience are also noteworthy. Very few seminaries reflect the racial and ethnic diversity of the United States. Very few have publicly self-identified lesbian and gay faculty members. Very few have found ways to incorporate working-class and poor persons' perspectives into the teaching or to honor them in the learners. Those schools and denominations that try to hold the levees against the waters of society's diversity will find the future flooding in, washing away their entrenched power that held out for so long against the many others.

Feminist theologians and ethicists who work with their own tools but in institutions not established on feminist principles often work under great stress. Their courses draw disproportionately many students (inspiring barely concealed resentment among other faculty). They spend another full-time life in conferences and counseling with students. The publish or perish syndrome conspires with their own self-doubts, socialized as they are into sexism and racism. Many feminist theologians are also bereft of other institutional support or even besieged by intense opposition, since their theology is radically critical of traditional church theologies. For ethicists, this theological clash may be similarly stress-producing or, in nontheological feminist ethics, happily irrelevant.

Women in the ordained ministry, for another example, are often separated from each other, caught up in overworking and care-giving, alienated from the theology of their denomination, and yearning for support. But while clergywomen organized their own support system in the first decade of being admitted to ordination, the increase in numbers obscures the even greater need now. The need is greater because the denominations are still run on nonfeminist principles, and the more women participate in leadership, the more women will feel torn, conflicted, and worn out. Working in an institution that does not truly believe in the full humanity of women and in justice as defined by women cannot be good for women's health.

Changing these institutions depends on political organizing that the university and church have simultaneously used and condemned. That is, organizing by men for their purposes is called good administration or following the leading of the Spirit. Organizing by women is called obstructive or faithless. Organized political action by men is called doing the work of the church. Organized political action by women is called special interest politics. Establishing an all-male priesthood or church council is following Jesus' command. Establishing a quota system to redress centuries of injustice is not believing the gospel.

Sustaining justice-oriented groups of women beyond the initial stages of consciousness-raising and superficial institutional reform is difficult when the institution itself runs on competitive individualism, as university, seminary, and even church tend to do. Working to make the church more just brings into the open misogyny, racism, homophobia, and a host of other personal prejudices and structural oppressions. Until the critical analysis (prophetic naming) of these conditions is matched by political savvy, alienation is a wise course. Engagement in these institutions without alienation leads to co-optation and spiritual erosion.

Women who care about religion are still, in the majority, attached to religious institutions — denominations, retreat centers, congregations, seminaries, etc. Only very rarely are these institutions established and run on feminist principles. Rarely is an explicit purpose of these institutions to serve women's well-being *as women define it.* Thus, feminists in these institutions are always engaged in a struggle against structures, policies, and theologies that were created to serve male-defined interests. Often these interests are contingent upon the subordinating and even oppressing of children and women. The costs of this inequitable distribution of benefits and burdens are disguised and justified as the burdens of faithfulness.

Many women have good reasons for continuing to participate in these institutions. For some the local congregation is home, community, and the most tangible form of a distinctive culture left. I have talked with many women for whom Lutheran theology is largely irrelevant but for whom the Lutheran congregations to which they belong are precisely where they feel they belong. Since growing up in a tradition creates a large part of who a woman is, a religious institution can be not only a place where your name is known but a place that is you. Other women stay because one central belief is what holds their life together, even while other teaching or rituals threaten to tear it apart. For whatever reason, millions of women will continue to live connected to religious institutions.

When academically based feminist theology and ethics lose touch with women in congregations and local communities, the action on which our reflecting is based is too narrow. The political work necessary to effect the goals that feminist theology and ethics urge is much less likely to succeed. At the same time, the desire and need for reform are so great that the goals may appear closer than they really are (like objects in the rearview mirror). The reform of long-lived institutions is dangerous work, for the temptation to see improvement is nearly irresistible. The temptation is to mistake political temporizing for hope, tokenism for acknowledgment of capability, smiling spite for collegiality, and rhetorical rejection of abuse for an increase of justice.

Within feminism as well, increased diversity has raised new opportunities and challenges. The feminist movement has become explicitly the *mujerista* movement, the womanist movement, the lesbian movement. It is not Euro-American simply or even primarily, but rather grows in the daily struggles of the most oppressed women the world over. Much of the best feminist theory and theology is thus still in the oral traditions of women organizing around the most basic of human rights: food, bodily integrity, education, contraception, shelter. If the world economy and ecological integrity do not decline too far, these oral traditions will grow and spread and combine into a feminist movement truly global.

But on whose terms will this combining happen? The success of feminism in the future also depends on attention to the interconnection of the many kinds of oppression women face. I have learned so much from the Women's Theological Center in Boston in this regard. The WTC is alternative theological education, education for community action and social justice, and public programs and publications keeping the interstructuring of many forms of oppression in focus. The center presupposes that a critical analysis of sexism is not only incomplete but also dangerous if it does not treat the complexity of privilege and oppression in which women live. The center presupposes that in order to obtain justice, organized cooperation of communities and groups is essential. But prior to cooperation across difference, confrontation and conflict across difference must be acknowledged and engaged.

Four years ago I joined the center as a facilitator of learning in feminist theology and theory in the Study/Action Program. I have come to understand much better the nature of privilege and oppression, as I have worked with African American women, Euro-American women, Asian American women, women from Korea, Ireland, New Zealand; bisexual, lesbian, and heterosexual women; Jewish women, pagan, post-Christian, never religious, and spiritually hungry women; unemployed women, working-class, very affluent, and marginally paid women; victims and survivors of abuse.

The temptation for white, middle-class, heterosexual, Christian women such as myself is to leap to commonality with all women, thinking it possible to set aside racism, classism, heterosexism, anti-Semitism, etc., as problems for "the next stage" of our work, at best. At worst, attention to race and class and sexual orientation are viewed as too divisive and conflictual, best avoided so that the women's movement can make at least some progress. The "women's movement" then is women who have the privileges of being white, middle-class, heterosexual, and Christian. This is not to minimize the reality of sexism, the suffering it causes, and the necessity of struggling against it. But no woman is only gendered. Coming to critical awareness and action regarding one's participation by virtue of being a white woman in the structures and organizations of racism is as important in the feminist movement as are the struggles of anti-sexism. The same holds with regard to sexual orientation and class.

Lately, slinging the PC label as a new scarlet letter has been one more attempt to close down critical analysis and organizing in this country. And simply listing "isms" does not in itself constitute resistance against any of them. However, millions of women are oppressed not only because they are female, but also because they are old. Others are attacked or neglected not only because they are female, but also because they are disabled. Sex, race, class, sexual orientation, age, physical ability, mental condition — even this is the short list of all the categories by which the subordinated other, the subjugated inferior is defined in this country. Rejecting and resisting this organized devaluing of persons may be "politically correct." In the old days it was called doing justice. Now and in the future, I hope it is the meaning of the feminist movement.

The struggle for community-based, action-reflection models of feminist theology and theory is energy-intensive. The struggle against racism seems to be getting more sharply angled uphill every day. So too with all liberation movements. The present emphasis on spirituality makes sense. The wells of hope run dry too quickly if fed by springs running only with statistics, footnotes, and committees. The spirit-springs are rising to the surface again, nourishing, refreshing, and, in combination, they are a tide of liberating lives.

~ 2 ~

The Positionality of Women in the African American Church Community

Katie Geneva Cannon

Introduction

The positionality of women in the African American church community cannot be understood and explained adequately apart from the sociohistorical context that called the black church into existence. One year before the Pilgrims arrived on the Mayflower, at least three women were among the twenty Africans on the Dutch frigate that landed in August 1619 at Jamestown, Virginia. By 1625, one of the couples became the parents of the first African child born in English America. The child, a boy named William, was baptized before the cedar chancel in the Church of England in Jamestown.[1] "That child, historians reason, was freed by the act of baptism since the English law in effect in Virginia at that time enfranchised any person baptized or christened."[2] Colonists were not long in changing the statutes and the laws so that Christianization did not require emancipation. Race and servitude thus created a religious barrier at the onset.[3]

Historical Background

From the standpoint of sheer logic it is rather remarkable that enslaved African American Christians, relegated to marginal status within colonial Protestantism, created an antebellum black church whose positionality was at the center of black life.[4] With justice denied, hopes thwarted, and dreams shattered, black women and men believed that it was God who gave them spiritual poise and balance in the midst of chattel slavery. According to the scanty records available, some slave women were successful in the area of preaching and evangelism. One of the most zealous and vigilant of these worthy and faithful churchwomen was Aunt Hester.

> Aunt Hester of Franklin, Louisiana, preached and prayed so constantly that she influenced all of the slaves bought by her master. The master sold her but soon bought her back again. She continued to spread the word, causing even the young mistresses in the house to become serious about religion. Aunt Hester was sold. But there was so much consternation in the household that the master bought her back once again, complaining that he would have to put up with her religion and spoiling of the Negroes.[5]

More complete records would likely disclose dozens of Aunt Hesters whose duties of oversight, direction, and watchcare were quite prophetic in nature and extent.[6]

During the postbellum years, the African American church community continued to operate for the most part in secrecy. The expository and religious discourse enabled the adherents of the faith to understand the interplay of historical events and societal structures. Not buried from sight were the pains and lessons from bondage.

In particular, the relationship of power dynamics remained much as it had before the war. The standardized land-tenure contract was structured so as to maintain the hegemony of the antebellum slave-owning aristocracy. As a result of the crop lien laws passed in 1865, African Americans were financially unable or not allowed to purchase land. The black woman and her family's legal emancipation trapped them in a grossly unequal poverty cycle of debt peonage. Every year the white landowners and commissary merchants provided black sharecroppers with credit at high rates of interest to purchase seed, tools, food, fuel, and other necessities. At the end of the harvest season, the sharecroppers were compelled to accept a settlement of their share of the crop minus charges according to the landlord's rendition of the farm accounts. This type of perpetual indebtedness resulted in involuntary servitude and a severe spiritual plight for an overwhelming majority of African American families.

Even with newly won civil rights, economic opportunities and religious equality for blacks tottered between dependency and despair. Two decades after the Civil War, large numbers of African American Christians found themselves legally bound to labor for payment on trumped-up debt-charges, assigned to benches in balconies of congregations controlled by paternalistic whites, restricted to special times to kneel and pray, and denied Holy Communion until all white congregants were served.

In general, the theology of the black church community after emancipation continued to be dominated by a tradition that emphasized "equality in inequality."[7] Women in the church worked side by side with men to develop ministerial activities related to the socioeconomic and political context in which black people found themselves. In every sphere where African Americans were circumscribed and their legal rights denied, the black church called its members, both females and males, to a commitment of exacting social change and righteousness here on earth.

Hence, the after-effects of slavery and their consequence called the black church forth as the oldest and largest institution controlled by African Americans. Even with diverse and amorphous characteristics, the African American church occupied a unique and central place in both the North and the South. As such, it came to be the channel outside the home where black women, men, and children could express themselves freely, composing and singing new songs and thereby giving to America one of its few indigenous art forms. With the increasing growth in population and intensified discrimination in white churches, the black church community became the basic organization of African American life.

Structural Developments

The advent of the Freedmen's Aid Societies signaled a shift in the positionality of women in the African American church. The Freedmen's Relief Association, the American Freedmen's Union, the Western Freedmen's Aid Commission — in all fifty or more active organizations — launched a massive, never-to-be-forgotten venture to elevate the dignity of freed African Americans into a self-sustaining place in the body politic. In the most noticeable manner women were excluded from administrative boards and ecclesiastical decision-making processes.

It was not until the nineteenth century — when all–African American denominations began to appear, a prototype of hierarchal structural organization that also prevailed in African American congregations affiliated with predominantly white ecclesiastical establishments — that antifemale black cultural nationalist theological rhetoric was publicly espoused. The majority of African American men maintained that they had to exert a more prominent leadership role in their negotiations with patriarchal representatives from the dominant white culture. Jacquelyn Grant sums it up this way:

As we move further away from the slave culture, however, a dualism between black men and women increasingly emerges. This means that black males have gradually increased their power and participation in the male-dominated society.... By self-appointment, or by the sinecure of a male-dominated society, black men have deemed it proper to speak for the entire community, male and female.[8]

Women's Auxiliary Groups

Supplementing rather than duplicating the program of the Freedmen's Aid Societies, the women used their church auxiliary groups to address the education of black children, child care, nutrition programs, general evangelism, and the establishment of industrial homes — a network of residential centers offering training of head and heart for black females migrating from rural areas to northern cities. Many of the names of the noble African American women who visited, prayed with, and exhorted the sick, rebuked the impenitent, counselled the troubled, and conducted social meetings during this period have slipped from memory and record.[9]

As tens of thousands of black people moved from South to North and from rural to urban areas seeking relief from stifling circumstances, the black church community was the citadel of hope.[10] During this colossal movement of African American people, women were instrumental in helping the black church continue to serve as the focal point for acquainting African Americans with major social issues affecting them. The church served as a bulwark against laws, systems, and structures that rendered black people as nonentities. In essence, African American churchwomen touched the lives of the weary travelers in all their ramifications.

As segregation laws and practices continued to cut African Americans off and prohibit their participation in most of the societal institutions — eliminating blacks from educational distinctions, judicial justice, and economic opportunities — black women worked to build the church community from within. Churchwomen were actively involved in the enormous effort to organize health clinics, sewing classes, mothers' clubs (to reduce the frightful rate of African American infant mortality), and community centers. As home missionaries they itinerated, taught, interpreted, organized, trained, and cultivated leadership skills. More than any other component in the African American church, the women's laity groups attracted and engaged people in wide-ranging community activities. The successes of women in establishing these organizations, so that many of them are still active and popular with junior and senior branches in the African American church today, were the result of hard and eager striving.

World Wars I and II brought about the most visible changes in black people's existential reality. Under coercive pressure from the African American community, the federal government was forced to take definite steps to halt racial discrimination in war industries. In segregated plants and factories, African American women attained semi-skilled, skilled, and supervisory positions. Most black women, however, were assigned the most arduous tasks, worked in the least skilled jobs, and received lower wages than their white counterparts. Because labor reserves were depleted, large numbers of black men and women were hired to manufacture ammunition and iron and steel products. This employment policy was gradually repeated in other industries.

After World War II, there was a rise in the number of black lawyers, physicians, politicians, and businesspersons, who took their place alongside of preachers, teachers, and factory workers in the urban ghettoes. At the same time, many women became heads of households. Marital instability, low remarriage rates, and an increase of out-of-wedlock births resulted in large numbers of African American women becoming dependent on the social welfare system. Thus, the forming and solidifying of new class strata in the overall community changed the roles of women in the black church. Organized ostensibly to provide services to the membership of the local parish, working-class and middle-strata Christian women extended their areas of mission to incorporate the needs of the wider urban community: care of the handicapped, understanding of the alcoholic, concern for public school education, search for integrity in political leadership, and interpretation of public economic concerns in order to influence social policy.

African American churchwomen also developed service guilds in order to deepen the integration of faith and praxis. These guilds presented numerous interdenominational programs to which members of neighboring churches were invited; they promoted various types of creative fundraising activities for the financial support of the church; and many of them sponsored annual social and recreational activities that were quite popular throughout their geographical regions.[11] The majority of this work was done in Christ's name as sacrificial giving. It was not so much that African American churchwomen had no money; the majority simply had little beyond that required for the necessities of life.

In the early 1960s, like the late 1950s, there was considerable segregation in public and private facilities. Major civil rights organizations — National Association for the Advancement of Colored People, the National Urban League, Congress of Racial Equality, Southern Christian Leadership Conference, and the Student Nonviolent Coordinating Committee — designed direct civil rights activities to end legal racial segregation, to increase African American political activities and representation, and to institutionalize a series of statutory and constitutional rights for black people in the U.S. Thus, the African American church emerged as the prime training ground and staging area for struggles against racial injustice.

Many churchwomen with outstanding abilities and skills were active in civil rights organizations. With the black church as the centralized, institutional base, women combined their Christian commitments with action strategies. Hundreds upon hundreds of African American women participated in sit-in campaigns, prayer marches, freedom rides, and voter registration projects.[12] In addition to continuing the work of the historical auxiliaries and service guilds, churchwomen also understood their mission in the 1960s to consist of coalition-building with black men and members of other racial communities in order to eschew agitation for persuasion against calculated racist policies in education, in industry, and in politics. The impact of churchwomen in the overall African American community has been nothing short of astonishing.

Womanist Concerns[13]

Womanist religious scholars argue that human rights for African American women in contemporary society is still a situation of struggle, a struggle to survive collectively and individually in the continuing harsh historical realities and pervasive adversities in today's world. The existential circumstances in which churchwomen find ourselves in the 1990s are little better than the situation in the 1890s. The Korean, Vietnam, and Persian Gulf wars, federal government programs, civil rights movements, and voter education programs have all had a positive impact on the civil rights of African Americans, but they have not been able to offset the negative effects of the inherent inequalities that are tied to the history and ideological hegemony of racism, sexism, and class elitism. The persistent obstacles of poverty, gender discrimination, and racial prejudice continue to enslave the majority of African American women and our families to hunger, disease, and the highest rate of unemployment since World War II. Education, housing, health care, and other necessities that were gained during the mid- and late 1960s are deteriorating faster now than ever before.

Womanist scholars are aware that we cannot retain allegiance to the pivotal history and theology around which the African American church community defines itself unless androcentrism and the social consequences of patriarchal hegemony are debunked, unmasked, and disentangled. As theologically trained African American women with a strong commitment to eradicate oppression, we need to be in dialogue with active laywomen in order to analyze critically and creatively the strengths and limitations of women's auxiliaries and service guilds in the contemporary church. Womanist analyses that are compatible with active Christian faith praxis — however varied — incorporate what is best in churchwomen's organizations and reject what is damaging and oppressive. Informed critical power analyses reveal the current positionality of African American women as working at the center of the black church and yet pushed to the margins of malestream decision-making processes. In essence, womanist scholars address the occupancy of the "in but still out" position, challenge the structures of ecclesiastical androcentricity, and create resistance against domination that signals co-equal discipleship.

No Defect Here:
A Black Roman Catholic Womanist
Reflection on a Spirituality
of Survival

Toinette M. Eugene

The majority of the findings of this extremely significant and sociolog-
ically relevant report reflect almost entirely the personal experiences
and empirical summary expressions of white women in Roman Catholic or liberal Protestant churches who want to change the religious
institutions in which they are or have been members. I make my response to these findings and offer my vision of a justice-loving church
from the perspective of a black Catholic social ethicist, that is to say,
from a very "different"[1] form of womanist[2] religious scholarship and
worldview.

What is it that has allowed or persuaded a majority of black Catholic women *not* to "defect in place," as the findings of this report
indicate as the choice of many women, but at the same time also to
remain and to resist the negative, dehumanizing images that both the
Roman Catholic Church and society in general have maintained of
them? The lives and words of black Catholic women point to a "spirituality of survival" that they have developed and nurtured and by
which they have been strengthened. There are at least two aspects to
this Roman Catholic womanist spirituality of survival: it fosters an
empowering self-esteem[3] and it overwhelmingly affirms the presence
of God in the day-to-day praxis of justice and in struggle for survival.[4]

What does the significance of a "spirituality of survival" for black
Catholic women mean in the context and hermeneutic of this report,
which does not include any extended reference to black women in
either mainstream (white) Protestant or Roman Catholic traditions or
from within the more traditionally defined black church? It means
that womanist spirituality and theology must continue to find ways

to engage in religio-cultural analyses that are inclusive of them, as well as to continue to articulate a separate analysis of themselves for the purposes of integrity and clarity.

Both kinds of analyses must endeavor to include and to highlight those aspects of black culture and religion that foster self-esteem for black Catholic women as well as men, and that help them to transcend the negative images of themselves that a racist, sexist, classist, and heterosexist Roman Catholic Church and dominant secular culture project. These dual analyses must also confront those aspects within black culture and religion that limit self-esteem and transcendence for its women. Essentially, such religio-cultural analyses will point to the necessity of a spirituality of survival for the larger religious and civic black community in which black Roman Catholic women surely participate and share.

The feminist movement, both in society and within Christian churches, has been one of white women — usually educated, middle-class women — with freedom and privilege to become militant without fearing the consequences that a woman of color or lower-class white woman would be subject to. In the Roman Catholic Church, as this report has strongly emphasized and indicated, the greater number of white women advocating equality have been women religious with similar education, freedoms, and privileges. The result has been that the experience of white women has been presented as universal, incorporating and speaking for the experience of all women. It is not that women of color are assumed to be incapable of speaking for themselves; rather, their silence or absence is simply not even acknowledged.[5]

Black men, ordained and lay, have also had the dubious distinction of occupying similar roles as oppressors of women, especially their own, for it must be acknowledged that sexism exists in the black church and world. This leaves black Catholic women, in particular, on the bottom of church and society, stigmatized and condemned for both their strengths and their weaknesses and too often denied a space in which to grow, explore, and develop. It also leaves them, paradoxically, with a challenging freedom, not simply to "defect in place," but rather to describe and to define a new "spirituality of survival" as well as a theology and ethic of care, which is in essence a theology and ethic of justice/love. This is a decidedly different option and contraindication than that of either intentionally or by default "defecting in place" — the option of choice for the majority of women who are reported in the conclusions of the social researchers who authored these findings.

As this report has indicated in its salient findings, the situation in the Roman Catholic Church is fraught with problems that pose a challenge to women, including black women, within its embrace. Black Catholic women are challenged to be our truest "womanist" selves, for we are called, as Mary was called, to recognize our own vocation in bearing witness to Jesus, the Liberator of humanity. We can, as black women, react to oppression, whether of race, class, or sex, by leaving the official Roman Catholic Church in frustrated anger or pain, or we can remain and, together with our alienated white sisters who are "defecting in place," serve as a thorn in its patriarchal, institutional, bureaucratic side.

We can also make the sad and futile mistake of those who seek not to change the structures themselves but only their outward manifestation, resulting in empowerment for only a few — a few more black priests and bishops and, in time, a few black women priests, but leaving the hierarchical, authoritarian entity intact. Or we can remain to work actively from within to restructure this institution and make it truly inclusive as a model for and an experience of a discipleship constituted of equal human beings. It is this direction that my own vision looks toward and focuses on as an empowering experience of a more normative "Just Church" that pastorally supports and ministers with oppressed communities of disenfranchised persons who long for and who indeed initiate this kind of public prophetic witness. For alienated white women, this intentional prophetic action may be referred to as "defecting in place." For black women, it is a "spirituality of survival."

Given black women's ability to survive under the worst of circumstances and their active commitment to their extended families' and communities' survival, a black Roman Catholic womanist spirituality must be more than simply a form of generic liberation spirituality. It must highlight God's role as a principal sustainer of oppressed, struggling, or marginated black women. It must examine the sustaining presences of the Holy Spirit[6] in all black women's lives.

Such utilization of black Catholic women's paradigmatic experience in living out such a "spirituality of survival" can graphically illustrate additional ways in which womanist spirituality and theology are distinct from black theology. Both are concerned with the black community's freedom and God's role in the freedom struggle. Womanist spirituality and theology, however, go beyond black theology as well as beyond the stated confines of this report, important as it is, for understanding the ways in which women's communities of support and inspiration give an essential grounding for survival and success in keeping hold of the Divine economy of grace and goodness.

A truly authentic black Catholic womanist spirituality is an important but often forgotten or discounted facet of the larger womanist community's daily struggle to survive domestically and economically as well as ecclesially in an often hostile environment and ecology. All authentic womanist spiritualities also utilize more comprehensive sociopolitical analyses for understanding the black community's efforts to exist in as well as to resist the powerful dynamics of dominance and subordination so prevalent in both church and society. The current challenge is for black Catholic women, in concert with all other womanist theologians, ethicists, pastors, and parishioners who continue to respond to diverse but indispensable forms of religious leadership, to move forward with the task of bringing womanist spirituality, theology, and ethical praxis to full fruition.

~ 4 ~

Spiritual Movements of Transformation? A Critical Feminist Reflection

Elisabeth Schüssler Fiorenza

In her letter of March 24, 1993, Miriam Therese in the name of Adair and Allison invited us to write a "vision statement on the future of the church from your perspective and in relationship to your scholarly discipline and/or your own sociopolitical situation, a statement influenced by the widespread phenomenon of women's spiritual support groups within and beyond our current definitions of church." Since the letter was quite clear that we were not to write a reflection on the project, but rather a brief statement on what we "see/think/feel about this phenomenon of women's groups in the U.S. (and globally)," I will limit my remarks to this task. As long as the feminist-religious politics and vision of these groups are not decided, I must resist the temptation to elaborate my hermeneutical, theological articulation of the *ekklesia* of women/women church. To locate such spirituality groups just because they are groups of women within the discursive space of the *ekklesia* of women would mean either to subscribe to an uncritical universalizing notion of woman or to undermine the political power and spiritual space that this theological articulation seeks to identify and generate for feminist movements of liberation in biblical religions.

Since I have just published a book on my "vision of the church,"[1] I will focus here more narrowly on developing criteria for assessing the significance that the "phenomenon of women's spiritual support groups" has for transforming patriarchal church into the "discipleship of equals" or the "ekklesia of wo/men." I approach this task from the perspective of a critical feminist theology of liberation. This perspective compels me to underscore the crucial difference between women's spirituality groups that are feminist and those that are not.

What do I mean by "feminist" and why do I insist on using this contested term?[2] The expression "feminist" is often shunned because it evokes negative reactions, emotions, and prejudices. Recent polls in the U.S. have shown that almost 70 percent consider the term "feminist" to be a negative label, although they subscribe to many goals of the feminist movement and have benefitted from its achievements. Moreover, the term "feminism" carries a negative connotation not only on the popular level but also in the academy. Because feminism espouses political values and the interest to change patriarchal institutions, feminist studies are often rejected as "ideological" and therefore "unscientific," whereas academic research on women or gender is integrated more easily into the dominant framework of academic scholarship that purports to produce value-free, disinterested, and objectivist scientific knowledge.

Nevertheless, the notion of feminism as a movement and theory doesn't just provoke negative reactions in society, academy, and church. It also connotes a rich variety of theoretical perspectives and practical goals. However, the diverse theoretical articulations of feminism generally agree in their critique of masculine supremacy and hold that gender roles are socially constructed rather than innate or ordained by God. The "root experience" of feminism brings to the fore that cultural "common sense," dominant perspectives, scientific theories, historical knowledge, and religious revelations are androcentric, i.e., male biased, and therefore not objective accounts of reality, but rather, ideological mystifications of patriarchal structures.

Although Euro-American feminist gender discourses have questioned cultural androcentrism and asymmetric gender dualism, they have not radically displaced essentialist gender conceptualization. Rather they have reinscribed Western patriarchal discourses. Such discourses have defined Woman in analogy and opposition to universal Western Man and understood women's nature either as inferior to, superior to, or the same as that of men.

Euro-American feminist discourses generally have used categories such as "androcentrism," "patriarchy," or "gender dualism" as synonymous and overlapping concepts. In feminist gender discourses the term "androcentrism" refers to a linguistic structure and theoretical perspective in which man or male stands for human. Insofar as Western grammatically masculine languages function as so-called generic languages, they use male terms either as gender specific or as inclusive of women and understand the pronoun "he" as inclusive of "she." Insofar as Euro-American feminist discourses have tended to valorize women and femininity over and against men and masculinity, they have reproduced this androcentric symbolic construction of male-female gender polarity and compulsory heterosexuality that are constitutive of the patriarchal order.

Feminist liberation movements and theorists around the globe have unmasked the universalizing and essentializing gender discourse on woman as mystifying and reproducing patriarchal or, better, *kyriarchal* (master) relations of domination. Their historical analyses have pointed out that not only the nature of elite women but also that of subordinated and colonialized peoples has been construed as the devalued and deficient "other" of elite Western Man. Whereas Western philosophy has specified the "nature" of colonialized male "others" in analogy to that of the elite "women" and the "feminine," it has defined that of oppressed women as the opposite to that of the "white Lady." Hence the articulation of a "special" nature of elite women as well as oppressed women and men seeks to legitimate the exclusion of the subordinated "others" from the institutions of knowledge, culture, and religion in a democratic society that proclaims the equality of all its citizens but restricts equal rights and the power of ruling to elite, freeborn, educated men.

Feminists of color therefore have consistently maintained that an analysis of women's situation just in terms of gender does not suffice. The general understanding of patriarchy as gender dualism or as the domination and control of man over woman does not comprehend the complex systemic interstructuring of gender, race, class, and ethnicity that determines women's lives. Hence, a feminist liberationist perspective has to distinguish between the categories of linguistic *androcentrism* and ideological *gender dualism/kyriocentrism* on one hand and *patriarchy/kyriarchy* understood as a complex overarching social-religious system of elite male domination on the other. The patriarchal pyramid of domination and subordination (*kyriarchy*) is structured by the overlapping systems of racism, sexism, classism, and colonialist imperialism. Although cultural and religious *patriarchy/kyriarchy* as a sociopolitical "master" system has been modified throughout the centuries, its basic structures of domination and ideological legitimization are still operative today. Biblical religions and churches have played a central role in transmitting and legitimating the patriarchal social order as well as in socializing women into its cultural and religious values and mindsets.

Western cultural symbol-systems and religious discourses are not just *androcentric*, i.e., male-centered. Rather they are *kyriocentric*, i.e., master-centered. For instance, the nouns "Africans," "Europeans," "Asians," "the poor," or "minorities" can be understood as inclusive of women and men. However, when we list groups such as Africans, Americans, the poor, *and* women, our language functions in an exclusive masculine fashion, though as if on the one hand only men and not women belong to social-ethnic groups, and on the other hand women are exempt from ethnic, race, class, and other cultural definitions. Hence, by universalizing the notion of women such grammatical-linguistic androcentrism obscures the fact that women are not only defined by sex and gender but also by race, class, culture, religion, age, and ethnicity. Thus conventional masculine generic language makes women of minority groups totally invisible. Insofar as feminist discourses continue to use the universalizing and essentializing concept of woman, they reproduce the invisibility of women whose lives are determined by multiple structures of subordination. The neologisms "womanist" or "mujerista" as well as the qualifications of women's struggles with national-ethnic terms as "Asian," "European," "African," or "Latin American" rightly seek to particularize the universalizing notion of "woman" in the essentializing analysis of cultural gender-feminism. However, by restricting feminist theories and movements to Euro-American gender discourses they are in danger not only of relinquishing the rich multicultural international history of feminism as a political theory and emancipatory movement but also of reinscribing kyriarchal structural divisions among women by valorizing such divisions as feminist differences.

A critical liberationist theological perspective understands feminism as embodied in the visions and movements of those who seek to transform patriarchal/kyriarchal structures of domination and to eliminate the exploitation and marginalization of all women without exception. As one of the oldest maxims of the women's liberation movement states: as long as not every woman is free no woman is free. However, if there are no liberated women, there are also no liberated groups of women.

Hence, a critical feminist theology of liberation must insist that women's spirituality or faith-sharing groups have to be assessed as to whether and how much they aim to continue or seek to change patriarchal social and ekklesial frameworks and structures of domination. Such groups can function either as a spiritual safety valve for the patriarchal church and as a religious refuge, or as a training ground for patriarchal society by fulfilling the religious consumer needs of women. Or they can empower women struggling for spiritual survival and for the transformation of kyriarchal society and church. By constituting themselves as the *ekklesia*, the congress and assembly of women feminists acting in the power of the Spirit can claim their religious rights and spiritual authority to theological self-determination, ekklesial leadership, and human well-being.

Prayer circles, covens, and self-help groups of women either can exhaust themselves in individualistic, depoliticized forms of "new age" and fundamentalist, feminine forms of spirituality or gather for shaping critical consciousness, for articulating spiritual vision, and for celebrating women's survival, dignity, and struggle. Both consumerist and liberationist religious women's groups may resort either to biblical Jewish or Christian traditions and rituals, to those of other world religions, or to those of reconstructed "Goddess" spirituality. In other words, both spiritual feel-good groups and critical liberationist religious gatherings of women can utilize divergent theological and cultural resources for constructing religious meanings and developing liturgies and rituals. Both types of women's groups may either feel at home on the margins of the church, move out of the church, or understand themselves as exiles from organized religion and church. Both types of groups may identify with and locate themselves at the center of church either because they equate church with patriarchal church structures or because they want to change patriarchal forms of church and religion.

I do not want to be misunderstood here. I do not argue that women's spirituality groups are liberationist only if they eschew prayer and introspection and exhaust themselves in social action projects. Rather I argue that such spiritual self-help groups both mute and deepen women's insecurities, pain, and longing for spiritual sustenance if they insinuate that patriarchal alienation and exploitation are a mother- or self-inflicted disease from which women can recover by sheer force of will and be saved through therapy, ritual, and prayer.

Only when women's faith groups organize for bringing about institutional change and engage in systemic conscientization will they be able to practice the life of the Spirit who heals, strengthens, and empowers. Studies have shown that one of the most damaging signs of patriarchal oppression is low self-esteem, self-loathing, and self-sacrifice produced by internalized racism, sexism, classism, or colonialism. Only if religious groups of women learn to recognize kyriocentric mindsets and patriarchal exploitations as structural sin and evil will they be able to practice the self-respect and spiritual care of the self that sustains us in the long struggle for transformation.

Finally, we must ask in whose interest academic studies of women are done, why they are financed, and what ends they will serve. Are such studies conceived as orientation and tool that will help religious women's groups in their struggle for survival and liberation, or are they studies that will reify and legitimate the patriarchal status quo? Such inquiry is necessary because androcentric/kyriocentric science and knowledge reify women as study objects and produce "data" about women that can be utilized for patriarchal ends. Hence feminist critical debates that seek to change patriarchal knowledge production have to insist that studies of women must enable women who have been silenced and subordinated by patriarchal religious institutions for centuries to become theological subjects and religious agents. To that end such studies must be contextualized within women's struggles for survival in and transformation of institutionalized socioreligious kyriarchal mindsets and structures.

A mere description of women's spirituality or faith-sharing groups, I have argued here, is not able to tell us whether these groups are feminist harbingers of self-esteem and institutional change. Only if such studies adopt a critical feminist theology of liberation as their organizing theoretical framework of research are they able to provide the insight and knowledge that will allow us to assess whether women's faith groups will have an impact on patriarchal church and religion, and, if so, what kind. Without such a critical feminist assessment our visions of a just and liberated church are bound to remain empty dreams.

Women-Church and Similar Spiritual Support Groups in Mainline Protestant and Catholic Churches: Comments on the Hartford Study

Beverly W. Harrison

The results of the study reported here are intriguing, and to this interpreter simultaneously surprising and predictable. What is surprising is the clear testimony garnered of the not inconsiderable impact of feminism, in a variety of ideological guises, on women's spiritualities within "oldline" (European-root churches) and "mainline" U.S. Christian communities. Over the last two decades much of the male leadership of the Roman Catholic and Mormon denominations has been officially and systematically hostile to feminism, while "oldline" Protestant leadership has been, at best, ambivalent, giving lip-service to women's needs for recognition and ecclesiastic inclusion while resisting substantive feminist calls for the reimaging of the Christian faith itself. What is predictable is that none of the denominations central to this study has taken to heart feminist assessments of Christian complicity in women's historical oppression.

In spite of this, however, the Hartford study attests that feminism has touched and to some degree reshaped the imaginations and spiritual longings of women who still participate in these churches. Even in the face of massive, predictable resistance to change and a well-orchestrated backlash against feminism, this study documents that women sympathetic to feminism have found ways to gain spiritual support within their communities of faith and sometimes to organize effectually for change. As a Christian feminist woman who has struggled to alter this "official" state of affairs, the persistence and extent of success of women identified here is not only surprising but gratifying.

Year after year I have observed the effectualness of the official resistance to feminism as it takes its toll. I have seen numerous gifted and caring women move outside of Christianity altogether, convinced that the death-dealing fearfulness that characterizes what is here termed "mainline" Christianity makes it impossible for these churches to participate in shaping the sort of spiritual revolution required for our violence-drenched world. Many feminists believe that visions of a radical spirituality of mutual respect and cosmic reverence required for planetary survival demand an active repudiation of patriarchy, not merely the reluctant accommodation to women's most modest complaints.

We are living in a time when the social forms of religious life are undergoing dramatic change, and given the strong refusal to hear women, it might be expected that this study would reveal more anger and disaffection among self-identified feminists in the churches than appears to be the case. One possible reason for these findings may be that many of the women's groups in this study are based in those sectors of Christianity that are "oldline" groups shaped by European roots. Elsewhere I have argued that it is precisely those denominations that were most dramatically if reluctantly impacted by the earlier feminist movement. The theologically "liberal" or bourgeois Christianity that stems from Europe (which in the late twentieth century includes Roman Catholicism), while resistant to justice-centered feminism, accommodated almost in spite of itself to "soft feminism," with the result that the culture of oldline Christianity was altered profoundly. Some critics of this transformation have dubbed this contemptuously as the "feminization of Christianity," a shift that, it is contended, led to the "sentimentalizing" of faith. Pejorative characterizations of these changes notwithstanding, what was involved was a shift to a more experience-centered and less "leader as authority" centered form of communal life, a move to a parish or congregational system where nurturance and personal support came to be expected dimensions of Christian communal life. In a culture where bureaucratic efficiency, utilitarian rationalism, and personal autonomy were dominant public norms, oldline liberal Christianity came to reflect the alternative values of the presumed "privatized" world of women and children—community, participation, and interdependence.

Appreciation for these changes and commitment to these values may well account for the persistence, even tenacity, of women's loyalty to local Christian communities and to churches that are still powerfully contemptuous of them.

What this study may suggest is that many parishes and local communities of Christians are more genuinely affected by feminism than the cautious and fear-filled leadership of these churches imagine. Many of us who have argued the need for a genuine theo-ethical embrace of justice-centered feminism as a necessary condition for the revitalization of liberal Christianity may at least take some small comfort from these findings. Even as the media-manipulated readings of contemporary Christian dynamics seek to persuade us that papal, neo-orthodox, and neo-fundamentalist versions of Christianity reign unchallenged, it may just be that the genuine spiritual life of oldline Christianity really is being renewed in the expressions of alternative faith by women, including feminist women who no longer need permission to envision God in their image. If so, the survival and prosperity of these churches may turn out to have far more to do with hospitality to feminist spirituality than to the successful reimposition of the Master Narratives that characterize patriarchal Christianity, whether authored by cardinals and popes, neo-fundamentalists, or neo-liberal and neo-orthodox refurbishers of earlier twentieth-century modernist patriarchal piety.

All efforts to reconstitute a Powerful Voice of Truth that seeks to enable mainline Christianity to "compete" with the new, modernist fundamentalism so different from earlier traditionalist resistance to modernity (also sometimes labeled "fundamentalist") are doomed to failure. The new neo-fundamentalism is totally identified with the myths of National Imperium and it is passionately *anti-historical* and *anti-particular*. It involves an embrace of very modernist scientific Master Narrative theories of truth. Since the future spirituality of this culture will never again be shaped imperialistically by oldline Christian traditions, imitating fundamentalism is silly. The imperative of placing the well-being of women and children and marginated men at the center of our spirituality and challenging and exposing this fundamentalist dominant public Christianity is what is needed.

Ours is a world whose very survival depends upon our learning, and quickly, very different notions of truth and spirituality than those generated by Eurocentric dominant modernist epistemologies, whether these privilege "Revelation" or "Science." The imperative is to recognize that truth is pluriform, complex, changing, and unfolding, that true spirituality is about "learning to learn" (Segundo), about movement, about creating new solidarities, about resisting, together, the Master Narratives of those who wish to keep their power in place.

The feminism generated by the largely white, middle-strata women included in this study is hardly sufficient in itself to bring out the needed paradigm shift. Fortunately the search for alternative spiritualities is aided by powerful emerging Third World feminisms and by womanist and *mujerista* theologies that demand a more complex and radical analysis of oppression. These voices are deepening and reshaping white feminist spiritualities and pushing us to a deeper sense of justice as well.

Even so, among Christians in the "oldline" traditions shaped by European spirituality, the feminisms described here in their varied guises do provide a genuine critical opening toward spiritualities that correct the distortions of the Eurocentric episteme. We must learn to ground our spirituality in what European theological traditions most fear — physical embodiment, cultural particularity, and the unavoidable reality of multifaceted interdependence and cosmic interconnection.

~ 6 ~

A *Mujerista* Perspective on the Future of the Women's Movement and the Church

Ada Maria Isasi-Diaz

For generations Hispanic women have been doing what feminists seem to be doing today: we have determined how to relate to the Catholic Church instead of allowing the church to impose on us how to do it. Oh, it is not that they have not tried; for example, one of the commandments of the Catholic Church is that we are to go to Mass Sundays and holy days under pain of mortal sin. But, as the crudest of church attendance statistics will show, Latinas have not considered that essential to being Catholic. Yes, in a culture that is still a religious culture, we have learned to separate our religion from the church and relate to the church insofar as we need it to maintain and/or celebrate our faith and our daily struggles for survival.

But the fact is that the way Hispanic women relate to the church, our quiet rebellion — a "defecting in place," if you want — has had little or no impact on the institutional church. The church continues to give little importance to the lives of Latinas and it pays little if any attention to our religious understandings and practices, to our faith traditions, and to our moral struggles. It seems to me that the strategy of defecting in place that Hispanic women have followed for centuries and that many other women also follow at present has been mostly ineffectual. For example, not long ago the local TV news reported that the cardinal of New York had used the Sunday homily to insist that the Catholic Church would endure until the end of time. It was obvious that what he meant was that the church would not change, that the hierarchy would not consider any changes regarding birth control, lesbian and gay rights in the church, the full participation of women in the official ministry of the church—no matter what, the church would continue the way it is.

Strategies are conceived in order to accomplish something. Strate-

231

gies have to be evaluated from, among other things, the perspective of effectiveness. Yes, our vision of a fully inclusive church has indeed influenced many church-goers, but it has brought about no systemic change in the church. Therefore, since the strategy of defecting in place that Latinas have followed for centuries has been mostly ineffectual, it is time for *mujeristas* and all other feminists to consider other ways of letting the hierarchy of the church know who we are, what we feel, how we think about the lack of justice for women in the church. I think this is precisely what has to become the agenda of feminist groups for which religious faith and the gospel message of justice and peace are generative. I understand how our need to survive as women in the midst of religious institutions that are so oppressive and alienating has lead us to concentrate on supporting each other instead of giving priority to what we need to do to change the institutional church. But the fact is that if feminist support groups do not become feminist *action* groups, and if our women's communities do not preoccupy themselves with struggling against oppression in the church as much as with struggling against injustices in society, I am afraid the church will never change. And, what is saddest of all, many of us do not seem to comprehend that as long as the church is a patriarchal, hierarchical institution, it will continue to uphold societal structures that are oppressive precisely because they are patriarchal and hierarchical.

I believe three things need to happen for feminist religious groups to become feminist religious *action* groups. First, we need to recognize that most of us continue to promote all sorts of false dichotomies between the so-called spiritual and the corporeal, between prayer and action, between society and church. As long as we do this we will be helping the hierarchy by giving them grounds to argue that they can be preoccupied about justice in the world without working to establish justice for all in the church. I have heard bishops and priests in several different countries ardently defend the right of the poor and the oppressed to define what constitutes justice for them. And I have also heard some of those very same men ardently deny women the right to define what constitutes for us justice in the church. I remember years ago when a U.S. bishop wrote a pastoral in which he denounced sexism as a sin. We were so elated; then we talked to him. He told us that the church's insistence on denying ordination to women has nothing to do with sexism — it is not a sin.

I think the time has come for *mujeristas* and all other feminists to proclaim boldly that justice is a seamless garment, that the bishops cannot expect to be taken seriously when they champion the oppressed ones of society while they continue to be oppressors of women in the church. It is time that *mujeristas* and all other feminists take very seriously the fact that action on behalf of justice for women in church and society is prayer and that real prayer is not possible apart from justice-seeking in all realms of life. It is time for us to understand and proclaim that we cannot be about supporting each other apart from actively engaging in struggling against what oppresses us in church and societal structures.

Second, and a corollary of my first point, *mujeristas* and all other feminists have to understand that the church is a historical reality, a sociological institution. Therefore, one of the most effective ways we can pressure it is by using our economic power. It is an established fact that in the majority of the homes women are the ones who decide how much money to contribute to the church. It is also a well-known fact that women are extremely reticent about using our economic power to pressure the church. For centuries it has been Hispanic women who have kept the church going. For centuries we have made *tortillas*, *pasteles*, and *tamales* to feed the clergy, to repair churches, to pay for church programs. But when women are asked to join an economic boycott of the church, we become guilt-ridden and refuse to do so. And yet, what more effective way could we speak to the church than with the power of the purse? What other way can we make the church pay attention to women's just demands? Many studies, including this present one, show that the majority of those polled feel women should be ordained in the Catholic Church. But I am convinced we could get not even 10 percent of those women to withhold their church contributions. The time has come for that to change. The time has come for *mujeristas* and all other feminists to understand that it is not illegal nor immoral to join an economic boycott of an oppressive structure: the church.

Third, *mujeristas* and all other feminists have to be much more vocal about the oppression we suffer in the church. Recently I went to lunch with a friend. The young woman who waited on us kept calling us "you guys." I sheepishly kept quiet, not wanting to embarrass the young waitress. But my friend simply said to her, "First of all, we are not guys." When the young woman left my friend said to me, "I feel my whole life is a big CR — one constant consciousness-raising effort." That is precisely what all of us justice-seeking women have to do. We have to take our struggle for justice in the church so seriously that we will use every single opportunity to make people aware of the sexism that exists in the church. Initially we might feel embarrassed, but soon we will realize that our consciousness-raising efforts are moments of affirmation for ourselves, women who are made in the image and likeness of God.

And the church, what about the Catholic Church? I continue to believe in miracles; I continue to believe in the presence of God among us. I believe that change is possible, that it will happen. But that does not excuse the church for its present-day deafness, for its lack of willingness to listen to the *sensus fidelium*, to the belief of the majority of the people through which the Holy Spirit makes herself present in the church. I believe that the church will endure until the end of time, but I believe that it is up to each and every one of us, the clergy and hierarchy included, to see to it what role the church will play in shaping the future of our world. I believe that unless the church changes radically and ardently pursues justice within its structures as well as in society at large, the role of the church in our world will diminish more and more.

When it comes to women's issues the church has abdicated its responsibility. When it comes to women's issues the church is a rear-guard prophet, if a prophet at all. An old Spanish saying proclaims, "El profeta que va a la cola no merece el pan que come," "rear-guard prophets are not worthy of the bread they eat." *Mujeristas* and other feminists rightfully say to the church today: "I am hungry for justice; have you fed me? I am suffering oppression and injustice; have you struggled with me for justice?" It is up to the hierarchy and to the clergy, those who have power in the church, to act in such a way that the church will be an active participant in the unfolding of the kindom of God instead of being a stumbling block to the establishment of justice and peace for women and all peoples in our world.

Feminism: A Critique from a Sociohistorical Perspective

Marie Augusta Neal

Feminism is the name currently accorded, by design, to what was formerly generalized as the "Women's Movement." The latter term now brings to mind the older struggle of women for the right to vote. The names of Elizabeth Cady Stanton and Lucretia Mott mark the initiation of that struggle at Seneca Falls, New York, in 1848. There followed several decades of demand for the right to participate in the economy, supported by the work of Charlotte Perkins Gilman in the 1890s. The demand for entry into educational institutes for advanced degrees accelerated in the 1920s, and for equal pay for equal work in 1963 with the Kennedy Commission on the Status of Women, thanks to the persistence of Esther Peterson. In general, this struggle for equality is the agenda associated with NOW, the National Organization for Women.[1] The goal of this early activity was the elimination of inequality in access to a share in society's channels to power and wealth or, more simply, to a measure of freedom and security for women.

The early phase of the women's movement claimed that women can do what men can do and that work so done should be similarly recognized by appointment to similar jobs leading to access to power, wealth, and status. Trying to achieve this access constituted the theme of the historic struggle. Working out these demands, however, led to the discovery of hidden networks of resistance to women's competing for these channels of reward. This suggested the need of a much more complex framework for the next stage of development of movements for the liberation of women.

Resistance was embedded in the culture of society caught in historical processes associated not only with nature but also with nurture. The change of wording in the name of the movement from "women's" to "feminist" indicated new functions, including a questioning of the value of merely participating in a ruthless struggle for power, wealth, and status. Something more was happening as women discovered the structures that kept male dominance in place: the "old boy" network and the lackey roles of younger men, for example. Some women concluded they could add humanizing qualities to a somewhat unscrupulous system. They could work toward changing the goals to include the making of a more humane society by introducing from their experience in family life the transformation of political and economic structures to operate as community rather than hierarchy, as solidarity more than conflict, cooperation over competition. But would it work? Such goals sound naive to those convinced that might makes right and that market competition is of human nature.[2] The feminist movement, however, found the challenge worth a try.

In trying, however, they changed some of the goals women had organized to achieve within the system. They also changed the assumptions about the nature of women to "equal as human beings" but speaking "in a different voice."[3] This assumption could be rooted in nature and/or nurture. It opened, for some, the hope of changing the system to one that is more humane. It also opened the movement to reform-minded men and initiated differences in point of view among the membership, as yet only loosely organized for these new emphases.

Currently, the feminist movement also emphasizes denouncing the practice of aggressive and hostile sexual relationships like rape, whether within or outside marriage, and making them punishable as crime. Achievement of peer relationships as colleagues in the workplace highlighted the incongruity of tolerating invasive sexual behavior without peer consent. Furthermore, recognition of women as peers in the workplace raised to consciousness the need to demand similar relationships within the institutions of family and recreation and the need to put all sexual practice into the same moral perspective of respect for the individual's human rights.

Affirming the choice to generate families and to control family size as equally the right of both partners is current agenda for feminists. The new norm is "the right to choose." The societal imperative derives from the expanding pace of world population and the need for voluntary restraint. This affirmation disassociates expressive sexual behavior from reproduction and introduces the agenda of contraception, abortion, and lesbian relationships into the movement to protect a woman's right to choose family making as a way of life. This is a far different distribution of decision-making power from that of old Roman patriarchal law, which gave the father full power of life or death over his subordinates, named as wives, children, and slaves. The responsibilities of this division of right are currently poorly understood and practiced. The implications only slowly reveal themselves. The responsibilities are many; the implications, culture-changing.

Consider one case. Only recently has the model of patriarch as landlord been challenged in church and society. It is still operative in canon law with respect to property ownership. Its link to homelessness, work, and ownership, to human rights, health, education, and social welfare for the dispossessed are only now becoming evident, generating new insights regarding human rights and the common good.[4] However, the recognition of this agenda as linked to the right to choose is slight. Though rich in biblical reference, it still evades commitment even on the part of women who have defined this content as feminist. It challenges a masculine culture of claiming possession of wealth in private property through family-name–linked inheritance with obligations only of charity and not of justice toward those who have worked the land over a lifetime of underpaid or unpaid labor. The extended implication of this reality for housing is yet to be explored.

Consider another case. Once they become a professionally skilled work force not needing support as women, many women question their loss of identity in the change of name at marriage. This factor adds to the growing instability of marriage and family life, given the practice of sexual permissiveness outside of marriage, guided only by an outmoded set of rules resting on assumptions of patriarchy. Why choose father's name? Why not mother's, depending on which partner is more stable? The critical analysis of several outmoded rules is suggested here. The "glass ceiling" functioning in both church and state gradually reveal to newly enfranchised women the control that men still have over their lives, a control no longer tolerable once they become equal in trained competence yet remain outside the system of decision-making, respect, and rewards simply because they are not men.

Commitment to the creation of a just global society puts forth the realization of social justice in global perspective as the commitment of those dedicated to fostering the stability and integrity of family life. The question posing itself is this: What grounds these rights that challenge institutional structure? The research dares to claim religion as a grounding factor for the retention or reinstatement of those practices whose symbolic expression reinforces beliefs about God's steadfast love and abiding care and God's relationships with the world as Creator, Redeemer, and Sanctifier. Hence, liturgy has a place in the struggle for human rights, social justice, and peace. This constitutes a faith position that links the feminist movement with the struggles against racism and classism and the subtle siding of science versus religion in addressing issues of equal worth and suggests the link of these latter "isms" with the coming crises in ageism, healthism, and environmentalism. The questions, Who shall live? Who shall die? and Who shall decide? are the ultimate questions of inequality. The ancient structures no longer satisfy a woman's right to know how to share responsibility for life and death as peer.

The Hartford evidence shows that women's groups are meeting for a range of reasons, from prayer in new forms and the practice of inclusive liturgies around images of God unfamiliar to the Christian traditions, to demands for leadership roles in the church on the basis of the right to participate in decisions that affect not only their own lives but also those of the global community. The feminist movement is recently more awakened to action to change unjust systems in the direction of satisfying the needs of the poor as a special option. Although the Hartford study found only a third of their sample intensely aware of that priority, the evidence points to a future development in this direction.

The Hartford Seminary study of feminist spirituality groups raises many questions about the significance of women's support groups for the future of church and society. The evidence indicates that such groups are increasing and that they have some common agenda regarding critique of the church in its present patriarchal structure. Furthermore, there is evidence that some institutionalized dimensions of church structure are already being effectively challenged by these women: namely, the continued use of sexist language in prayer and scripture reading and the predominance of a single-sexed leadership in liturgy, as well as in church governance. Many of the women meeting in feminist spirituality groups see themselves as really different from most women. They experience alienation from the church, even though, for the most part, they remain participating members of a local congregation. Some experience anger and alienation from the church sufficiently strong to cause defection, but in general they decide to "defect in place." This expression will probably become more familiar as the movement picks up momentum and organizational structure. Am I assuming that it will so do? Yes. Why? Because in many respects the findings of this exploratory study using purposive and snowball techniques reinforce and, in some cases, confirm the Sisters' Survey, which used a longitudinal and probability sample of American Catholic Sisters at three time periods beginning in 1966.[5]

New Responsibilities for Social Justice Agenda

Historically, the commitment of the Catholic Church to the social justice agenda accelerated from 1891 through 1991 and is marked by the publication of Pope Leo XIII's *Rerum Novarum* in 1891, followed by anniversary documents in 1931, 1961, 1971, 1981, and 1991.[6] Each of these documents was followed by a major movement toward the liberation of some group suffering from lack of the resources needed for life. The labor movement occupied *Rerum Novarum* and *Quadragesimo Anno*, 1931. Third World countries were the focus of *Mater et Magistra*, 1961, and *Octogesima Adveniens*, 1971; *Laborem Exercens* in 1981 took up the groundbreaking claims to ownership related to work with all their implications of human rights to health, education, and welfare. Documents within each decade developed the implications for rights of the poor to share the resources of the world until the Catholic Church formally in the 1970s declared "an option for the poor" as mandated by Vatican II. The World Council of Churches from 1910 has followed a similar development of the social justice agenda and much of this movement was done together. The United Nations Bill of Human Rights follows this development but expresses in its final published format the unresolved conflict that characterized the debate and the vote for its adoption finally in 1976. The West could accept a covenant that protected human freedom but saw the right to human services as goals to strive for rather than rights to demand, while the East recognized the human services as rights but not the human freedoms.[7]

The presence of communism supporting human services with an atheistic ideology generated resistance to the adoption of the bill and drew suspicion on the implementation of this social justice agenda in the United States. Here it was viewed as part of a communist plot against capitalism, naively supported by old Catholic countries unable to throw off their feudal past, rooted in a tradition of patriarchy and endangering the development of democracy. With a phase of this historic struggle coming to a close, consider the activities of the United States Conference of Bishops. Since the 1976 Call to Action national gathering in Detroit, the bishops have been able to produce pastorals on racism, the economy, and peace but, after two tries, they have failed to speak as a body to sexism in the church. In his 1988 encyclical *Sollicitudo Rei Socialis*, Pope John Paul II condemns capitalism equally with communism as ideologies exploiting poor people and equally godless in orientation.

Women, aware of the oppression of patriarchal systems making fathers privileged ones, are moving to the justice agenda in global perspective. Democracy is the route chosen. We are a global society in the making. We are a violent world attempting to resolve differences by winning wars, i.e., by might. Many have lost confidence in that process because it destroys innocent bystanders and leaves as winners only those with greater firepower. We delete prayers extolling violence, yet new religious movements defy this selected reading of scripture and put violence back in. God gets lost in this patriarchal struggle of violence.

The challenge today is in the realization of the social justice agenda. How do you claim the land when the parties at war have all experienced it as their own? What replaces a no longer effective patriarchy? How name God in this dilemma so that the lion can lie down with the lamb and we know war no more? This is the challenge to women, the primary victims of patriarchy.

~ 8 ~

Women-Church
on the Road to Change

Diann L. Neu

Women-church communities and women's spiritual support groups are emerging across the United States and throughout the world because patriarchal religions have failed women, children, and women-identified men. Participants are in search of a sense of meaning and purpose that can direct our thoughts and actions for personal growth and social change. We are interested in being church, not simply in leaving or staying in churches that do not meet our needs. Even the most far-reaching reform is not sufficient to the need we have to be religious on our own terms.

I look at women-church both as a member of a local base community and as a professional dedicated to its enhancement through my role as co-founder and co-director of WATER, the Women's Alliance for Theology, Ethics and Ritual. WATER is a feminist nonprofit educational center, a network of justice-seeking people that began in 1983 as a response to the need for serious theological, ethical, and liturgical development for and by women. We work locally, nationally, and internationally doing programs, projects, workshops, retreats, counseling, and liturgical planning that have helped people be part of an inclusive church and society. WATER works in coalition with the Women-church Convergence, a network of thirty-five women-church organizations and groups rooted in the Catholic tradition but encompassing a spiritual arena far beyond it.

Trained both for Catholic priesthood and for social work, I understand my vocation as liturgist and therapist to be the kind of ministry that future generations will undertake as part of women-church rather than as ordained clergy in denominations or as social workers in secular agencies. While this combination makes for an exciting and creative career, it also entails an extra measure of frustration through lack of definition in structural and institutional terms. In short, we at WATER create as we go in a now ten-year-old organization that has women-church at its center. The women-church movement needs dozens more such organizations providing regional support, creative ideas and education, children's programs, and kindred projects to bring it to fruition and to achieve social and ecclesial change.

From my vantage point, women-church is alive, healthy, and well on the road to making a real difference both for individuals and for the larger religious community. Women-church encourages the development of local groups where the movement is most vibrant. Nationally, women-church is developing vehicles for communicating, like the Women-church Convergence and organizational newsletters such as *WATERwheel* and *New Women/New Church*. Internationally, the movement has made connections among U.S. women-church, counterparts in New Zealand, Australia, and Korea, *frauen-kirche* in Germany and Switzerland, Latin American *mujer-iglesia* groups, and others in Southeast Asia and Africa. The lives and actions of women who are part of the movement leave the strong impression that something important is afoot.

My reflections are hopes as well as projections; my approach is that of an advocate as well as an observer. I expect that the results of the survey material will go some way toward enlightening and encouraging people about a movement that I believe plays an important part in reshaping the religious landscape.

The study results show that women-church as a movement and phenomenon is here to stay. For growing numbers of people, especially women, it has set in motion a dynamic alternative to patriarchal Christianity, something that no mere "women and" addendum could accomplish. Many others have found women-church to be a lifeline to maintaining some tie to their faith traditions without compromising themselves. Internal denominational changes have been more far-reaching because of fundamental challenges from women-church to Christianity, calling not simply for cosmetic overhaul but for deep structural shifts. Without the witness of nonordained but sacrament-celebrating Catholic women in women-church, ordained women in sacramental denominations would not have the strong inspiration and encouragement they need to rethink their own styles of ministry.

Women-church proclaims through sacrament and solidarity, story and song that women are church. This is different from merely belonging to a church or even leaving a church, since it signals that women are essentially what patriarchy has denied, namely, religious protagonists able to shape and create the reality called church. Women-church recognizes that from generation to generation feminists work for a new dawn when "justice will roll down like water," when patriarchy will be transformed into circles of equality, and when diversity will be treasured. Women-church as a movement is evidence of just how much work must be done on all of these fronts. As Mary E. Hunt says in her introductory remarks to *Women-Church Sourcebook*, published by WATER,

> Defining women-church in the negatives, saying what women-church is not, will help to clarify what I mean. Women-church is not an organization with members, elected officials, even with its own clergy. It is not a club from which men are excluded and in which children are tolerated if they keep quiet. It is not the women's auxiliary of the larger church. Nor it is simply a place where women who have been wounded by patriarchy can find comfort.

And she calls women-church, "a global, ecumenical movement made up of local feminist base communities of justice-seeking friends who engage in sacrament and solidarity."

The biblical Mary spoke in the Magnificat of a justice-based spirituality when she experienced God/ess acting to feed the hungry, bring the powerful out of their hierarchies, and offer liberation to those who live under oppression. Women-church communities live this justice-based spirituality by designing rituals that are inclusive, creating myths that portray women as strong doers, not passive receivers, using symbols that express women's life experiences, and encouraging relationships that value women and all oppressed peoples as equals.

The women-church movement is in process of defining itself in a range of ways: theological, liturgical, political, and social action, among others. In terms of constituency, women-church is a global ecumenical movement, first named and claimed in the U.S. by Catholic women, but now having a global reach on its own terms in many countries throughout the world. Men are beginning to seek ways to affiliate as women-church; children's parents and care sharers are asking how children can *be* women-church, that is, participate in communities in ways that are age- and situation-appropriate. Adults seek ways to help children bypass the experiences producing the direct confrontation with patriarchal religion that has brought so many women to the movement in the first place.

Liturgy and community, social justice and solidarity are what most women want when they become part of a women-church community or a women's spiritual support group. I devote considerable time and attention to developing liturgies that speak to, for, and about women's lived experiences as religious expression. Women come to these groups because we are starved for a language that sustains us spiritually, for a symbol system we can call our own. We yearn for rituals that speak to our concerns, needs, desires, dreams, and practices.

We seek to be part of an intentional community that worships in a way that embraces our sense of ourselves as religious, that does justice, and that does not offend our political sensibilities in a world that is slowly but surely becoming more inclusive despite the backlash of the late twentieth century.

Women-church groups are comprised of women of faith who in a patriarchal culture must create the context of our own spirituality. Women-church groups recognize the historical and contemporary oppression of women, especially poor women and women of diverse racial and ethnic backgrounds, as well as dependent children. Women-church groups seek to change social structures and personal attitudes to stop oppression, but we recognize that no one can sustain such efforts without a strong, firm basis in faith. It is that basis that the groups seek to undergird, not by rescuing patriarchal notions but by rediscovering and, if need be, inventing new dimensions of faith.

Likewise, I find a women-church strand in the counselling and supervision I do, the feminist spiritual direction and feminist therapy that I combine to help women cope with and make sense out of their lives. Many women who come to me for counseling regarding abuse, violence, reproductive choice, self-esteem, separation, and death have turned away from patriarchal churches. Many of them are veterans of long struggles to wrest recognition, acceptance, even a crumb of acknowledgment from the denomination of their upbringing, struggles that they cannot expect to win because of patriarchal odds. Further, given that some of the very issues women are dealing with have been provoked or caused by the churches — Catholic women seeking ordination, women told to stay with abusive spouses for religious reasons, women embodying an image deemed "not good enough" — it is important to provide real alternatives grounded in a different theological view. These women hunger and thirst after right-living, a human right, but something that they have not found in the religious traditions of their birth. They demand, crave, savor liturgies of affirmation, support, and healing that offer new words and new ways to express their holiness, liturgies that provide a strong supplement to their therapy.

WATER sponsors a monthly women-church group that is much like the dozens of such groups that exist all over the country. Participants find at WATER a place where they can be church once again, where they can pay quality attention to their spirituality, and where they can participate in the creation of an intentional community in which they do not have to translate language, rehearse presuppositions, or explain their needs. As an added plus, they can borrow books and tapes from an extensive resource center, attend seminars and workshops where the intellectual dimensions of their growing feminist faith will be expanded, and network with like-minded justice seekers.

WATER's *Women-Church Sourcebook* describes ways to start a group. It includes names and addresses of women-church groups around the country for networking purposes. It describes the history and liturgical life of the movement, offers guidelines for planning a women-church liturgy, and provides sample liturgies. WATER has been connecting women-church groups for the past ten years. Letters and calls come from individuals, organizations, the media, for everything from worship planning, research and writing, and counselling referrals to background information and interviews — in short, connections between and among people and groups seeking to be women-church, to understand women-church, and to bring its theological flavor to mainline churches as well.

More such agencies are needed to attend to the needs of women for whom the parallel resources of institutional churches are inadequate. The Mautner Project for Lesbians with Cancer is one such agency for which WATER provides spiritual resources, resources that frankly no other religious group seems as well suited to offer. Women living with serious illness do not need the additional indignity of inadequate religious support that condemns their lifestyle. Besides accompanying women with cancer and their partners and families, we invite people to bring attention to the spiritual side of illness and death. Without emphasizing one particular faith tradition and in the spirit of women-church's openness to the range of ways women choose to be religious, we provide spiritual resources.

The study at hand shows women voting with their feet against institutional churches that seem capable only of minimal accommodation rather than openness to real changes in power models, understandings of ministry, and the like that are at the heart of women-church. Still, it would seem easier to reform old models than to create whole new ways of being church, primarily because institutions will provide the resources for their own transformation but surely not for their competition. Nonetheless, more than 1200 attended the 1983 women-church gathering in Chicago, "From Generation to Generation: Woman Church Speaks"; more than 3200 attended the 1987 gathering in Cincinnati, "Women-Church: Claiming Our Power"; and more than 2400 women attended the 1993 gathering in Albuquerque, "Women-Church: Weavers of Change." These gatherings of women-church demonstrate the vitality of the movement. It is not, however, seamless: we know problems of racism, class differences, and the like plague the U.S. movement. Yet, consider the fact that Christianity is two thousand years old and suffers from the same problems, while women-church is a mere ten years old and already focusing such issues. Much work needs to be done to build an inclusive movement, but at least we can see efforts made and progress, though small, on the horizon.

Women-church as a movement raises the question whether the time and energy women spend on reforming institutional churches is really a trap. Does it keep women working on an agenda they did not set and therefore co-opt or at least retard progress toward religious agency? It raises the question whether institutional churches are really capable of or interested in changes, or whether such efforts as the World Council of Churches' Ecumenical Decade in Solidarity with Women are merely ways to keep women busy while churches go their patriarchal way. There are no definitive answers yet, but at least women-church presents an option for autonomous ways of being religious that shift the burden from deconstruction to construction, from responding and reshaping to creating and confirming.

The theological foundation of women-church as articulated by Elisabeth Schüssler Fiorenza in her recent volume *Discipleship of Equals* involves "a liberation theological integration of biblical roots both with Western notions of liberty and democracy and with the radical egalitarian vision of the 'Grandmothers' society...'" (372). This approach is both global in its vision and particular in its application so that U.S. women are merely one piece of a much larger, more colorful mosaic that is women-church in many places on terms set by those many contexts. There is discussion of an international synod for the turn of the century, but details and logistics remain to be imagined, since the variety alone presents a daunting task. Meanwhile, communication and networking between and among women-church communities and with women's spiritual support groups is essential. WATER's resource center is a repository for many of the publications of these groups, the newsletters, flyers, and lists of events that are evidence of the movement's growth and vitality.

Women-church is on the road, making a difference in women's lives and, therefore, creating change in all those that women touch — children, loved ones, families, friends, neighborhoods, churches, organizations. It is unfair to expect more from a ten-year-old movement than from a two-thousand-year-old church. Women-church cannot solve all problems overnight, nor invent immediately *ex nihilo*, especially considering women's economic and social/political status in a patriarchal culture. Rather, we can rejoice in what we have created thus far and at how it is leavening the rest of the churches and society at large. The more important task is getting on with the day-to-day work, as we do at WATER, of responding to women's various physical and spiritual needs, and empowering women to be church for perhaps the first time in history.

9

Defecting in Place: Reflections on Women's Spiritual Quest and New Support Groups

Rosemary Radford Ruether

The study of women from the Christian traditions who are seeking spiritual support groups, in addition to their regular parish assemblies, points to a significant phenomenon in late twentieth-century North America and also globally (although the international aspect of this phenomenon goes beyond the limits of the study). A significant number of women from Catholic, liberal Protestant, and, to a lesser extent, conservative Protestant traditions feel deeply alienated from their existing institutional churches specifically as women. In other words, they feel that these churches fail to affirm them sufficiently as women, not only in terms of using their talents for leadership, but also theologically and spiritually, i.e., affirming an understanding of God and God's relation to creation that is inclusive of women and women's experience.

Such women then are seeking and forming alternative communities that do affirm their capacities for initiative and leadership and that do allow the expression of women's experience theologically and spiritually. Yet by and large these women are not choosing the familiar schismatic solution. They do not definitively leave all affiliation with historical Christianity or their particular branch of it and found a new feminist church. Instead, they combine attendance at a women's support group with some relation to and membership in a historical church, ranging from attending its assemblies in a dissatisfied mood to actually being official leaders of such churches, i.e., ordained clergy.

What is the meaning of this combination of strategies, this "defecting in place"? Is it simply a temporary or transitional solution until a compelling new feminist church arises that such people can join? Or is it a more long-term pattern in which women (and some men) will shape new community forms to have the freedom to experiment and live a new vision now, while continuing to witness to the institutional church, eventually creating a new synthesis, a sufficiently transformed institution so that most of the demands of the movement for feminist communities can be satisfied in the regular parish assemblies?

This question cannot be answered at the moment, not simply because the research accumulated contains insufficient data to answer it, but because what is being uncovered here is a process whose future is still unrealized. Depending largely on whether the institutional churches respond to women's demands, or refuse to respond and even turn reactionary and repressive toward such demands, either of these two directions or even some combination of both of them may shape the future.

The study is limited by the methodology chosen, namely, by the decision to gather random answers from a pool of people whose relation to certain journals and centers indicated their likelihood to have interests in feminist spirituality. This method was useful in showing a certain spread of such interests, but it also allowed the phenomenon to remain rather anonymous. A more targeted methodology, such as going specifically to groups that affiliate with the Women-church network, would have yielded a narrower sample, primarily Catholic, but also a group that is more conscious of creating a specific movement with an emerging history and identity.

My remarks in this reflection will focus on my experience with the Women-church network and how it compares with the findings of the study.

The chief difference between the subjects reported in the grant survey and the Women-church movement is that the latter does not only impel the formation of feminist spiritual communities on the local level, but also has constructed a national network. This network has rubrics for affiliating with it and has a history of assembling national conferences at roughly five-year intervals. The first national conference was held in Chicago in 1983, the second in Cincinnati in 1987, and the third in Albuquerque in 1993. In addition there are local affiliates, such as Women-Church Massachusetts, which have established their organization on a regional basis and have yearly assemblies, a newsletter, and a fund for supporting women's ministries.

The Women-church movement thus has taken on some of the apparatus of a feminist church organization. At the same time it has also refused to be a distinct "church." It has rejected the creation of any national office or leadership in favor of being a network of local organizations that may range from being simply a single local group, to being an umbrella organization of groups in a region (like

Women-Church Massachusetts or Chicago Catholic Women), to being a feminist caucus within a national movement (such as the Grail Women's Taskforce), to even being a national organization, such as Catholics for a Free Choice. By refusing to link these distinct groups into a superstructure or to provide any ongoing central office for the movement, other than a clearing house for the coordination of the distinct groups, Women-church also refuses to become an institution in itself.

This refusal to institutionalize itself as a church also means that Women-church refuses to define itself in terms of a set of polarized options. It does not direct its members either to stay within their local churches or to leave them. It does not mandate that they remain defined as members of a particular denomination. It does not limit its members to being Christian or demand that they be post-Christian. It consciously refuses these either-ors in favor of a process approach that allows a variety of options along a spectrum.

This spectrum might include a feminist support group of women who all belong not only to the same denomination but also to the same parish. Whether officially sanctioned or not, such a group is a parish-based subcommunity. Some women-church groups that affiliate with regional networks, such as Women-Church Massachusetts, may be of this type. More commonly women-church groups draw from a region, e.g., a city such as Chicago or Baltimore, and bring together women from a number of neighborhoods. In some cases these women are almost entirely Catholic; in other cases, such as those who worship in the Women of Faith Center in Chicago, they may come from both Catholic and Protestant backgrounds and may even include an occasional Jew.

Women-church groups also adopt a worship style that, while predominantly Christian, does not feel the need to be exclusively so. It may also draw prayers or rituals from Goddess groups, Native Americans, and other religious traditions. It is thus ecumenical both within and beyond Christianity, while rejecting the schismatic insistence that one must either be exclusively Christian or else reject Christianity altogether as hopelessly patriarchal and inimical to women.

While much of historical Christianity may be judged as deeply patriarchal and alienating, this judgment is not extended to its founder, Jesus, who is claimed as an advocate of justice, including justice for women. Thus women-church remains within a reforming strategy, although a radical one. It claims the original foundations of Christianity as in line with a feminist transformation and calls on the historical churches to reform themselves in order to be authentically faithful to the one they claim as their founder.

This both-and strategy of women-church groups, both in and beyond the church, both in and beyond a particular denomination, both in and beyond Christianity, is jeopardized by polarizing forces in the churches and beyond the churches who reject this bridging process as inconsistent or wrong. Within both Catholicism and conservative Protestantism they are groups claiming to be representatives of an immutable orthodoxy that reject in principle inclusive language and understandings of God and spirituality that include female, particularly bodily, experiences, and sometimes reject women's ordination.

These "orthodox" groups insist that any group that goes beyond these limits is heretical and "pagan." They have not only ceased to be orthodox Christians of a particular tradition; they have ceased to be Christians at all. They are covert, if not overt, advocates of a false religion of nature worship, i.e., paganism. Since paganism in Christian rhetoric is associated not only with wrong thought but in some sense also with devil worship, such groups do not hesitate to label women's church groups "witches," thus using the language of demonizing a religious enemy as ones who are fundamentally evil and deserve to be purged from the church, if not killed.

Clearly such demonizing rhetoric could be the force that impels some feminist spiritual groups to despair of church reform and to side with those who claim that Christianity is not only deformed historically by patriarchy, but it, in its every essence, is patriarchal. They will be forced to conclude that women, in order to find a spiritual home, must desert Christianity for a women's religion, either one that is to be created now or one that revives an ancient women's religion that supposedly was crushed thousands of years ago with the rise of patriarchy.

Feminist spiritual groups on the inside and outside edge of the churches face polarizers on the left as well as on the right. The post-Christian polarizers identify with all that the "orthodox" vilify, namely, with "paganism," "witches," and "nature religion." Only for them, this has nothing to do with devils or evil, but is in fact the true healing religion for humans and all nature that was repressed by evil religions that reflect evil social systems, namely, patriarchy. For them Christianity is the evil religion, and paganism is the good "old time" religion.

Feminist spiritual communities who "defect in place" thus are faced with polarizing groups who insist on an either-or: either totally in a particular historical Christian tradition or else totally out of it. The one group wishes to push them out of their remaining claims on Christianity and the other group wishes to pull them out by demanding they recognize their "inconsistencies" and the hopelessness of their hopes for reform.

The outcome of this process is still in the future. But in my opinion it is the option of the "defectors in place" that is both more creative and more authentic than that of the polarizers of either right or left, for they remain faithful to a dialectical, transformative process and affirm both the good elements and also ambiguity in all our human traditions. But in order to sustain their both-and option, they will have to become much more mature in their understanding of this option, much more able to face their accusers of both right and left without fear or guilt and to give reasons for rejecting their mutually exclusive alternatives.

10

Searching for a
Church in the Round

Letty M. Russell

I have always found it difficult to walk away from the church, but I have also found it difficult to walk with it! This sort of love/hate relationship with the church was established at an early age. I was baptized and raised in the Presbyterian Church of Westfield, New Jersey. From the time I was in kindergarten until I went to college I was expected to be at church school or church every Sunday. However, there were times when I found it rather unexciting. For instance, when I was in kindergarten I ran away from church school and walked home to announce to my astonished and horrified mother that my class was boring! Some sixty years later I still find that attending church is often boring, but now I find that it is also alienating. It is this alienation that I face as I begin a journey to seek out what church might mean from a feminist perspective.

The alienation is shared with many other women and men whose pain and anger at the contradictions and oppression of church life lead them to challenge the very idea of talking about a feminist interpretation of the church. It is also increased by the knowledge of the disdain and anger of those theologians and church officials who consider women like me to be the *problem* rather than the church itself. It is impossible for me and for many other alienated women and men to walk away from the church, however, for it has been the bearer of the story of Jesus Christ and the good news of God's love. It seems rather that we have to sit back and ask ourselves about what is happening among us when two or three gather in Christ's name and begin to think through possible ways of being church that affirm the full humanity of *all* women and men.[1]

Ways of Being Church

Women and men are beginning to do just this in many parts of the world. What they are learning about new forms of partnership in the church provides us with many examples of faith and struggle for survival in the midst of oppressive ecclesial and social settings. Among these are the feminist Christian communities included in the Hartford Seminary study of the "Effects of Women's Communities of Support and Inspiration on Participants and Congregations in Catholic and Protestant Traditions" [the study's working title]. Those of us who share in both alienation and hope for transformation are greatly appreciative of the work of those who conducted this study and the Lilly Foundation's funding of the process. As a white, Protestant theologian I have been seeking out clues to new understandings of ecclesiology and testing these against the actual accounts of such groups, and I have been greatly helped by being part of the Hartford Seminary study as a consultant. I expect that further analysis of the report will provide additional insights into possibilities for transformation.

I myself am particularly interested in ways that feminist and liberation communities seek to live out a vision of new creation in which there is a possibility of wholeness in relationship among women and men of all races, classes, sexual orientations, and abilities, as well as the whole of creation. This vision of a transformed Christian community is what I have called "Church in the Round."[2] To speak of "church in the round" is to provide a metaphorical description of a church struggling to become a household of freedom, to become a community where walls have been broken down so that God's welcome to those who hunger and thirst for justice is made clear.

Clues to this unknown reality may be discovered in the new formations of women's spiritual support groups who gather in the round, searching for new connections: to themselves and to the world, to God and to their communities of faith. Church in the round describes a community of faith and struggle working to anticipate God's New Creation by becoming partners with those who are at the margins of church and society. In this brief reflection on women's spiritual support groups and their challenge to the churches I will be discussing the possibility of alternative structures for Christian communities that express advocacy for the full humanity of _all_ women together with men and provide clues for new ways of being church.

Feminist Christian Communities

Liberation structures in the church emerge out of liberation movements in society, and are associated in some way with both Protestant and Roman Catholic churches. They too are not always accepted by larger church institutions, but they lay claim to be fully *church* and even to be working, in the words of Leonardo Boff, to "reinvent the church."[3] These church structures reflect their contexts of struggle and are not of any one uniform type. They have many particular forms of organization that share in a common commitment to Christ and to sharing Christ's ministry on behalf of God's jubilee.

Feminist communities are not the only kind of liberation structures that are working to provide alternative structures for spiritual growth and social transformation. For instance, there are other communities of women and men who are committed to such a spiritual journey through the renewal of a more established congregation. All over Latin America and around the world basic Christian communities have been contributing to the development of liberation theologies and the transformation of church and society. On the other hand, women's spiritual communities are not necessarily Christian, and sometimes they are not feminist. This diversity is noted by the Hartford Study, although 74 percent of the 3,746 respondents were members of a local church, and 80 percent "responded in ways that are more or less 'feminist.' "[4] These women are *defecting in place*, in that they remain in their churches but also seek alternatives outside those churches that enable them to keep up the struggle within.[5]

As a Christian theologian I am particularly interested in feminist Christian communities and their implications for feminist interpretation of the church, but this does not mean that I would want to limit the movement of feminist spirituality to any one type of faith journey or confine the Holy Spirit to working only through women's support groups. The Hartford Study was focused on women connected with predominantly white mainline Protestant and Roman Catholic churches. The design leaves for another study spirituality groups that identify themselves as "post-Christian" or "post-Jewish," and it does not represent the variety of ways women of color and women who are poor and less educated may choose to "defect" in or out of place.

In discussing predominantly white and middle-class feminist Christian communities I am interested in their connections both to the faith traditions of the church and to the struggles for justice and life of which they are a part. My observations and comments are not limited to the research of the Hartford Study, but are intended to provide a series of clues to church in the round that can be tested, expanded, and corrected in the light of this exciting new study. With Leonardo Boff, I assume that these groups *are* church when they gather as church and ask about how they are seeking to show this faithfulness in their structures and mission. What makes them distinctive are not the traditional gifts of church life that they share, but their willingness to be connected to the struggle of particular groups for freedom and full humanity. Thus these communities become liberation and/or feminist churches of faith *and* struggle.

Whatever self-designation is used by these feminist Christian communities they form a movement for transformation and renewal of the church, made up of women and men who find themselves alienated by the patriarchal structures, liturgies, and theologies of the churches. Some groups come together in relation to a social justice issue such as battered women and families, ecology, women's health, etc. Many are formed around the need of women to find mutual support and new naming of their reality and of their own identity. Others band together to transform a local or national church around issues such as women's ordination, reproductive rights, human sexuality, or inclusive language. Some groups come together primarily for study or for celebration of inclusive liturgies making use of female imagery for the deity as well as human persons. Frequently the groups serve a variety of needs and move to new areas as the needs of the group change.[6]

Like many other Christian feminists I am connected to a variety of such groups and have experienced the way they grow, change, and disband as the tasks are accomplished, or are transformed into other areas of need. For twenty years I have been a member of the Ad Hoc Group on Racism, Sexism and Classism, meeting monthly in New York City in the winter, and at my home for an "Advance" weekend each June. This group is always changing and is maintained by a mailing list that keeps members informed of the program events that are planned ahead each June.

As we look at the wide variety of such groups it is difficult to draw generalizations. Yet it is possible to discern that the basic functions of the feminist Christian communities are not all that different from other church structures. Rosemary Ruether suggests that Women-Churches continue a variety of functions that make up church life, such as collective study, liturgy, social praxis on behalf of others, and collective community.[7] These suggestions are not difficult to recognize as functions in the life of Christian churches often spoken of as *kerygma, leiturgia, diakonia,* and *koinonia*. It would seem that wherever Christians gather, the presence of the Spirit of Christ is made known by these simple acts of shared word, liturgy, service, and community.

These very different communities find their commonality not only in marginality to the churches, but in their connection to the feminist movement and its protest against patriarchy. Their tasks are varied but usually include both a spiritual search for meaning and self-identity among women and advocacy for justice for women. The constituency remains predominantly white and middle class, but other forms of feminist Christian communities are emerging among women of many different cultures and races. The vision or goal of these communities is that of Galatians 3:28: a church and a society in which there is no longer division between persons because of race, class, or gender.

Clues to Church in the Round

Having had an opportunity to look at many examples of communities of faith and struggle and at the many and various ways they are connected to movements and to the Christian tradition, I would like to suggest a few clues for church in the round. These clues are drawn from the witness of feminist Christian communities as well as from other alternative forms of liberation communities.

First, as they participate in God's sending and liberating work in the world, feminist Christian communities require a *justice connection*. There is no way to be an advocate for partnership beyond patriarchy without working for justice. Solidarity requires that persons and their communities share in the struggle for full humanity and human dignity for all people and especially those too poor and powerless even to think beyond the need to find some food for the family gathering. In the Hartford Study this connection is clear, for 74 percent of the women surveyed "give at least a little time to social justice activities related to structural change."[8] It is not clear, however, how many groups see the justice struggle as part of their collective calling.

Secondly, the witness of the church is *rooted in a life of hospitality* when bounded communities (who have sought to gain identity behind their particular walls of tradition) find themselves broken open by the gospel invitation of hospitality to the stranger in their midst. Communities of hospitality become a living invitation to God's welcome table and, in turn, are developed by those who have found a new openness and welcome in the gospel message. Feminist communities such as those in the Hartford Study are most often "located outside of a single congregation" and welcome members from different faiths as well as secular traditions.[9] However, those studied were overwhelmingly well educated and white in their background and did not represent the diversity for which feminist Christian communities must struggle if they are to be open to women of different classes, races, and sexual orientations.

Lastly, we can see even from a cursory reading of the data on women's spiritual support groups that the life of feminist Christian communities involves the nurture of _spirituality of connection._ The women's support groups find room to survive and to support one another in the practice of liturgy that is inclusive and open to many different forms of spirituality.[10] Like other communities of faith and struggle, they practice the presence and connection to God and to the people on the margins of society through the study of the Bible and its interpretation and celebration in the round table community of Christ. In such settings there is an opportunity for life to come together in a way that both transcends and includes the bits and pieces that make up the struggle for wholeness, freedom, and full humanity.

It may be that the gift of faith and struggle in the life of the church today is one of the ways God's Spirit is at work to renew the church as well as the whole earth. This has happened before in the history of the church and perhaps God will again do a new thing in our midst. Only God knows if this can transform the church, but in the meantime feminist communities can contribute to this struggle for the mending of creation and provide us with a sign of hope.

Tables

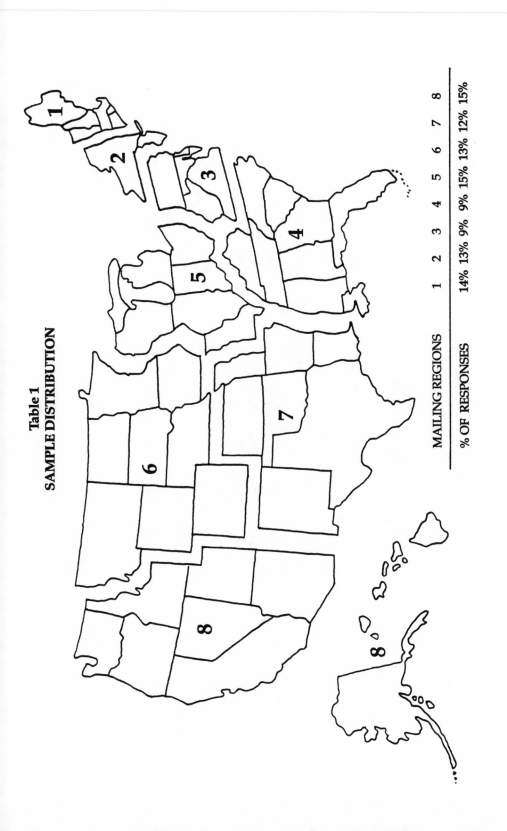

Table 1
SAMPLE DISTRIBUTION

MAILING REGIONS	1	2	3	4	5	6	7	8
% OF RESPONSES	14%	13%	9%	9%	15%	13%	12%	15%

Table 2
AREA DISTRIBUTION OF DENOMINATIONS

	% of Total	Mailing Region								=100%	(Number)
		1 %	2 %	3 %	4 %	5 %	6 %	7 %	8 %		
Catholic	32%	16%	13%	7%	7%	16%	12%	17%	11%	=100%	(1213)
Baptist	3%	9%	16%	12%	20%	16%	8%	11%	11%	=100%	(120)
Brethren	2%	0%	17%	22%	3%	34%	5%	8%	12%	=100%	(65)
Episcopalian	9%	19%	16%	15%	10%	6%	7%	14%	13%	=100%	(347)
Lutheran	5%	6%	10%	5%	6%	14%	38%	10%	11%	=100%	(176)
Mennonite	2%	2%	24%	11%	6%	13%	14%	25%	5%	=100%	(64)
Methodist	10%	7%	10%	8%	13%	20%	16%	14%	11%	=100%	(370)
Mormon	5%	6%	9%	2%	5%	6%	1%	1%	70%	=100%	(181)
Presbyterian	8%	4%	18%	17%	12%	14%	10%	11%	14%	=100%	(310)
UCC & Disciples	8%	34%	8%	4%	7%	12%	12%	9%	14%	=100%	(311)
Unitarian/Universalists	2%	12%	10%	9%	12%	5%	16%	21%	15%	=100%	(76)
Other Denomination/ Religion	5%	11%	18%	12%	6%	20%	10%	11%	12%	=100%	(169)
None (and no answer)	9%	22%	10%	10%	10%	12%	14%	7%	12%	=100%	(344)
Total Responses	100%										(3746)

Table 3

ALIENATED FROM THE INSTITUTIONAL CHURCH

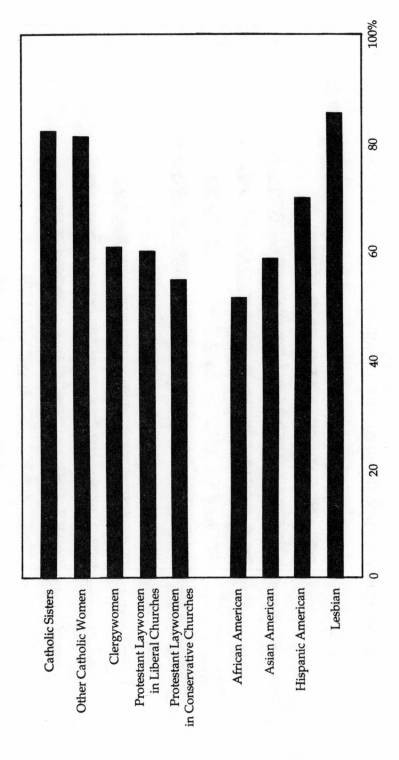

Table 4

PROPORTION OF THE ALIENATED WHO ARE MEMBERS OF LOCAL CHURCHES

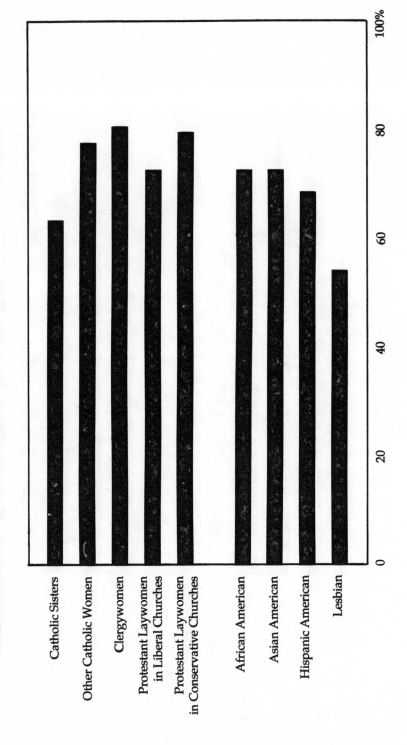

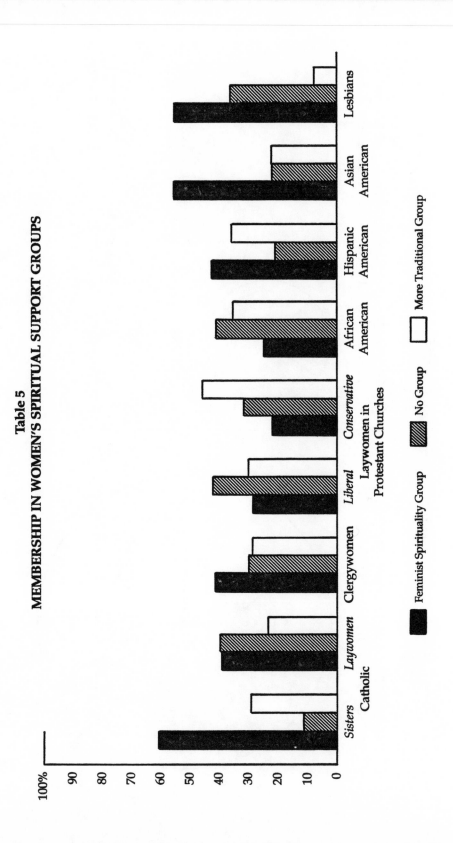

Table 5

MEMBERSHIP IN WOMEN'S SPIRITUAL SUPPORT GROUPS

Feminist Spirituality Group

No Group

More Traditional Group

Table 6

PROPORTION OF THOSE IN WOMEN'S SPIRITUAL SUPPORT GROUPS WHO OFTEN FEEL ALIENATED

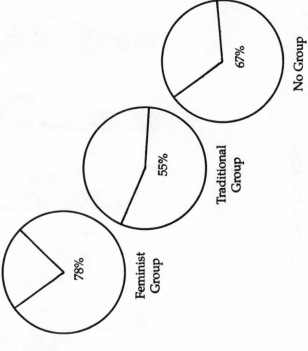

Feminist Group — 78%

Traditional Group — 55%

No Group — 67%

PROPORTION OF THE ALIENATED WHO ARE IN WOMEN'S SPIRITUAL SUPPORT GROUPS

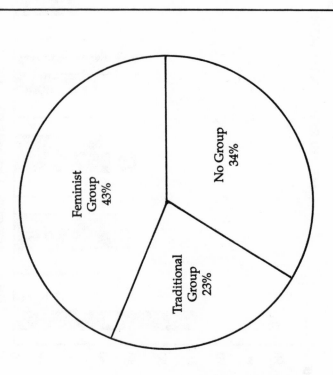

Feminist Group 43%

Traditional Group 23%

No Group 34%

Table 7
IMAGES OF GOD

Major Image of God		Most Important Image of God
83%	Creator	8%
80%	Spirit	10%
78%	Wisdom	3%
75%	Healer	4%
74%	Encompassing presence	18%
68%	Mystery	8%
63%	Friend	6%
60%	Liberator	6%
57%	Help	1%
52%	Emerging connection	5%
51%	Protector	1%
50%	Elemental force	2%
46%	Jesus	3%
37%	Father-Mother	4%
36%	Father, Son, Holy Spirit	5%
34%	Lover	3%
27%	Father	4%
19%	Mother	2%
20%	Goddess	3%
18%	Master	1%
12%	Creator-Destroyer	1%
12%	Judge	1%

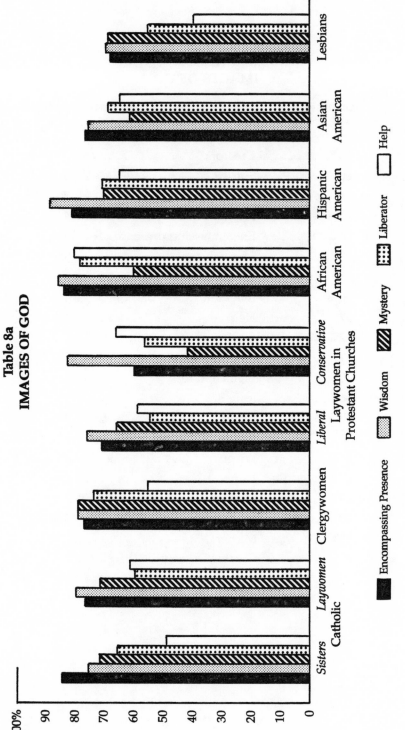

Table 8a
IMAGES OF GOD

% = % responding this is "much" a part of their image of God.

Legend: ■ Encompassing Presence   ▨ Wisdom   ▧ Mystery   ⦙ Liberator   □ Help

Categories (left to right): Sisters / Laywomen (Catholic), Clergywomen, Liberal / Conservative Laywomen in Protestant Churches, African American, Hispanic American, Asian American, Lesbians

Table 8b
IMAGES OF GOD

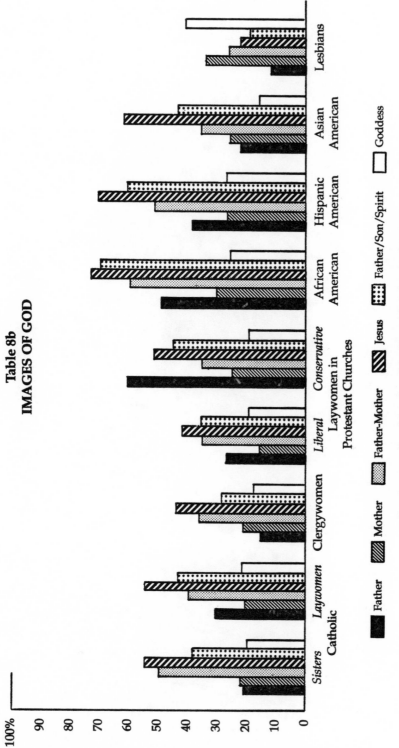

% = % responding this is "much" a part of their image of God.

Notes

Abbreviations

AA	African American
A	Asian American
C	Caucasian
H	Hispanic/Latina
M	Mixed
NA	Native American
U	Unknown

Geographical Designations. To assure that the respondent's identity is kept confidential and at the same time to give some indication of where the response is coming from, the respondent's home state has been placed in one of fourteen geographically descriptive regions, which sometimes overlap: New England, Northeast (New York, New Jersey), East, Mid-Atlantic, Southeast, South, Southwest, Midwest, North Central, Central, South Central, West, West Coast, Pacific Northwest (except for Alaska and Hawaii, which, if included, are named).

Introduction

1. See Lang, 1989–90, 1987; McLoughlin, 1989–90; Selma Williams, 1981.
2. See Demos, 1982; MacHaffie, 1986; Ruether and Keller, 1981, 1983; Ruether and McLaughlin, 1979.
3. Ruether and Keller, 1983:142.
4. Ibid:142–43.
5. MacHaffie, 1986:86.
6. Chafetz and Dworkin, 1986:1.
7. Ibid.
8. Ibid:1–2.
9. See also Simon and Danziger, 1991.
10. Chafetz and Dworkin, 1986:106.
11. Ibid:164; Benokraitis and Feagin, 1986:161–70.
12. Lerner, 1993:274.

13. Feminist/womanist/*mujerista* theological interpretation is rooted in the pioneering work of Fiorenza (1992, 1984, 1983) and other feminist biblical scholars. See Newsome and Ringe, 1992; Russell, 1985; Schneiders, 1991b; Trible, 1989, 1984, 1979; Wainwright, 1991; and Weems, 1988.

14. Fiorenza, 1992:5.

15. Ibid:39–40.

16. For an understanding of women-church, see Fiorenza, 1984; Halligan, 1990; Hunt, 1990; Neu, 1993; Ruether, 1985; Trebbi, 1991; Winter, 1989; and Ziegenhals, 1989.

17. Ruether, 1985.

18. Boff, 1986.

19. Russell, 1993, 1987, 1981, 1979.

20. Andolsen, 1986; Chung, 1990; Grant, 1989; hooks, 1981; Joseph and Lewis, 1981; Lorde, 1984; Isasi-Diaz, 1993, 1988; Thistlethwaite, 1991; Townes, 1993; Weems, 1988; and Delores Williams, 1993.

21. Feminist/womanist/*mujerista* theology addresses women's reality and is influencing women worldwide. See Bennett, 1989; Brock, 1992; Chopp, 1989; Chung, 1990; Fiorenza, 1993; Grant, 1989; Hampson, 1990; Hunt, 1991; Isasi-Diaz, 1993; Johnson, 1993, 1992; Loades, 1990; McFague, 1993, 1987; Moltmann-Wendel, 1988; Pobee and von Wartenberg-Potter, 1986; Ruether, 1992a, 1983b; Russell, 1985; Russell et al, 1988; Schaberg, 1990; Soelle, 1990, 1984; Tamez, 1989; Townes, 1993; von Wartenberg-Potter, 1987; Welch, 1989, 1985; Delores Williams, 1993; and Young, 1990.

22. Morton, 1985:17.

23. Ibid:18.

24. Daly, 1973, 1968; Schaef, 1981; Gilligan, 1982; Belenky et al, 1986; Christ and Plaskow, 1979; Kolbenschlag, 1979.

25. Studies on women's experience include: Belenky et al, 1986; Bolen, 1984; Carr, 1988; Chicago, 1985; Chittister, 1990a; Estés, 1992; Gilligan, 1982; Kolbenschlag, 1988, 1979; Kramer, 1992; Lawless, 1993; Pagels, 1988; Rhodes, 1987; Schaef, 1981; Torjesen, 1993; and Ulanov, 1988.

Chapter 1: The Women in this Study

1. Woman over sixty (C), Catholic, in New England.
2. Woman in her thirties (C), unaffiliated, in the Pacific Northwest.
3. Woman in her thirties (C), Presbyterian, in the South.
4. Woman in her forties (C), Episcopal, in the Southwest.
5. Catholic Sister in her forties (C), in the Midwest.
6. Woman in her fifties (C), Catholic, in the South Central region.
7. Woman in her forties (C), Episcopal, in the Northeast.
8. Clergywoman in her forties (C), Presbyterian, in the South Central region.
9. Woman in her twenties (AA), Episcopal, in the Midwest.
10. Woman in her forties (C), Catholic, in the Southeast.
11. Woman in her forties (C), United Methodist, in the South.

12. Catholic Sister in her forties (C), in New England.

13. Woman in her fifties (C), Southern Baptist, on the West Coast.

14. Woman in her sixties (C), Presbyterian in a Baptist congregation, in the Northeast.

15. Catholic Sister in her fifties (C), in the Mid-Atlantic region.

16. Woman in her fifties (C), Methodist, in the Pacific Northwest.

17. Woman in her fifties (C), Catholic, in the Southwest.

18. Woman in her forties (C), Episcopal, on the West Coast.

19. Woman in her forties (C), United Church of Christ, in the North Central region.

20. Woman in her forties (C), United Methodist, in the Northeast.

21. Clergywoman in her fifties (C), Church of the Brethren, in the Southeast.

22. Woman in her forties (C), Catholic, in the Southeast.

23. Clergywoman in her forties (C), United Methodist, in the Midwest.

24. Clergywoman in her forties (C), Episcopal, in New England.

25. Catholic Sister in her sixties (C), in the Mid-Atlantic region.

26. Woman in her fifties (H), Catholic, in the Northeast.

27. Woman in her fifties (C), formerly Seventh-day Adventist, in the North Central region.

28. Woman in her fifties (C), Catholic, in the Central region.

29. Woman over sixty (C), Catholic, in New England.

30. Woman in her forties (M), Catholic, in New England.

31. Woman in her fifties (C), United Methodist, in the Midwest.

32. Woman over sixty (C), Jewish, on the West Coast.

33. Woman in her fifties (C), unaffiliated, in the Midwest.

34. Woman in her thirties (C), United Methodist, in the Central region.

35. Woman in her thirties (C), Church of the Brethren, in the Midwest.

36. Woman in her forties (C), United Methodist, in the Mid-Atlantic region.

37. Woman in her fifties (C), unchurched, in the South Central region.

38. Woman in her thirties (C), Episcopal, in the Northeast.

39. Woman over sixty (C), United Methodist, in the Midwest.

40. Woman in her seventies (C), Church of the Brethren, on the West Coast.

41. Woman over sixty, Episcopal (C), in the Southeast.

42. Catholic Sister in her fifties (C), in the Northeast.

43. Clergywoman in her thirties (C), United Methodist, in the Mid-Atlantic region.

44. Woman in her fifties, Episcopal (C), in the South Central region.

45. Woman in her thirties, Episcopal (C), in the Southeast.

46. Clergywoman in her forties (C), Episcopal, in the Midwest.

47. Woman in her forties, Episcopal (C), in the South.

48. Woman (C), Quaker, in New England.

49. Woman in her forties (C), United Church of Christ, in the Central region.

50. Clergywoman in her thirties (AA), United Methodist, in the Southeast.

51. Woman over sixty (C), Episcopal, in the South.

52. Woman in her fifties (C), Presbyterian, in the Southeast.

53. Clergywoman in her fifties (C), United Methodist, in the Northwest.

54. Woman in her fifties (C), Episcopal, in the South.

55. Clergywoman in her thirties (C), United Church of Christ, in New England.

56. Woman in her thirties (C), Lutheran, in the North Central region.

57. Woman over sixty (C), Episcopal, in New England.

58. Woman in her forties (C), Episcopal, in the Mid-Atlantic region.

59. Woman in her forties (C), Lutheran, on the West Coast.

60. Woman in her forties (C), Latter-day Saints, in New England.

61. Woman (C), Presbyterian, in the Central region.

62. Clergywoman in her forties (C), Episcopal, on the West Coast.

63. Woman in her thirties (C), Lutheran, in the North Central region.

64. Woman in her thirties (C), Latter-day Saints, in the Southwest.

65. Woman in her forties (C), Unitarian, in the South Central region.

66. Catholic Sister in her fifties (C), on the West Coast.

67. Catholic Sister in her forties (C), in New England.

68. Woman in her forties (C), Presbyterian, in the South.

69. Clergywoman in her fifties (C), Episcopal, in the Northwest.

70. Woman in her forties (C), Latter-day Saints, in the Southwest.

71. Catholic Sister in her fifties (C), in the Central region.

72. Clergywoman in her forties (C), Presbyterian, in the Southeast.

73. Woman over sixty (C), Mennonite, on the West Coast.

74. Woman over sixty (C), Lutheran, in the Northwest.

75. Woman in her thirties (AA), in the South.

76. Woman in her twenties (C), Latter-day Saints, in the Southwest.

77. Clergywoman in her fifties (C), Presbyterian, in the Mid-Atlantic region.

78. Clergywoman in her thirties (C), Lutheran, in the Central region.

79. Woman (C), Mennonite, in the Southeast.

80. Catholic Sister in her fifties (C), in the South.

81. Catholic Sister over sixty (C), in the North Central region.

82. Catholic Sister in her thirties (C), in the Midwest.

83. Anonymous.

84. Clergywoman in her forties (C), Lutheran, in the Northeast.

85. Clergywoman in her fifties (C), United Church of Christ, in New England.

86. Woman in her forties (C), Catholic, in the Southeast.

87. Woman in her fifties (C), Catholic, in the North Central region.

88. Woman in her forties (C/M), United Methodist, in the South Central region.

89. Clergywoman in her fifties (C), Presbyterian, in the Southeast.

90. Woman in her thirties (C), Catholic, in the Southeast.

91. Catholic Sister in her fifties (C), in the Midwest.

92. Woman in her fifties (C), Catholic, in the Midwest.

93. Woman in her forties (C), Quaker, in the South.

94. Woman in her forties (H), Catholic, in the South Central region.

95. Woman in her fifties (C), Congregationalist, in New England.

96. Woman in her thirties (C), Latter-day Saints, in the Mid-Atlantic region.

97. Woman over sixty (C), Catholic, in New England.

98. Clergywoman over sixty (C), Presbyterian, on the West Coast.

99. Clergywoman in her forties (C), United Church of Christ, in the Northeast.

100. Catholic Sister over sixty (C), in the Midwest.

101. Catholic Sister in her fifties (C), in the Central region.

102. Woman in her forties (C), unaffiliated, in the Midwest.

103. Woman in her forties (C), former Catholic, in the Northeast.

104. Woman in her fifties (AA), Episcopal, in New England.

105. Catholic Sister in her fifties (C), in the North Central region.

106. Woman in her thirties (C), Latter-day Saints, on the West Coast.

107. Woman in her thirties (C), Catholic, in the Midwest.

108. Woman over sixty (C), Episcopal, in the South.

109. Woman in her sixties (C), Presbyterian, in the Midwest.

110. Woman in her fifties (U), unaffiliated, in New England.

111. Clergywoman in her thirties (C), Disciples/United Church of Christ, in the Midwest.

112. Catholic Sister in her thirties (C), in New England.

113. Woman in her forties (H/M), Catholic, in the Midwest.

114. Woman in her fifties (C), Catholic, in the Northeast.

115. Morton, 1985:17–18.

116. To help ensure geographical representation, the United States was divided into eight mailing regions and sampling from these lists was done geographically.

117. A first mailing of six thousand questionnaires was sent out in the summer of 1991 and resulted in a 62 percent return. A supplemental mailing to strengthen minority representation was sent out the following spring. Approximately seven thousand questionnaires were mailed in all. About two hundred were sent intentionally to a sample of men.

Our limited study consists primarily of white feminist groups in essentially white, fairly liberal denominations, and we have been exceedingly careful to interpret our findings within these limitations. Our work remains incomplete until similar studies of African American, Native American, Hispanic/Latina, and various Asian and other ethnic groups are carried out by women who are part of those cultures and the results are compared with our own. Delores Carpenter, Cheryl Gilkes, and Jacquelyn Grant are already doing research targeted to women in the African American community; Ada Maria Isasi-Diaz and Yolanda Tarango continue to study Hispanic *mujeristas;* and preliminary work has begun among Korean women in the U.S.

118. This designation was proposed by Roof and McKinney (1987) to replace the term "mainline" in recognition of changing realities within the Protestant Church in America. Their categorization of denominations as "lib-

eral," "moderate," and "conservative," while descriptively helpful, did not work for this sample.

119. The Baptist sample includes American Baptist, Southern Baptist, and a variety of independent Baptist denominations and churches. There are also very small numbers affiliated with African Methodist Episcopal, Assemblies of God, Christian Methodist Episcopal, Church of God in Christ, Church of the Brethren, Evangelical Covenant Church, Mennonite, Reformed Church in America, Seventh-day Adventist, Society of Friends (Quaker), United Evangelicals, and a variety of pentecostal and evangelical churches. Among those who belong to other religious traditions, 5 percent are Mormon and 2 percent are Unitarian. For many of these groups, the numbers were too few to run a separate percentage distribution. The sample also includes twenty women who define themselves as Protestant or Christian without any specific denominational affiliation, seven Jewish women, twenty-one women from Eastern religions, and eight women who say they are New Age, wicca, or pagan. In this sample, 9 percent of the women surveyed profess no religious affiliation.

120. Only five Native Americans were identified in the sample, too small a number to factor into our data analysis.

121. The term "feminist" can be defined a number of ways. For example, see Riley, 1989:43–63. For an overview of feminism and feminist thought, see Bettenhausen, 1990, 1985; Bunch, 1981; Daly, 1990; Donovan, 1992; Freeman, 1989; Fuss, 1989; Harrison, 1985; Lerner, 1993; Mudflower Collective, 1985; Pearsall, 1993; Ruether, 1983a; Scanzoni and Hardesty, 1992; Schneiders, 1991a; Schneir, 1972; Shulamit, 1992; Storkey, 1985; Thistlethwaite, 1991; Tong, 1993; and Wallace, 1989.

For the "womanist" perspective, see Cannon, 1985; Eugene, 1988; Grant, 1989; Townes, 1993; and Delores Williams, 1993. For the *mujerista*, see Isasi-Diaz, 1993, and Isasi-Diaz and Tarango, 1988.

122. In this study, the term "inclusive language" means language that includes women and women's experience. When used by respondents in their narratives, the distinction between inclusive language and non-sexist language, which avoids gender references, may not always be clear.

123. See Roof's *A Generation of Seekers* (1993) for support on the growing separation between religion and spirituality.

Chapter 2: Women in Protestant and Related Traditions

1. Woman in her thirties (C), American Baptist, in the Northeast.
2. Woman in her fifties (C), Disciples of Christ, in the Central region.
3. Woman in her fifties (C), United Methodist, in the Midwest.
4. Woman in her forties (C), Presbyterian, in the Mid-Atlantic region.
5. Clergywoman in her forties (C), Church of the Brethren, in the Midwest.
6. Woman in her fifties (C), Quaker, in the Northeast.

7. Clergywoman in her fifties (C), United Methodist, in the Pacific Northwest.

8. Woman in her fifties (C), Latter-day Saints, in New England.

9. Woman in her thirties (C), Episcopal, in New England.

10. Woman in her twenties (C), United Methodist, in the Southeast.

11. Woman in her forties (C), American Baptist, in the Midwest.

12. Woman (U), Lutheran, in the Midwest.

13. Clergywoman in her forties (C), American Baptist, in the Midwest.

14. Clergywoman in her fifties (C), Episcopal, in the North Central region.

15. Clergywoman in her fifties (C), Disciples of Christ, in the Northeast.

16. Woman in her fifties (C), Episcopal, in the South Central region.

17. Woman over sixty (C), Lutheran, in the Central region.

18. Woman in her thirties (C), Mennonite, in the Mid-Atlantic region.

19. Clergywoman in her fifties (C), Episcopal, in New England.

20. Woman in her thirties (C), Mennonite, in the Southwest.

21. Clergywoman in her thirties (C), Presbyterian, in the South.

22. Woman over sixty (C), Episcopal, in the Pacific Northwest.

23. Clergywoman, United Methodist, in the Southwest.

24. Woman in her fifties (A), Latter-day Saints, on the West Coast.

25. Clergywoman in her thirties (C), Lutheran, in the Northeast.

26. Clergywoman in her thirties (C), Presbyterian, in the Pacific Northwest.

27. Woman in her forties (C), Episcopal, in the Central region.

28. Woman over sixty (C), Presbyterian, in the Southeast.

29. Clergywoman in her thirties (C), Lutheran, in the North Central region.

30. Clergywoman over sixty (C), United Methodist, in the North Central region.

31. Woman in her forties (C), Episcopal, in the South Central region.

32. Woman in her fifties (C), Presbyterian, in the Southeast.

33. Clergywoman in her thirties (C), Episcopal, in the Northwest.

34. Woman in her forties (C), Disciples of Christ, in the Midwest.

35. Clergywoman in her fifties (C), United Methodist, in the Pacific Northwest.

36. Woman over sixty (A), Presbyterian.

37. Clergywoman in her fifties (C), Church of the Brethren, in the Midwest.

38. Woman over sixty (C), United Methodist, in the Northeast.

39. Clergywoman in her forties (C), Presbyterian, on the West Coast.

40. Woman in her forties (C), Quaker, in New England.

41. Clergywoman in her thirties (C), United Church of Christ, in New England.

42. Woman in her forties (C), Southern Baptist, in the Midwest.

43. Woman in her fifties (C), Presbyterian, in New England.

44. Woman in her fifties (C), Unitarian, in the South Central region.

45. Woman in her forties (C), United Methodist, in the Northeast.

46. Clergywoman in her thirties (C), United Church of Christ, in the Southwest.

47. Clergywoman (U), Presbyterian, in the Midwest.

48. Woman in her fifties (C), United Church of Christ, in the Midwest.

49. Woman in her forties (C), United Methodist, in the Southeast.

50. Clergywoman over sixty (C), Presbyterian, in the North Central region.

51. Clergywoman in her thirties (C), United Methodist, in the Mid-Atlantic region.

52. Clergywoman in her thirties (C), United Methodist, in the Northwest.

53. Clergywoman in her forties (C), Quaker, in the Southeast.

54. Woman in her forties (C), United Methodist, in New England.

55. Woman in her thirties (C), Evangelical Free Church, in the North Central region.

56. For an overview of American Protestant religion, see Roof and Mc-Kinney, 1987. For an overview of religion in America, see Wuthnow, 1994, 1988. Studies of individual traditions include: Bentley, 1990, and Cornwall and Howe, 1990 (Mormon); Elisabeth Brown, 1989 (Quaker); Brubaker, 1985 (Brethren); and Prelinger, 1992 (Episcopal).

57. See Brown and Bohn, 1989, and Lerner, 1986.

58. See the following studies of clergy wives, which depict the difficulties women confront as spouses of pastors: Greenbacker and Taylor, 1991; Lee and Balswick, 1989; Lummis and Walmsley, 1993.

59. See Carroll et al, 1983; Lehman, 1985; Royle, 1982.

60. Research on job realities for clergywomen as compared with clergymen can be found in Carroll et al, 1983; Lehman, 1985; Nesbitt, 1993, 1992; and Royle, 1987, 1982. There is even some evidence that the greater the number of ordained women in a denomination, the worse clergywomen fare in comparison with clergymen in going from entry level church or chaplaincy positions to better paying positions in larger churches. See also Nesbitt, 1992. For a different perspective on women pastors, see Stokes, 1993.

Chapter 3: Women in the Roman Catholic Church

1. Woman in her thirties (C), in the Southeast.

2. Woman in her forties (H), in the Southwest.

3. Woman in her thirties (H), in New England.

4. Woman in her forties (H/M), in New England.

5. Woman in her forties (H), unaffiliated, in the South Central region.

6. Woman in her fifties (C), in the Southeast.

7. Woman (U) in the North Central region.

8. Woman in her seventies (C), in the Pacific Northwest.

9. Woman in her forties (C), in the Midwest.

10. Woman in her forties (C), in the Southeast.

11. Woman in her forties (C), in the Midwest.

12. Woman in her forties (C), in the Mid-Atlantic region.

13. Woman in her thirties (C), in New England.

14. Sister in her forties (C), in the South Central region.
15. Sister over sixty (C), in the Northeast.
16. Sister in her fifties (C), in New England.
17. Woman in her fifties (C), in the Southeast.
18. Noncanonical Sister in her fifties (C), in the Southwest.
19. Woman in her twenties (C), in the Southeast.
20. Woman in her fifties (C), in the Midwest.
21. Sister in her fifties (C), in the Northeast.
22. Woman in her fifties (C), in the North Central region.
23. Sister in her forties (U), in the Midwest.
24. Sister in her fifties (U), on the West Coast.
25. Woman in her fifties (C), in New England.
26. Woman in her fifties (C), in the Southwest.
27. Woman over sixty (C), in the South Central region.
28. Woman in her fifties (C), in the Midwest.
29. Sister in her fifties (H), in the Northeast.
30. Sister in her fifties (C), in the Midwest.
31. Sister in her forties (H), in the South Central region.
32. Woman in her forties (C), in New England.
33. Sister in her forties (U), in the Midwest.
34. Woman in her fifties (H), in the Southwest.
35. Woman in her forties (H), in the Southeast.
36. Woman in her forties (C), in the Midwest.
37. Woman in her fifties (C), in the Mid-Atlantic region.
38. Sister in her thirties (C), in the Central region.
39. Sister in her forties (H), in the South Central region.
40. Woman in her forties (C), in the Southeast.
41. Sister in her forties (C), in the Midwest.
42. Woman over sixty (C), in the Midwest.
43. Sister (C) in her forties.
44. Woman in her forties (C), in the Southeast.
45. Woman in her fifties (C), in New England.
46. Woman in her fifties (C), in the Central region.
47. Woman in her forties (C), in the Pacific Northwest.
48. Woman in her forties (C), in the Northeast.
49. Woman in her forties (C), in the Southeast.
50. Woman in her forties (C), in the Midwest.
51. Woman (U) on the West Coast.
52. Woman in her fifties (C), in the Mid-Atlantic region.
53. Woman in her forties (C), in the Southeast.
54. Woman in her fifties (C), in the Central region.
55. Woman in her fifties (C), in the Southeast.
56. Woman in her thirties (C), in the Southeast.
57. Woman in her fifties (C), in the Midwest.
58. Woman in her fifties (C), in the Northeast.
59. Woman in her thirties (C), in the Midwest.
60. Sister in her forties (C), in New England.

61. Woman in her forties (C), in the North Central region.
62. Woman in her fifties (C), in the Mid-Atlantic region.
63. Woman in her fifties (C), on the West Coast.
64. Sister in her forties (C), on the West Coast.
65. Sister in her thirties (C), in the North Central region.
66. Sister in her fifties (C), in New England.
67. Woman in her fifties (C), in New England.
68. Woman in her forties (C), in the North Central region.
69. Sister in her fifties (C), in the Midwest.
70. Sister over sixty (C), in the Midwest.
71. Woman in her forties (C), on the West Coast.
72. Woman in her thirties (C), in New England.
73. Woman in her forties (C), in the South Central region.
74. Woman in her fifties (C), in the Northeast.
75. Woman in her fifties (C), in the Southeast.
76. Woman over sixty (C), in the Mid-Atlantic region.
77. Sister in her fifties (H/M), in the Midwest.
78. Woman in her forties (C), in the Southeast.
79. Woman in her thirties (C), in the North Central region.
80. Woman in her forties (C), in the Mid-Atlantic region.
81. Woman in her fifties (C), in the West.
82. Woman in her thirties (C), on the West Coast.
83. Woman in her forties (C), now United Church of Christ, in New England.
84. Woman in her twenties (C), in the North Central region.
85. Woman in her forties (C), now Episcopal, in the Southeast.
86. Woman over sixty (C), in New England.
87. Woman in her forties (C), in New England.
88. Woman in her forties (C), in the Mid-Atlantic region.
89. Woman in her fifties (C), in the Pacific Northwest.
90. Woman in her forties (C), in the Southwest.
91. Woman in her fifties (C), in the Southeast.
92. Woman in her forties (C), in the Southwest.
93. Woman in her forties (C), in the Pacific Northwest.
94. Woman in her forties (C), in the Southwest.
95. Woman in her thirties (C), in the Southeast.
96. Woman (U) in the West.
97. Woman in her fifties (C), in the North Central region.
98. Woman in her forties (C), in the Central region.
99. Woman in her forties (C), in the Southeast.
100. Woman in her thirties (C), in New England.
101. Woman in her forties (C), in the North Central region.
102. Woman in her fifties (C), in the Mid-Atlantic region.
103. Woman in her fifties (C), in the South Central region.
104. Woman in her forties (C), in the South.
105. Sister in her forties (C), in the East.
106. Sister in her forties (C), in the Northeast.

107. Woman in her thirties (C), in Alaska.
108. Woman in her forties (C), in New England.
109. Woman in her forties (C), in the North Central region.
110. Woman in her forties (C), in New England.
111. Woman over sixty (C), in the Northwest.
112. Sister in her forties (C), in the Midwest.
113. Sister in her forties (H), in the West.
114. Sister in her thirties (H), in the Central region.
115. Sister over sixty (U), in the Central region.
116. Sister in her fifties (C), in the North Central region.
117. Woman in her fifties (C), in the South.
118. Woman in her forties (H), in the Southwest.
119. Woman in her forties (C), in the West.
120. Sister in her forties (C), in New England.
121. Sister in her thirties (H), in the Midwest.
122. Sister in her forties (H), in the Southwest.
123. Woman in her thirties (H), in the South Central region.
124. Sister in her forties (H), in the West.
125. Sister in her fifties (H), in the West.
126. Sister in her fifties (H), in the East.
127. Woman in her forties (C), in the Mid-Atlantic region.
128. Woman in her forties (C), in the Southeast.
129. Sister in her forties (C), in the Central region.
130. Woman in her fifties (C), in the Southeast.
131. Sister in her fifties (C), in New England.
132. Woman in her fifties (C), in the Northeast.
133. Sister in her fifties (C), in the Mid-Atlantic region.
134. Woman in her sixties (C), in New England.
135. Woman in her fifties (C), in the Midwest.
136. Woman in her fifties (C), in the Southeast.
137. Sister in her forties (C), in the Southwest.
138. Sister in her fifties (C), in the East.
139. Woman in her forties (H), in the South Central region.
140. Woman over sixty (C), on the West Coast.
141. Woman in her forties (C), in the Mid-Atlantic region.
142. Woman in her forties (C), unaffiliated, on the West Coast.
143. Sister in her forties (C), in the Midwest.
144. Woman in her forties (U), unaffiliated, in New England.
145. Woman in her forties (C), in the South Central region.
146. Woman in her forties (C), in the Southeast.
147. Woman over sixty (C), on the West Coast.
148. Woman in her fifties (C), on the West Coast.
149. Woman in her fifties (C), on the West Coast.
150. Woman in her fifties (C), in the Midwest.
151. Woman over sixty (H), in the West.
152. Woman in her thirties (C), in the Pacific Northwest.
153. Woman in her thirties (U), in the Midwest.

154. Woman in her forties (C), in the South Central region.
155. Woman in her forties (C), in the North Central region.
156. Woman in her forties (C), in the North Central region.
157. Woman in her forties (C), in the North Central region.
158. Sister in her forties (C), in the Midwest.
159. Woman in her fifties (C), in the Midwest.
160. Woman in her fifties (C), in the North Central region.
161. Sister in her fifties (C), in the Northeast.
162. Woman in her fifties (H), in the Midwest.
163. Woman in her fifties (C), in the Northeast.
164. Woman in her forties (C), in the Northeast.
165. Woman in her fifties (C), in the Southeast.
166. Woman in her thirties (C), in the Mid-Atlantic region.
167. Woman in her thirties (C), in the Central region.
168. Woman in her thirties (C), in the Midwest.
169. Woman over sixty (C), in the Central region.
170. Sister in her fifties (C), in the Southeast.
171. Anonymous.
172. Woman in her thirties (C), in the South.
173. Woman in her thirties (C), in the West.
174. Woman in her fifties (C), in the Mid-Atlantic region.
175. Sister in her forties (C), in the Mid-Atlantic region.
176. Sister in her forties (C), in the North Central region.
177. Woman in her fifties (C), in the Central region.
178. Woman in her thirties (C), in the Midwest.
179. Sister in her fifties (C), in the South.
180. Sister in her forties (C), in New England.
181. Woman in her forties (H), in the South Central region.
182. Laywoman with vows, in her forties (C), in the Central region.
183. Woman in her sixties (C), in the Southeast.
184. Sister in her fifties (C), in the Midwest.
185. Woman in her sixties (C), in the North Central region.
186. Strictly speaking, Catholic Sisters are laywomen with religious vows. In this study, there will be two terms used to describe Catholic women: "Sisters" (to mean women with religious vows, also known as women religious or nuns) and "laywomen" (to mean all other Catholic women). The term "sisters" (lower case) will refer to the global sisterhood of all women.
187. To understand just how much the Catholic Church has changed in recent years, see Bianchi, 1993; Boff, 1986; Ebaugh, 1991; Greeley, 1990; Hoge, 1986; Kaufman, 1992; Kennedy, 1988; Kennelly, 1989; Osiek, 1986; Riley, 1989; Schneiders, 1991a; Wallace, 1993, 1992; and Weaver, 1985.
188. Riley, 1989:55.
189. Kennedy, 1988:3–4.
190. Schneiders, 1986:268–69.
191. Hoge, 1986:289, 297.
192. Ibid:298.
193. Murphy, 1992:14.

194. Ibid:13.

195. See Burns, 1992, 1990; Chittister, 1990b; Ebaugh, 1993; Collins, 1991; Leddy, 1990; Lieblich, 1992; Neal, 1991, 1990a, 1984; Nygren and Ukeritis, 1992; Quinonez and Turner, 1992; Schneiders, 1986; and Wittberg, 1991, 1989.

196. The Leadership Conference of Women Religious (LCWR) developed these transformative elements together with the Conference of Major Superiors of Men (CMSM) in 1989. See LCWR, 1989.

197. Marie Augusta Neal's surveys of Catholic Sisters indicate the following response to the question of ordination for Catholic women: in 1967, definitely yes=14 percent; definitely no=80 percent; in 1989, definitely yes=47 percent; definitely no=52 percent.

198. Carmody, 1986; Collins, 1991; Ebaugh 1993, 1991; O'Connor, 1993; Quinonez and Turner, 1992; Schneiders, 1991a, 1986; Swidler and Swidler, 1977; Wallace, 1993, 1992; and Weaver, 1985.

199. See statements by the Vatican's Sacred Congregation for the Doctrine of the Faith (1976) and by John Paul II (1993, 1988).

200. In 1975 the Women's Ordination Conference (WOC) launched a national initiative focused on achieving ordination for women in the Catholic Church, giving impetus to the "women-church" movement. It maintains visibility through political action, a newsletter, and periodic events, such as the three national conferences in solidarity with the Women-church Convergence in 1983, 1987, and 1993.

201. Sacred Congregation for the Doctrine of the Faith, 1976: art. 16, 19.

202. Title of the first draft of the U.S. bishops' pastoral letter on women's concerns. See National Conference of Catholic Bishops, 1988.

203. See Wallace, 1992. This revealing study on Catholic women as pastors of parishes was funded by a grant from the Lilly Endowment.

204. Wallace, 1993:32.

205. See Michael J. Sheehan, "Sunday Celebrations: The Priestless Community Worships," *Parish Ministry LINK* 3 (January–February, 1990), 1.

206. John Paul II, 1993: art. 3.

207. Wallace, 1993:40.

208. Andrew Greeley, "Catholics Go Their Own Way," *Hartford Courant*, August 25, 1993; reprinted from the *Los Angeles Times*.

209. Greeley, 1990:2.

210. Greeley, 1993. See also Kaufman, 1992.

211. The Notre Dame Study of Catholic Parish Life reveals these statistics. Over 80 percent of the CCD teachers and catechumenate sponsors in Catholic parishes are women. Over 75 percent of those who lead or participate in adult Bible studies or religious discussion are women. Over 70 percent of those who are active in parish renewal and spiritual growth and 80 percent of those who join with prayer groups are women. Over 85 percent of those who lead or assist in ministries designed to help the poor, visit the sick, comfort the grieving and minister to the handicapped are women. Involvement in efforts for justice and peace is also heavily female. Parish council composition is 52 percent female, and 60 percent of the Eucharistic ministers are women. When asked how they felt about the presence of women in liturgi-

cal roles, 80 percent of core Catholics responded that they either welcomed or had adjusted to women in the sanctuary. See Leeg, 1985:52, 56–57.

212. Murphy, 1992:15. Feminists also applaud Archbishop Rembert Weakland for his ongoing public support.

Chapter 4: Feminist Spirituality Groups for Support and Alternative Liturgy

1. Woman in her twenties (C), Catholic, in New England.

2. Woman in her thirties (C), United Church of Christ, in the South.

3. Clergywoman in her twenties (C), Lutheran, in the Central region.

4. Clergywoman in her forties (C), United Methodist, in the Pacific Northwest.

5. Woman in her thirties (C), Lutheran, in the North Central region.

6. Woman in her thirties (C), Episcopal, in the South.

7. Woman in her forties (C), Mennonite, in the Mid-Atlantic region.

8. Woman in her fifties (C), unaffiliated, in the North Central region.

9. Woman in her thirties (C), nondenominational, in Alaska.

10. Woman in her forties (C), United Church of Christ, in the Pacific Northwest.

11. Woman in her forties (C), Lutheran, in the Midwest.

12. Clergywoman in her thirties (C), Lutheran, in the North Central region.

13. Woman in her forties (C), Latter-day Saints, in the Southwest.

14. Woman in her forties (C), Presbyterian, in the North Central region.

15. Woman in her forties (C), Catholic, in the Southwest.

16. Woman over sixty (C), Lutheran, in the Northeast.

17. Woman in her forties (C), Catholic, in the Southwest.

18. Woman in her fifties (C), Presbyterian, in the Midwest.

19. Woman over sixty (C), unaffiliated, in the North Central region.

20. Woman in her forties (C), Catholic, in the Midwest.

21. Woman in her fifties (C), Christian Reformed, in the Northeast.

22. Woman over sixty (C), Presbyterian, in the Mid-Atlantic region.

23. Woman in her fifties (C), American Baptist, in the Midwest.

24. Woman in her fifties (C), Lutheran, in New England.

25. Woman in her thirties (C), Catholic, in the Pacific Northwest.

26. Woman in her fifties (C), Presbyterian, in the Northeast.

27. Woman over sixty (C), Catholic, in the Central region.

28. Woman in her thirties (C), Presbyterian, in the Northeast.

29. *Among the local, regional, and national organizations that surfaced in this study:* Women's Walk to Emmaus (Un. Meth.); Theresians (R.C.); Women's Theological Collective; Ecumenical and Evangelical Women's Caucus; Mormon Women's Forum; Exponent II; National Black Sisters Conference; United Methodist Korean Womenclergy Association; Las Hermanas (R.C.); Eastern North Dakota Women's Board (END); Houston Catholic Women's Forum; Justice for Women (Presb.); WATER (Women's Association for Theology,

Ethics and Ritual) in Washington, D.C.; C.L.O.U.T. (Christian Lesbians Out Together); Leadership Conference of Women Religious (LCWR); National Association of Women Religious (NAWR); Women's Ordination Conference (WOC); Women-church Convergence (a network of organizations supportive of women-church); Mary's Pence; United Church of Christ Coordinating Center for Women; Council of Women's Ministries of the Episcopal Church; Kansas Area Women; Church of the Brethren Women's Caucus; Concerned Catholic Women of Oregon; Louisville Women's Group; Women for Meaningful Summits; Minnesota Women's Consortium; Alexandria Women's Consortium; Women's Network of the Association for the Sociology of Religion; Midwest Association of Religious Talent, Inc. in Milwaukee (MART: a collaborative organization promoting the creative and artistic ministry of women religious); and the Seventh-day Adventist Gender Inclusiveness Task Force.

Some of the centers that surfaced in this study: Women's Theological Center in Boston; Grailville in Loveland (Ohio); Center for Women and Religion at the Graduate Theological Union in Berkeley (Calif.); Resource Center for Women and Ministry in the South (Durham, N.C.); Women's Institute of Theology at Nebraska Wesleyan University; Women's Research Institute at Brigham Young University; Degrees of Freedom, a women's retreat center in Ohio; Center for Women, the Earth, the Divine in Connecticut; Women in Ministry/Wesley Foundation in Urbana (Ill.); and the Women's Center in the Divinity School at Duke University in Durham (N.C.).

30. See Scott, 1992, and Zikmund, 1993.

31. See Cady et al, 1989; Duerk, 1989; Eller, 1993; Hunt, 1990; Morton, 1985; Neu, 1993; Ruether, 1985; Russell, 1993; Welch, 1985; and Winter, 1989.

32. Gilkes, 1986, 1985.

33. Southard and Brock, 1988.

34. Isasi-Diaz and Tarango, 1988.

35. Quinonez and Turner, 1992.

36. Hunt, 1990a:1.

Chapter 5: Feminist Spirituality

1. Woman in her thirties (C), in the Midwest.

2. Woman in her thirties (C), Presbyterian, in the Southeast.

3. Woman over sixty (C), Episcopal, in the Southeast.

4. Woman in her fifties (C), Episcopal, in the Northeast.

5. Clergywoman in her thirties (C), American Baptist, in the Midwest.

6. Woman in her forties (C), unaffiliated, in the Southwest.

7. Clergywoman over sixty (C), Presbyterian, in the Midwest.

8. Woman in her forties (C), Episcopal, in the North Central region.

9. Woman in her thirties (C), unaffiliated, in the Northwest.

10. Woman in her forties (C), Catholic, in New England.

11. Woman in her fifties (C), Catholic, in the South Central region.

12. Woman in her forties (C), Catholic, in the South.

13. Woman in her forties (C), United Methodist, in the South.
14. Woman in her fifties (C), United Methodist, in New England.
15. Clergywoman in her thirties (C), United Methodist, in the Northeast.
16. Catholic Sister in her forties (C), on the West Coast.
17. Woman in her twenties (C), Lutheran, in New England.
18. Woman in her thirties (C), Latter-day Saints, in the Southwest.
19. Woman in her thirties (C), Latter-day Saints, on the West Coast.
20. Woman in her fifties (C), United Church of Christ, in New England.
21. Woman in her thirties (C), Episcopal, in New England.
22. Woman in her thirties (C), Moravian, in the Southeast.
23. Woman in her thirties (A), Latter-day Saints, in the Southwest.
24. Woman in her forties (C), Unitarian, in the South Central region.
25. Woman in her twenties (C), Presbyterian, in the Southeast.
26. Woman in her forties (C), Presbyterian, in the Mid-Atlantic region.
27. Woman in her forties (C), Catholic, in New England.
28. Woman over sixty (C), Mennonite, in the Northeast.
29. Woman in her forties (C), Catholic, in the Southeast.
30. Woman over sixty (C), Catholic, in the Pacific Northwest.
31. Woman in her fifties (C), Episcopal, in the Northeast.
32. Woman in her forties (C), unaffiliated, in the Central region.
33. Woman in her forties (C), Episcopal, in the Southeast.
34. Clergywoman in her forties (C), American Baptist, in New England.
35. Clergywoman over sixty (C), Episcopal, in the South Central region.
36. Catholic Sister in her fifties (C), in the Northeast.
37. Woman in her fifties (C), Catholic, in the North Central region.
38. Woman in her forties (C), Catholic, in New England.
39. Catholic woman (C) in New England.
40. Woman in her fifties (C), American Baptist, in the Midwest.
41. Woman in her forties (C), Catholic, in the West.
42. Woman in her thirties (C), ecumenical, in the Midwest.
43. Woman in her thirties (C), Catholic, in the Midwest.
44. Woman in her forties (NA/M), Catholic, on the West Coast.
45. Clergywoman in her thirties (C), Episcopal, in the South.
46. Catholic Sister in her fifties (C), in the Southwest.
47. Clergywoman over sixty (C), United Church of Christ, in New England.
48. Clergywoman (C), United Church of Christ, in New England.
49. Woman in her forties (A), United Methodist, in the South Central region.
50. Clergywoman in her thirties (C), Presbyterian, in the Southeast.
51. Woman in her thirties (C), Episcopal, in the South.
52. Woman in her twenties (C), Catholic, in the Southeast.
53. Woman in her forties (C), Catholic, in the South Central region.
54. Catholic Sister in her thirties (C), in the Central region.
55. Woman in her thirties (C), Episcopal, in the South.
56. Woman in her fifties (C), United Methodist, in New England.
57. Woman in her twenties (C), Presbyterian, in the South.

58. Woman in her forties (C), Presbyterian, in the North Central region.
59. Clergywoman in her fifties (C), Presbyterian, in the Southeast.
60. Woman in her thirties (C), United Methodist, in New England.
61. Woman in her forties (C), Catholic, in the West.
62. Woman in her forties (C), Catholic, on the West Coast.
63. Woman in her thirties (C), Disciples of Christ, in the Midwest.
64. Woman in her fifties (C), American Baptist, in the Pacific Northwest.
65. Woman in her twenties (C), Lutheran, in New England.
66. Woman in her thirties (M), Catholic, in the Southeast.
67. Woman in her thirties (C), Mennonite, in the West.
68. Clergywoman in her fifties (C), Presbyterian, in the Northeast.
69. Clergywoman in her forties (C), United Methodist, in New England.
70. Woman in her forties (C), Episcopal, in the South Central region.
71. Woman in her fifties (C), Disciple of Christ, in the South.
72. Woman in her fifties (C), Episcopal, in the Pacific Northwest.
73. Woman in her thirties (C), Episcopal, in the South.
74. Clergywoman in her twenties (C), Lutheran, in the Central region.
75. Clergywoman in her fifties (C), Episcopal, in the Midwest.
76. Woman in her forties (C), Presbyterian, in the Southeast.
77. Clergywoman in her forties (C), Episcopal, in the South Central region.
78. Clergywoman in her thirties (C), Presbyterian, in the South Central region.
79. Woman in her forties (C), United Church of Christ, on the West Coast.
80. Woman in her thirties (C), Quaker, in New England.
81. Catholic Sister in her fifties (C), in New England.
82. Clergywoman in her forties (C), Presbyterian, in the East.
83. Woman in her forties (C), unaffiliated, in the Northeast.
84. Clergywoman in her forties (C), Episcopal, in the Midwest.
85. Woman in her thirties (C), Southern Baptist, in the Southeast.
86. Clergywoman in her thirties (C), United Methodist, in the Central region.
87. Woman in her forties (C), former Disciples of Christ, in the Pacific Northwest.
88. Clergywoman in her fifties (C), United Methodist, in the East.
89. Woman in her thirties (C), Catholic/Episcopal, in the Northeast.
90. Woman in her forties (C), Unitarian, in the South.
91. United Methodist Woman (U), in the North Central region.
92. Woman in her forties (C), unaffiliated, in the Southeast.
93. Woman in her thirties (C), Catholic, in New England.
94. Clergywoman in her forties (C), Episcopal, on the West Coast.
95. Woman in her forties (C), Presbyterian, in the Northeast.
96. Woman in her thirties (C), in the South.
97. Woman in her twenties (C), Presbyterian, in the Central region.
98. Woman in her forties (C), Unitarian, in the Central region.
99. Woman in her fifties (C), Catholic, in New England.
100. Woman in her twenties (C), unaffiliated, in the North Central region.
101. Woman in her forties (C), unaffiliated, in New England.

102. Woman in her twenties (C), unaffiliated, in the North Central region.

103. Woman (C), unaffiliated, in the Midwest.

104. Woman in her fifties (C), Episcopal, in New England.

105. Clergywoman in her fifties (C), Methodist/Science of Mind, on the West Coast.

106. Clergywoman over sixty (C), Presbyterian, in the South.

107. Anonymous.

108. Woman in her forties (C), Presbyterian, in the Southeast.

109. Woman in her thirties (C) in the Midwest.

110. Woman in her forties (C), Congregational, in New England.

111. Catholic Sister in her forties (C), in the Northeast.

112. Catholic Sister in her forties (C), in the Central region.

113. Woman in her thirties (C), unaffiliated, in the Mid-Atlantic region.

114. Woman in her forties (C), United Church of Christ, in the North Central region.

115. Woman in her forties (C), Unitarian, in New England.

116. Clergywoman over sixty (C), Presbyterian, in the Northeast.

117. Woman in her forties (C), unaffiliated, in the Southeast.

118. Catholic Sister in her forties (C), in the Mid-Atlantic region.

119. Woman in her thirties (C), Roman Catholic, on the West Coast.

120. Clergywoman in her forties (C), Presbyterian, in the Midwest.

121. See Berger, 1985; Clanton, 1990; Collins, 1985; Craighead, 1986; Duck, 1991; Eisler, 1987; Eller, 1993; Engelsman, 1979; Frymer-Kensky, 1992; Gadon, 1989; Gimbutas, 1989; Heeren and Mason, 1984; Johnson, 1993; Luke, 1986; McFague, 1987; Mollenkott, 1984; Neitz, 1991; Rae and Marie-Daly, 1990; Ramshaw, 1982; Roberts, 1993; Ruether, 1992a, 1983b; Saussy, 1991; Sjoo and Mor, 1987; Soelle, 1990; Stone, 1979, 1976; Trible, 1978; Ulanov, 1986; Wilshire, 1994; and Winter, 1987.

122. Brown and Stuard, 1989; Chicago, 1979; Fiorenza, 1983; Lang, 1987; MacHaffie, 1986; Ruether and Keller, 1986, 1983, 1981; Ruether and McLaughlin, 1979; Trible, 1989; and Winter, 1992, 1991, 1990.

123. *Liturgies, rituals, resources:* Linda Clark, 1981; Susan Clark, 1992; Froehle, 1992; Henry, 1992; Jacobs, 1991; Keene, 1991; Mitchell and Ricciuti 1991; National Council of the Churches of Christ, 1985, 1984, 1983; Neu, 1989, 1985; Neu and Hunt, 1993; Schaffran and Kozak, 1986; Starhawk, 1987, 1982, 1979; Swidler, 1974; Barbara Walker, 1990, 1988, 1985, 1983; Winter, 1993, 1992, 1991, 1990, 1987; and the World Council of Churches, 1988. *Feminist theory of liturgy and worship:* Collins, 1985; Duck, 1991; Goudey, 1993; Ramshaw, 1988; Procter-Smith, 1991; and Procter-Smith and Walton, 1993.

124. Mitchell, 1991, 1988, 1985, and Smith, 1992, 1989.

125. Belenky et al, 1986; Chopp, 1989; Gilligan, 1982; Hardesty, 1987; Ramshaw, 1988, 1982; and Tannen, 1990, 1986.

126. See O'Connor, 1993. Her international research on Catholic women's perspective on ordination shows remarkable agreement among women in the four countries under study: Brazil, Bangladesh, Uganda, and the U.S.

127. See Adams, 1993; Allen, 1991, 1986; Cady, 1986; Christ, 1980; Conn, 1986; Fiand, 1987; Fox, 1991, 1988, 1983; Giles, 1982; Haney, 1989; Har-

ris, 1988; Luke, 1986; Lummis and Stokes, 1994; Meehan, 1991; MacNichol, 1993; Mollenkott, 1992; Muto, 1991; Ochs, 1983; Plaskow and Christ, 1989; Ochs, 1983; Giles, 1982; Ruether, 1992b; Sams, 1993; Sams and Nitsch, 1991; Spretnak, 1982; and Zappone, 1991.

128. See Anderson and Hopkins, 1991; Bolen, 1984; Craighead, 1986; Kyrouz, 1991; Meehan, 1994, 1991; Rae and Marie-Daly, 1990; Saussy, 1991; and Ulanov, 1986.

129. Steinem, 1992:308.

130. Ibid:185.

131. A small sample of men also filled out this questionnaire. The men responding are significantly more likely than women to give greater emphasis to the male images or masculine imagery, i.e., to "Father," "Jesus," "Father, Son, Holy Spirit," "Creator-Destroyer."

132. Rosemary Ruether, "Is Radical Feminism a Sin or a Caricature?" in *National Catholic Reporter,* September 18, 1992.

133. Carpenter, 1986; Sanders, 1986; Isasi-Diaz and Tarango, 1988.

134. Kyrouz, 1991; Marciano, 1991.

135. Grant, 1989; Ruether, "Is Radical Feminism a Sin or a Caricature?"

136. Grant, 1989:212–22.

137. Gilkes, 1985.

138. Kyrouz, 1991.

139. Ruether, "Is Radical Feminism a Sin or a Caricature?"

140. Schneiders, 1991a:80–81, 109–10.

141. Ibid:88.

142. Ibid.

143. A feminist slogan. See Sheila Collins, "The Personal Is Political" (1974), reprinted in Spretnak, 1982:362–67.

144. Schneiders, 1991a:88–89.

145. See Finley, 1991; Walters, 1985; and Weaver, 1985.

146. Neal, 1991.

147. *The American Catholic-Northeast,* August 1993, 10.

Conclusions

1. Although women who are not proponents of a feminist spirituality are also included in our sample, as are women who hold membership in more traditional women's groups, they were not the focus of this study. See Aidala (1985) and Davidman (1991) on why modern young women turn to patriarchal religions. See also Robbins and Bromley (1992). A very small number of women in our sample belong to feminist spirituality groups within the Wicca, Goddess, Pagan, and New Age traditions. For studies that focus on these groups, see Adler, 1979; Eller, 1993; Finley, 1991; Jacobs, 1991; Neitz, 1991; Porterfield, 1987; and Roberts, 1993.

2. From an address by Thomas W. Gillespie, president of Princeton Theological Seminary, in *Princeton Seminary Bulletin* 7 (n.s. 1986), 219.

3. See Eugene's reflection beginning on p. 217.

4. See Marler and Hadaway, 1993.

5. Catholic researchers who have found among feminist Catholic women this commitment to stay and work for change are Ebaugh, 1993, 1991; Greeley, 1990; Neal, 1991; Quinonez and Turner, 1992; Wallace, 1993, 1992; and Wittberg, 1991, 1989.

6. See p. 217.

7. See Beck, 1988; Carpenter, 1986; and Gilkes, 1985, 1986. Also Briggs (1987), Grant (1989), and Powell (1993) discuss the centrality of Jesus in the black church experience and how the fact that he was a man makes it difficult for a black woman to use inclusive language or to be accepted as senior pastor.

8. Bellah et al, 1985:221. Dubbed "Sheila Larson" to protect her identity, the subject of this study claimed for herself the kind of inner authority many of the respondents to our study claim.

9. Ibid.

10. Chafetz, 1989:138–52; citation:150, 152.

11. Lerner, 1986:6.

12. Lerner, 1993:275.

13. Ibid:282.

14. Riley, 1989:55.

2 ~ The Positionality of Women in the African American Church Community

1. Marianna W. Davis, 1982:xx.

2. Hoover et al, 1980(?):9.

3. Forrest G. Wood, *The Arrogance of Faith: Christianity and Race in America from the Colonial Era to the Twentieth Century* (New York: Alfred A. Knopf, 1990); Virgil Peterson, *Ham and Japeth: The Mythic World of Whites in Antebellum South* (Metuchen, N.J.: Scarecrow Press, 1978); and Winthrop Jordan, *White over Black: American Attitudes toward the Negro, 1550–1812* (New York: Penguin Books, 1969).

4. Albert Raboteau, *Slave Religion* (New York: Oxford University Press, 1978); Gayraud Wilmore, Jr., *Black Religion and Black Radicalism*, 2d rev. ed. (Maryknoll, N.Y.: Orbis Books, 1983); C. Eric Lincoln and Lawrence Mamiya, *The Black Church in the African American Experience* (Durham, N.C.: Duke University Press, 1990).

5. Albea Godbold, ed., *Forever Beginning 1766–1966* (Lake Junalaska, N.C.: Association of Methodist Historical Societies, 1967), 182. See also George P. Rawick, ed., *From Sundown to Sunup: The American Slave: A Composite Autobiography* (Westport, Conn.: Greenwood Publishing Co., 1972).

6. Henry L. Gates, Jr., ed. *Six Women's Slave Narratives* (New York: Oxford University Press, 1988); and William L. Andrews, *Three Black Women's Autobiographies of the Nineteenth Century* (Bloomington: Indiana University Press, 1986).

7. See Angela Davis, 1971:3–15.

8. Jacquelyn Grant, 1979:420–21.

9. Higginbotham, 1993.

10. Lemann, 1991.

11. Based on interview conversations with Corine L. Cannon and Wilma Powell, active leaders in the Catawba Synodical of the United Presbyterian Women for five decades.

12. Robinson, 1987; Crawford, 1990.

13. For an excellent discussion of womanist discourse, see "Part IV: Womanist Theology" in Cone and Wilmore, 1993; and Townes, 1993.

3 ~ No Defect Here

1. See Eugene, 1992a:91–98.

2. For purposes of contextualizing this response, it is vital to understand the definition of a "womanist" as developed by Alice Walker (1983:xi–xii). See Eugene (1992b:510–12 and 1993:1–11), the latter for a succinct theological and ethical elaboration on the term "womanist."

3. See Boyd, 1993.

4. Copeland, 1993:99–115.

5. Andolsen, 1986:102ff.

6. See Delores Williams, "Womanist Theology: Black Women's Voices," in Cone and Wilmore, 1993:271.

4 ~ Spiritual Movements of Transformation

1. Fiorenza, 1992.

2. For a fuller development of my theoretical feminist perspective see Fiorenza, 1992.

7 ~ Feminism: A Critique from a Sociohistorical Perspective

1. For a brief but good summary of the movement and NOW see Benokraitis and Feagin, 1985:161–70.

2. For example, see Edward O. Wilson, *On Human Nature* (Cambridge, Mass.: Harvard University Press, 1978).

3. For example, see Gilligan, 1982.

4. See USCC, NCC, and Synagogue Council, "The Common Good: Old Idea, New Urgency," *Origins* 24, no. 6 (June 24, 1993): 81, 83–86; and "Resolution on Health Reform," *Origins* 23, no. 7, 97, 99–102.

5. The Sisters' Survey, sponsored by the Leadership Conference of Women Religious, was conducted to prepare for the implementation of the decisions of the Second Vatican Council. It included a population survey in 1967 sent to all sisters reachable through the Leadership Conference of

Women Religious (LCWR). It had an 88 percent return on 158,000 questionnaires. It was updated in 1980 and again in 1989 with a random sample of 6,000 sisters with a 62 percent response. Other elements included two congregational reports on 391 congregations of sisters, 1966 and 1982, and a content analysis of 201 Constitutions or Chapter Decrees, 1974 and 1982. It is available for research at the LCWR archives at the University of Notre Dame. Besides research reports to all participating groups and several journal articles, it is reported in two books: Neal, 1984, 1990a.

6. For further development of this account of church teaching on social justice see my article: "The Context of Medellin and Puebla: World Church Movement toward Social Justice" in *Born of the Poor*, ed. Edward L. Cleary, O.P. (University of Notre Dame Press, 1990) and Neal, 1990b.

7. See *International Bill of Human Rights* (United Nations, 1978), 2, and Paula Dobriansky, "U.S. Human Rights Policy: An Overview," Current Policy no. 1091 (Washington D.C.: United States Department of State, Bureau of Public Affairs, 1988).

10 ~ Searching for a Church in the Round

1. The material for this essay is drawn from my book entitled *Church in the Round: Feminist Interpretation of the Church*, 1993. See especially "Preface," 11, and chapter 3, "Communities of Faith and Struggle," 80–111.

2. Russell, 1993:12.

3. Boff, 1986:5–6.

4. "Defecting in Place: Women's Spiritual Support Groups and Their Challenge to Churches," Summary of Grant Findings, Hartford Seminary, May 1993, 2–3.

5. Ibid:1.

6. This summary is based on a report by Sr. Rachelle Harper on "Women-Church" for my class on liberation ecclesiology, Yale Divinity School, April 1991. The report was based in part on Gretchen E. Ziegenhals, "Meeting the Women of Women-Church" (1989), 492–94, and Miriam Therese Winter, "The Women-Church Movement" (1989), 258–60. See also the preliminary research of Hartford Seminary.

7. Ruether 1985:91–94.

8. Summary of Grant Findings:3.

9. Ibid.

10. Ibid:2.

Works Cited

Adams, Carol J., ed.
   1993   *Ecofeminism and the Sacred.* New York: Continuum.
Adler, Margot
   1979   *Drawing Down the Moon. Witches, Druids, Goddess-Worshippers, and Other Pagans in America Today.* Boston: Beacon Press.
Aidala, Angela A.
   1985   "Social Change, Gender Roles and New Religious Movements." *Sociological Analysis* 46 (Fall): 287–314.
Allen, Paula Gunn
   1991   *Grandmothers of the Light: A Medicine Woman's Source Book.* Boston: Beacon.
   1986   *The Sacred Hoop: Recovering the Feminine in American Indian Traditions.* Boston: Beacon Press.
Anderson, Sherry Ruth, and Patricia Hopkins
   1991   *The Feminine Face of God: The Unfolding of the Sacred in Women.* New York: Bantam Books.
Andolsen, Barbara Hilkert
   1986   *"Daughters of Jefferson, Daughters of Bootblacks": Racism and American Feminism.* Macon, Ga.: Mercer University Press.
Beck, Carolyn S.
   1988   "Our Own Vine and Fig Tree: The Authority of History and Kinship in Mother Bethel." *Review of Religious Research* 29 (June): 369–84.
Belenky, Mary Field, Blythe McVicker Clinchy, Nancy Rule Goldberger, and Jill Mattuck Tarule
   1986   *Women's Ways of Knowing: The Development of Self, Voice, and Mind.* New York: Basic Books, Inc.
Bellah, Robert N., Richard Madsen, William M. Sullivan, Ann Swidler, and Steven M. Tipton
   1985   *Habits of the Heart: Individualism and Commitment in American Life.* New York: Harper and Row.
Bennett, Anne McGrew
   1989   *From Woman-Pain to Woman-Vision: Writings in Feminist Theology.* Minneapolis: Fortress Press.
Benokraitis, Nijole V., and Joe R. Feagin
   1986   *Modern Sexism: Blatant, Subtle, and Covert Discrimination.* Englewood Cliffs, N.J.: Prentice-Hall.

Bentley, Amy L.
1990   "Comforting the Motherless Children: The Alice Louise Reyn-
        olds Women's Forum." *Dialogue: A Journal of Mormon Thought*
        (Fall): 39–61.
Berger, Pamela
1985   *The Goddess Obscured: Transformation of the Grain Protectress from
        Goddess to Saint*. Boston: Beacon Press.
Bettenhausen, Elizabeth
1990   "Earth, Women, Church." In *Sequoia: News of Religion and Society*
        10 (October/November 1990).
1985   "Feminism, Human Rights, and the Global Mission of the
        Church." In *Human Rights and the Global Mission of the Church*,
        annual series, vol. 1. Cambridge: Boston Theological Institute.
Bianchi, Eugene C., and Rosemary Radford Ruether, eds.
1992   *A Democratic Catholic Church: The Reconstruction of Catholicism*.
        New York: Crossroad.
Boff, Leonardo
1986   *Ecclesiogenesis: The Base Communities Reinvent the Church*. Mary-
        knoll, N.Y.: Orbis Books.
Bolen, Jean Shinoda
1984   *Goddesses in Everywoman: A New Psychology of Women*. San Fran-
        cisco: Harper and Row.
Boyd, Julia A.
1993   *In the Company of My Sisters: Black Women and Self-Esteem*. New
        York: Dutton.
Briggs, Sheila
1987   "Women and Religion." Pp. 408–41 in Beth B. Hess and Myra
        Marx Ferree, eds. *Analyzing Gender: A Handbook of Social Science
        Research*. Newbury Park, Calif.: Sage Publications.
Brock, Rita Nakashima
1992   *Journeys by Heart: A Christology of Erotic Power*. New York:
        Crossroad.
Brown, Elisabeth Potts, and Susan Mosher Stuard, eds.
1989   *Witnesses for Change: Quaker Women over Three Centuries*. New
        Brunswick, N.J.: Rutgers University Press.
Brown, Joanne Carlson, and Carol R. Bohn, eds.
1989   *Christianity, Patriarchy, and Abuse: A Feminist Critique*. New York:
        Pilgrim Press.
Brubaker, Pamela
1985   *She Hath Done What She Could*. Elgin, Ill.: Brethren Press.
Bunch, Charlotte, ed.
1981   *Building Feminist Theory*. New York: Longman.
Burns, Helen Marie
1992   "Leadership: Making New Paths for Others to Walk In." *Origins*
        22 (September 17): 241–46.
1990   "Leadership in a Time of Transformation." *Origins* 20 (Septem-
        ber 13): 228–32.

Cady, Susan, Marian Ronan, and Hal Taussig
1989   *Wisdom's Feast: Sophia in Study and Celebration.* San Francisco: Harper and Row.
1986   *Sophia: The Future of Feminist Spirituality.* San Francisco: Harper and Row.

Cannon, Katie G.
1988   *Black Womanist Ethics.* American Academy of Religion Series, no. 60. Atlanta: Scholars Press.
1985   "The Emergence of a Black Feminist Consciousness." In Letty Russell, ed. *Feminist Interpretations of the Bible.* Philadelphia: Westminster Press.

Carmody, Denise Lardner
1986   *The Double Cross: Ordination, Abortion, and Catholic Feminism.* New York: Crossroad.

Carpenter, Delores Causion
1986   "The Professionalization of the Ministry of Women." *Journal of Religious Thought* 43 (Spring–Summer): 59–75.

Carr, Anne E.
1988   *Transforming Grace: Christian Tradition and Women's Experience.* San Francisco: Harper and Row.

Carroll, Jackson, Barbara Hargrove, and Adair Lummis
1983   *Women of the Cloth.* San Francisco: Harper and Row.

Chafetz, Jane Saltzman
1989   "Gender Equality: Toward a Theory of Change." Pp. 135–60 in Ruth Wallace, ed. *Feminism and Sociological Theory.* Newbury Park, Calif.: Sage Publications.

Chafetz, Jane Saltzman, and Anthony Gary Dworkin
1986   *Female Revolt. Women's Movements in World and Historical Perspective.* Totowa, N.J.: Rowman and Allanheld.

Chicago, Judy
1985   *The Birth Project.* Garden City, N.Y.: Anchor Books.
1979   *The Dinner Party: A Symbol of Our Heritage.* Garden City, N.Y.: Anchor Books.

Chittister, Joan
1990a   *Job's Daughters: Women and Power.* 1990 Madeleva Lecture in Spirituality. New York: Paulist Press.
1990b   *WomanStrength: Modern Church, Modern Woman.* Kansas City, Mo.: Sheed and Ward.

Chopp, Rebecca S.
1989   *The Power to Speak: Feminism, Language, God.* New York: Crossroad.

Christ, Carol P.
1980   *Diving Deep and Surfacing: Women Writers on Spiritual Quest.* Boston: Beacon Press.

Christ, Carol, and Judith Plaskow, eds.
1979   *Womanspirit Rising: A Feminist Reader in Religion.* San Francisco: Harper and Row.

Chung Hyun Kyung
1990   *Struggle to Be the Sun Again: Introducing Asian Women's Theology.*
        Maryknoll, N.Y.: Orbis Books.
Clanton, Jann Aldredge
1990   *In Whose Image? God and Gender.* New York: Crossroad.
Clark, Linda, Marian Ronan, and Eleanor Walker
1981   *Image-Breaking, Image-Building: A Handbook for Creative Worship
        with Women of Christian Tradition.* New York: Pilgrim Press.
Clark, Susan
1992   *Celebrating Earth Holy Days: A Resource Guide for Faith Communi-
        ties.* New York: Crossroad.
Collins, Mary
1991   "Women in Relation to the Institutional Church." Address given
        to the National Assembly of the Leadership Conference of
        Women Religious. Albuquerque (August).
1985   "Naming God in Public Prayer." *Worship* 59 (July): 291–304.
Cone, James H., and Gayraud S. Wilmore, eds.
1993   *Black Theology: A Documentary History.* Vol. 1: *1966–1979.* Vol. 2:
        1980–1992. Maryknoll, N.Y.: Orbis Books.
Conn, Joann Wolski, ed.
1986   *Women's Spirituality: Resources for Christian Development.* New
        York: Paulist Press.
Copeland, M. Shawn
1993   "African American Catholics and Black Theology: An Interpreta-
        tion." Pp. 99–115 in James H. Cone and Gayraud S. Wilmore,
        eds. *Black Theology: A Documentary History.* Vol. 2: *1980–1992.*
        Maryknoll, N.Y.: Orbis Books.
Cornwall, Marie, and Susan Howe, eds.
1990   *Women of Wisdom and Knowledge.* Salt Lake City: Deseret Book.
Craighead, Meinrad
1986   *The Mother's Songs: Images of God the Mother.* New York: Paulist
        Press.
Crawford, Vicki, ed.
1990   *Women in the Civil Rights Movement: Trailblazers and Torchbearers,
        1941–1965.* Brooklyn, N.Y.: Carlson Pub.
Daly, Mary
1990   *Gyn-Ecology: The Metaethics of Radical Feminism.* Boston: Beacon
        Press.
1973   *Beyond God the Father: Toward a Philosophy of Women's Liberation.*
        Boston: Beacon Press.
1968   *The Church and the Second Sex.* Boston: Beacon Press.
Davidman, Lynn
1991a   *Tradition in a Rootless World: Women Turn to Orthodox Judaism.*
        Berkeley: University of California Press.
1991b   "Women's Search for Family and Roots: A Jewish Religious Solu-
        tion to a Modern Dilemma." Pp. 385–407 in Thomas Robbins and
        Dick Anthony, eds. *In Gods We Trust: New Patterns of Religious*

Pluralism in America. 2d ed. New Brunswick, N.J.: Transaction Books.

Davis, Angela
1971   "Reflections on the Black Woman's Role in the Community of Slaves." *Black Scholar* 4 (December): 3–15.

Davis, Cyprian, O.S.B.
1990   *A History of Black Catholics in the United States.* New York: Crossroad.

Davis, Marianna W., ed.
1982   *Contributions of Black Women to America.* Vol. 2. Columbia, S.C.: Kenday Press.

Demos, John Putnam
1982   *Entertaining Satan: Witchcraft and the Culture of Early New England.* New York: Oxford University Press.

Donovan, Josephine
1992   *Feminist Theory: The Intellectual Traditions of American Feminism.* New York: Continuum.

Duck, Ruth C.
1991   *Gender and the Name of God: The Trinitarian Baptismal Formula.* New York: Pilgrim Press.

Duerk, Judith
1989   *Circle of Stones: Woman's Journey to Herself.* San Diego: LuraMedia.

Ebaugh, Helen Rose Fuchs
1993   *Women in the Vanishing Cloister: Organizational Decline in Catholic Religious Orders in the United States.* New Brunswick, N.J.: Rutgers University Press.
1991   "The Revitalization Movement in the Catholic Church: The Institutional Dilemma of Power." *Sociological Analysis* 52: 1–12.

Eisler, Riane
1987   *The Chalice and the Blade: Our History, Our Future.* New York: Harper and Row.

Eller, Cynthia
1993   *Living in the Lap of the Goddess: The Feminist Spirituality Movement in America.* New York: Crossroad.

Engelsman, Joan Chamberlain
1979   *The Feminine Dimension of the Divine.* Philadelphia: Westminster Press.

Estés, Clarissa Pinkola
1992   *Women Who Run with the Wolves: Myths and Stories.* New York: Ballantine Books.

Eugene, Toinette
1993   "Two Heads Are Better than One: Feminist and Womanist Ethics in Tandem." *Daughters of Sarah* 19 (Summer): 1–11.
1992a   "On Difference and the Dream of Pluralist Feminism. *Journal of Feminist Studies in Religion* 8 (Fall): 91–98.

| 1992b | "Womanist Theology." Pp. 510–12 in Donald Musser and Joseph Price, eds. *New Handbook of Christian Theology.* Nashville: Abingdon Press. |

1989   "Sometimes I Feel Like a Motherless Child: The Call and Response for a Liberational Ethic of Care by Black Feminists." Pp. 45–62 in Mary Brabeck, ed. *Who Cares? Theory, Research, and Educational Implications of the Ethic of Care.* San Francisco: Harper and Row.

1988   "Moral Values and Black Womanists," *Journal of Religious Thought* 44 (Winter/Spring): 23–34.

Fiand, Barbara

1987   *Releasement: Spirituality for Ministry.* New York: Crossroad.

Finley, Nancy J.

1991   "Political Activism and Feminist Spirituality." *Sociological Analysis* 52 (Winter): 349–62.

Fiorenza, Elisabeth Schüssler

1993   *Discipleship of Equals: A Critical Feminist Ekklesia-logy of Liberation.* New York: Crossroad.

1992   *But She Said: Feminist Practices of Biblical Interpretation.* Boston: Beacon Press.

1984   *Bread Not Stone: The Challenge of Feminist Biblical Interpretation.* Boston: Beacon Press.

1983   *In Memory of Her: Feminist Theological Reconstruction of Christian Origins.* New York: Crossroad.

Fox, Matthew

1991   *Creation Spirituality: Liberating Gifts for the Peoples of the Earth.* San Francisco: Harper and Row.

1988   *The Coming of the Cosmic Christ: The Healing of Mother Earth and the Birth of a Global Renaissance.* San Francisco: Harper and Row.

1983   *Original Blessing: A Primer in Creation Spirituality.* Sante Fe: Bear and Company.

Freeman, Jo, ed.

1989   *Women: A Feminist Perspective.* 4th ed. Mountain View, Calif.: Mayfield Publishing Company.

Froehle, Virginia

1992   *Called into Her Presence: Praying with Feminine Images of God.* Notre Dame, Ind.: Ave Maria Press.

Frymer-Kensky, Tikva

1992   *In the Wake of the Goddesses: Women, Culture, and the Biblical Transformation of Pagan Myth.* New York: Free Press.

Fuss, Diana

1989   *Essentially Speaking: Feminism, Nature and Difference.* New York: Routledge.

Gadon, Elinor W.

1989   *The Once and Future Goddess.* San Francisco: Harper and Row.

Giles, Mary E., ed.
1982   *The Feminist Mystic: And Other Essays on Women and Spirituality.*
        New York: Crossroad.

Gilligan, Carol
1982   *In a Different Voice: Psychological Theory and Women's Development.*
        Cambridge: Harvard University Press.

Gilkes, Cheryl Townsend
1986   "The Role of Women in the Sanctified Church." *Journal of
        Religious Thought* 43 (Spring–Summer): 24–41.

1985a   " 'Some Mother's Son and Some Father's Daughter': Gender
        and Biblical Language in Afro-Christian Worship Tradition" in
        Clarissa W. Atkinson, Constance H. Buchanan, and Margaret
        Miles, eds. *The Female in Sacred Image and Social Reality.* Boston:
        Beacon Press.

1985b   "Together and in Harness: Women's Traditions in the Sanctified
        Church." *Signs* 10: 678–79.

Gimbutas, Marija
1989   *The Language of the Goddess.* San Francisco: Harper and Row.

Goudey, June Christine
1993   "Atonement Imagery and Eucharistic Praxis in the Reformed
        Tradition: A Feminist Critique." Dissertation. Boston University
        School of Theology.

Grant, Jacquelyn
1989   *White Women's Christ and Black Women's Jesus: Feminist Christology
        and Womanist Response.* American Academy of Religion Series
        no. 64. Atlanta: Scholars Press.

1979   "Black Theology and the Black Woman." Pp. 420–21 in Gay-
        raud S. Wilmore and James H. Cone, eds. *Black Theology: A
        Documentary History, 1966–1979.* Maryknoll, N.Y.: Orbis Books.

Greeley, Andrew M.
1990   *The Catholic Myth: The Behavior and Beliefs of American Catholics.*
        New York: Charles Scribner's Sons.

Greenbacker, Liz, and Sherry Taylor
1991   *Private Lives for Ministers' Wives.* Far Hills, N.J.: New Horizons
        Press.

Halligan, Fredrica R.
1990   "WomanChurch: Toward a New Psychology of Feminine Spiri-
        tuality." *Journal of Pastoral Care* 44 (Winter): 379–89.

Hampson, Daphne
1990   *Theology and Feminism.* Cambridge, Mass.: Basil Blackwell.

Haney, Eleanor H.
1989   *Vision and Struggle: Meditations on Feminist Spirituality and Politics.*
        Portland, Maine: Astarte Shell Press.

Hardesty, Nancy A.
1987   *Inclusive Language in the Church.* Atlanta: John Knox Press.

Harris, Maria
1988   *Dance of the Spirit: The Seven Steps of Women's Spirituality.* New York: Bantam Books.
Harrison, Beverly Wildung
1985   *Making the Connections: Essays in Feminist Social Ethics.* Boston: Beacon Press.
Hayes, Diana L.
1991   "Feminist Theology, Womanist Theology: A Black Catholic Perspective." In William O'Brian, ed. *The Labor of Love: An Ignatian View of Church and Culture.* Washington, D.C.: Georgetown University Press.
Heeren, Donald B. Lindsey, and Marylee Mason
1984   "The Mormon Concept of Mother in Heaven: A Sociological Account of Its Origins and Development." *Journal for the Scientific Study of Religion* 23 (December): 396–411.
Henry, Kathleen M.
1992   *The Book of Ours: Liturgies for Feminist People.* Jamaica Plain, Mass.: Alabaster Jar Liturgical Arts.
Higginbotham, Evelyn Brooks
1993   *Righteous Discontent: The Women's Movement in the Black Baptist Church, 1880–1920.* Cambridge: Harvard University Press.
Hoge, Dean
1986   "Interpreting Change in American Catholicism: The River and the Floodgate." *Review of Religious Research* 27 (June): 289–99.
hooks, bell
1984   *Feminist Theory: From Margin to Center.* Boston: South End Press.
1981   *Ain't I a Woman: Black Women and Feminism.* Boston: South End Press.
Hoover, Theressa, et al.
1980?   *To a Higher Glory: The Growth and Mission of Black Women Organized for Mission in the Methodist Church 1940–1968.* New York: United Methodist Church.
Hunt, Mary E.
1991   *Fierce Tenderness: A Feminist Theology of Tenderness.* New York: Crossroad.
1990   "Defining 'Women-Church.'" *WATERwheel* 3 (Summer): 1–3.
Isasi-Diaz, Ada Maria
1993   *En la Lucha/In the Struggle: Elaborating a Mujerista Theology.* Minneapolis: Fortress Press.
Isasi-Diaz, Ada Maria, and Yolanda Tarango
1988   *Hispanic Women: Prophetic Voice in the Church.* San Francisco: Harper and Row.
Jacobs, Janet
1991   "Women-Centered Healing Rites: A Study of Alienation and Reintegration." Pp. 373–84 in Thomas Robbins and Dick Anthony, eds. *In Gods We Trust: New Patterns of Religious Pluralism in America.* 2d ed. New Brunswick: Transaction Books.

John Paul II
  1993   "On Parishes, Lay Ministry and Women. "Ad Limina" Address. *Origins* 23 (July 15): 124–28.
  1988   "On the Dignity and Vocation of Women." *Origins* 18 (October 6): 261–83.

Johnson, Elizabeth A.
  1993   *She Who Is: The Mystery of God in Feminist Theological Discourse.* New York: Crossroad.
  1992   *Consider Jesus: Waves of Renewal in Christology.* New York: Crossroad.

Joseph, Gloria I., and Jill Lewis
  1981   *Common Differences: Conflicts in Black and White Feminist Perspectives.* Boston: South End Press.

Kaufman, Philip S.
  1992   *Why You Can Disagree and Remain a Faithful Catholic.* New York: Crossroad.

Keene, Jane A.
  1991   *A Winter's Song: A Liturgy for Women Seeking Healing from Sexual Abuse in Childhood.* New York: Pilgrim Press.

Kennedy, Eugene
  1988   *Tomorrow's Catholics, Yesterday's Church.* San Francisco: Harper and Row.

Kennelly, Karen, ed.
  1989   *American Catholic Women: A Historical Exploration.* New York: Macmillan.

Kolbenschlag, Madonna
  1988   *Lost in the Land of Oz.* San Francisco: Harper and Row.
  1979   *Kiss Sleeping Beauty Good-Bye.* San Francisco: Harper and Row.

Kramer, Ross Shepard
  1992   *Her Share of the Blessings: Women's Religions among Pagans, Jews, and Christians in the Greco-Roman World.* New York: Oxford University Press.

Kyrouz, Elaina
  1991   "Of God and Gender: The Influences of Familial, Religious, Political, Educational, and Subcultural Socialization and Experience on the Adoption of Maternal Images of God." Revision of paper delivered at the annual meeting of the Association for the Sociology of Religion. Cincinnati (August).

Lang, Amy Schrager
  1989–1990 "Prophetic Woman: Anne Hutchinson and the Problem of Dissent." *New Conversations* 13 (Winter): 54–62.
  1987   *Prophetic Woman.* Berkeley: University of California Press.

Lawless, Elaine J.
  1993   *Holy Women, Wholly Women: Sharing Ministries through Life Stories and Reciprocal Ethnography.* Philadelphia: University of Pennsylvania.

Leadership Conference of Women Religious
  1989   "Transformative Elements for Religious Life in the Future."
           Principles developed at Joint Assembly of LCWR/CMSM in
           Louisville (August).
Leddy, Mary Jo
  1990   *Reweaving Religious Life: Beyond the Liberal Model*. Mystic, Conn.:
           Twenty-Third Publications.
Lee, Cameron, and Jack Balswick
  1989   *Life in a Glass House: The Minister's Family in Its Unique Social
           Context*. Grand Rapids, Mich.: Zondervan Publishing Co.
Leeg, David C., and Thomas A. Trozzolo
  1985   "Who Participates in Local Church Communities?" Notre Dame
           Study of Catholic Parish Life. *Origins* 15 (June 13): 50–57.
Lehman, Edward C.
  1993   *Gender and Work: The Case of the Clergy*. Albany, N.Y.: SUNY
           Press.
  1985   *Women Clergy: Breaking through Gender Barriers*. New Brunswick,
           N.J.: Transaction Books.
Lemann, Nicholas
  1991   *The Promised Land: The Great Black Migration and How It Changed
           America*. New York: Knopf.
Lerner, Gerda
  1993   *The Creation of Feminist Consciousness*. New York: Oxford Univer-
           sity Press.
  1986   *The Creation of Patriarchy*. New York: Oxford University Press.
Lieblich, Julia
  1992   *Sisters: Lives of Devotion and Defiance*. New York: Ballantine
           Books.
Loades, Ann, ed.
  1990   *Feminist Theology: A Reader*. London: SPCK.
Lorde, Audre
  1984   *Sister Outsider: Essays and Speeches*. Freedom, Calif.: Crossing
           Press.
Luke, Helen M.
  1986   *Woman, Earth and Spirit*. New York: Crossroad.
Lummis, Adair, and Allison Stokes
  1994   "Catholic Feminist Spirituality and Social Justice Actions." *Re-
           search in the Social Scientific Study of Religion* 6.
Lummis, Adair, and Roberta Walmsley
  1993   *Healthy Clergy, Wounded Healers: Their Ministries and Their Fami-
           lies*. Research monograph. Publication pending.
MacHaffie, Barbara J.
  1986   *Her Story: Women in Christian Tradition*. Philadelphia: Fortress
           Press.
MacNichol, Sally Noland, and Mary Elizabeth Walsh
  1993   "Feminist Theology and Spirituality: An Annotated Bibliogra-
           phy." *Women's Studies Quarterly* 21 (Spring/Summer): 177–96.

Marciano, Teresa Donati
  1991   "Why Have We Not Got Beyond God the Father? Prayer,
          Metaphor, and Social Structure as Creators of Male Godhead."
          Paper presented at the annual meetings of the SSSR. Pittsburgh
          (November).
Marler, Penny Long, and C. Kirk Hadaway
  1993   "Toward a Typology of Marginal Members." *Review of Religious
          Research* 35: 34–54.
McFague, Sallie
  1993   *The Body of God: An Ecological Theology.* Minneapolis: Fortress
          Press.
  1987   *Models of God: Theology for an Ecological, Nuclear Age.* Minneapolis:
          Fortress Press.
McLoughlin, William G.
  1989–1990 "Anne Hutchinson Reconsidered." *New Conversations* 13 (Win-
          ter): 37–45.
Meehan, Bridget Mary
  1994   *Delighting in the Feminine Divine.* Kansas City, Mo.: Sheed and
          Ward.
  1991   *Exploring the Feminine Face of God.* Kansas City, Mo.: Sheed and
          Ward.
Mitchell, Ella Pearson, ed.
  1991   *Women: To Preach or Not to Preach.* Valley Forge, Pa.: Judson Press.
  1988   *Those Preaching Women: More Sermons by Black Women Preachers.*
          Vol. 2. Valley Forge, Pa.: Judson Press.
  1985   *Those Preachin' Women.* Vol. 1. Valley Forge, Pa.: Judson Press.
Mitchell, Rosemary Catalano, and Gail Anderson Ricciuti
  1991   *Birthings and Blessings: Liberating Worship Services for the Inclusive
          Church.* New York: Crossroad.
Mollenkott, Virginia Ramey
  1992   *Sensuous Spirituality.* New York: Crossroad.
  1984   *The Divine Feminine: The Biblical Imagery of God as Female.* New
          York: Crossroad.
Moltmann-Wendel, Elisabeth
  1988   *A Land Flowing with Milk and Honey. Perspectives on Feminist
          Theology.* New York: Crossroad.
Morton, Nelle
  1985   *The Journey Is Home.* Boston: Beacon Press.
Mudflower Collective
  1985   *God's Fierce Whimsy: Christian Feminism and Theological Education.*
          New York: Pilgrim Press.
Murphy, Bishop P. Francis
  1992   "Let's Start Over: A Bishop Appraises the Pastoral on Women."
          Commonweal (September 25): 11–15.
Muto, Susan
  1991   *Womanspirit: Reclaiming the Deep Feminine in Our Human Spiritu-
          ality.* New York: Crossroad.

National Conference of Catholic Bishops
   1992   "One in Christ Jesus." Fourth draft of U.S. Bishops' Pastoral
            Response to Women's Concerns. *Origins* 22 (September 10).
   1988   "Partners in the Mystery of Redemption." First draft of U.S.
            Bishops' Pastoral Response to Women's Concerns. *Origins* 17
            (April 21).
National Council of the Churches of Christ in the U.S.A.
   1985   *An Inclusive Language Lectionary: Readings for Year C.* Philadelphia:
            Westminster Press.
   1984   *An Inclusive Language Lectionary: Readings for Year B.* Philadelphia:
            Westminster Press.
   1983   *An Inclusive Language Lectionary: Readings for Year A.* Philadel-
            phia: Westminster Press.
Neal, Marie Augusta
   1991   *A Report on the National Profile of the Third Sisters' Survey.* Boston:
            Emmanuel College.
   1990a   *From Nuns to Sisters: An Expanding Vocation.* Mystic, Conn.:
            Twenty-Third Publications.
   1990b   "The Church, Women, and Society." Third Annual Lecture in
            Catholic Studies. Saint Michael's College. Colchester, Vt.
   1984   *Catholic Sisters in Transition: From the 1960's to the 1980's.* Wilm-
            ington, Del.: Michael Glazier.
Neitz, Mary Jo
   1991   "In Goddess We Trust." Pp. 353–72 in Thomas Robbins and
            Dick Anthony, eds. *In Gods We Trust: New Patterns of Religious
            Pluralism in America.* 2d ed. New Brunswick, N.J.: Transaction
            Books.
Nesbitt, Paula D.
   1993   "Dual Ordination Tracks: Differential Benefits and Costs for Men
            and Women Clergy." *Sociology of Religion* 54: 13–20.
   1992   "Lamentations: The Politics of Gender and Ministry." Paper
            presented at the Society for the Scientific Study of Religion.
            Washington, D.C.
Neu, Diann L.
   1993   "Women-church Transforming Liturgy." Pp. 163–78 in Marjorie
            Proctor-Smith and Janet R. Walton, eds. *Women at Worship.*
            Louisville: Westminster/John Knox Press.
   1989   *Women and the Gospel Traditions: Feminist Celebrations.* Washing-
            ton, D.C.: WATERworks Press.
   1985   *Women-church Celebrations: Feminist Liturgies for the Lenten Season.*
            Washington, D.C.: WATERworks Press.
Neu, Diann L., and Mary E. Hunt
   1993   *Women-church Source Book.* Washington, D.C.: WATERworks
            Press.
Newsome, Carol A., and Sharon H. Ringe, eds.
   1992   *The Women's Bible Commentary.* Louisville: Westminster/John
            Knox Press.

Nygren, David, and Miriam Ukeritis
1992   "Future of Religious Orders in the United States." Executive summary of a study sponsored by Lilly Endowment, Inc. *Origins* 22 (September 24).

Ochs, Carol
1983   *Women and Spirituality*. Totowa, N.J.: Rowman and Allanheld.

O'Connor, Francis Bernard, C.S.C.
1993   *Like Bread, Their Voices Rise! Global Women Challenge the Church*. Notre Dame, Ind.: Ave Maria Press.

Osiek, Carolyn
1986   *Beyond Anger: On Being a Feminist in the Church*. New York: Paulist Press.

Pagels, Elaine
1988   *Adam, Eve, and the Serpent*. New York: Vintage Books.

Pearsall, Marilyn, ed.
1993   *Women and Values: Readings in Recent Feminist Philosophy*. 2d ed. Belmont, Calif.: Wadsworth Publishing.

Plaskow, Judith, and Carol P. Christ
1989   *Weaving the Visions: New Patterns in Feminist Spirituality*. San Francisco: Harper and Row.

Pobee, John S., and Barbel von Wartenberg-Potter, eds.
1986   *New Eyes for Reading: Biblical and Theological Reflections by Women from the Third World*. Oak Park, Ill.: Meyer-Stone Books.

Porterfield, Amanda
1987   "Feminist Theology as a Revitalization Movement." *Sociological Analysis* 48, no. 3: 134–244.

Powell, Annie Ruth
1993   "Hold On to Your Dream: African-American Protestant Worship." Pp. 43–53 in Marjorie Proctor-Smith and Janet R. Walton, eds. *Women at Worship*. Louisville: Westminster/John Knox Press.

Prelinger, Catherine M., ed.
1992   *Episcopal Women: Gender, Spirituality, and Commitment in an American Mainline Denomination*. New York: Oxford University Press.

Procter-Smith, Marjorie
1991   *In Her Own Rite: Constructing Feminist Liturgical Tradition*. Nashville: Abingdon Press.

Procter-Smith, Marjorie, and Janet R. Walton, ed.
1993   *Women at Worship: Interpretations of North American Diversity*. Louisville: Westminster/John Knox Press.

Quinonez, Lora Ann, and Mary Daniel Turner
1992   *The Transformation of American Catholic Sisters*. Philadelphia: Temple University Press.

Rae, Eleanor, and Bernice Marie-Daly
1990   *Created in Her Image: Models of the Divine Feminine*. New York: Crossroad.

Ramshaw, Gail
1988   *Searching for Language*. Washington, D.C.: Pastoral Press.

1982   "De Divinis Nominibus: The Gender of God." *Worship* 56: 117–31.

Rhodes, Lynn N.
1987   *Co-Creating: A Feminist Vision of Ministry.* Philadelphia: Westminster Press.

Riley, Maria
1989   *Transforming Feminism.* Kansas City, Mo.: Sheed and Ward.

Roberts, Wendy Hunter
1993   "In Her Name: Toward a Feminist Thealogy of Pagan Ritual." Pp. 137–62 in Marjorie Proctor-Smith and Janet R. Walton, eds. *Women at Worship,* Louisville: Westminster/John Knox Press.

Robbins, Thomas, and Dick Anthony, eds.
1991   *In Gods We Trust: New Patterns of Religious Pluralism in America.* 2d ed. New Brunswick, N.J.: Transaction Books.

Robbins, Thomas, and David Bromley
1992   "Social Experimentation and the Significance of American New Religions: A Focused Review Essay." Pp. 1–28 in Monty L. Lynn and David O. Moberg, eds. *Research in the Social Scientific Study of Religion* 4. Greenwich, Conn.: JAI Press.

Robinson, Jo Ann Gibson
1990   *The Montgomery Bus Boycott and the Women Who Started It.* Ed. David J. Garrow. Knoxville: University of Tennessee Press.

Roof, Wade Clark
1993   *A Generation of Seekers: The Spiritual Journeys of the Baby Boom Generation.* HarperSanFrancisco.

Roof, Wade Clark, and William McKinney
1987   *American Mainline Religion: Its Changing Shape and Future.* New Brunswick, N.J.: Rutgers University Press.

Royle, Marjorie H.
1987   "Using Bifocals to Overcome Blindspots: The Impact of Women on the Military and the Ministry." *Review of Religious Research* 28 (June): 341–50.
1982   "Women Pastors: What Happens after Placement?" *Review of Religious Research* 24: 116–26.

Ruether, Rosemary Radford
1992a   *Gaia and God: An Ecofeminist Theology of Earth Healing.* New York: Crossroad.
1992b   "Spirituality and Justice: Popular Church Movements in the United States." Pp. 189–206 in Eugene Bianchi and Rosemary Radford Ruether, eds. *A Democratic Catholic Church.* New York: Crossroad.
1985   *Women-Church: Theory and Practice.* San Francisco: Harper and Row.
1983a   *New Woman, New Earth: Sexist Ideologies and Human Liberation.* New York: Seabury Press.
1983b   *Sexism and God-Talk: Toward a Feminist Theology.* Boston: Beacon Press.

Ruether, Rosemary Radford, and Rosemary Skinner Keller
  1986   *Women and Religion in America.* Vol. 3: *1900–1968.* San Francisco: Harper and Row.
  1983   *Women and Religion in America.* Vol. 2: *The Colonial and Revolutionary Periods.* San Francisco: Harper and Row.
  1981   *Women and Religion in America.* Vol. 1: *The Nineteenth Century.* San Francisco: Harper and Row.
Ruether, Rosemary Radford, and Eleanor McLaughlin
  1979   *Women of Spirit: Female Leadership in the Jewish and Christian Traditions.* New York: Simon and Schuster.
Russell, Letty M.
  1993   *Church in the Round: Feminist Interpretation of the Church.* Louisville: Westminster/John Knox Press.
  1987   *Household of Freedom: Authority in Feminist Theology.* Philadelphia: Westminster Press.
  1981   *Growth in Partnership.* Louisville: Westminster/John Knox Press.
  1979   *The Future of Partnership.* Louisville: Westminster/John Knox Press.
Russell, Letty M., ed.
  1985   *Feminist Interpretation of the Bible.* Philadelphia: Westminster Press.
Russell, Letty M., Kwok Pui-lan, Ada Maria Isasi-Diaz, and
Katie Geneva Cannon
  1988   *Inheriting Our Mother's Gardens: Feminist Theology in Third World Perspective.* Philadelphia: Westminster Press.
Sacred Congregation for the Doctrine of the Faith
  1976   "Declaration on the Question of the Admission of Women to the Ministerial Priesthood." Pp. 1–9 in J. Gordon Melton, ed. *Women's Ordination: Official Statements from Religious Bodies and Ecumenical Organizations.* Detroit: Gale Research, Inc.
Sams, Jamie
  1993   *The Thirteen Original Clan Mothers: Your Sacred Path to Discovering the Gifts, Talents, and Abilities of the Feminine through the Ancient Teachings of the Sisterhood.* San Francisco: Harper and Row.
Sams, Jamie, and Twylah Nitsch
  1991   *Other Council Fires Were Here before Ours.* San Francisco: Harper and Row.
Sanders, Cheryl
  1986   "The Woman as Preacher." *Journal of Religious Thought* 43 (Spring/Summer): 6–23.
Saussy, Carroll
  1991   *God Images and Self-Esteem: Empowering Women in a Patriarchal Society.* Louisville: Westminster/John Knox Press.
Scanzoni, Letha Dawson, and Nancy Hardesty
  1992   *All We're Meant to Be: Biblical Feminism for Today.* 2d ed. Grand Rapids: Eerdmans.

Schaberg, Jane
  1990   *The Illegitimacy of Jesus: A Feminist Theological Interpretation of the Infancy Narratives.* New York: Crossroad.

Schaef, Anne Wilson
  1981   *Women's Reality: An Emerging Female System in a White Male Society.* Minneapolis: Winston Press.

Schaffran, Janet, and Pat Kozak
  1986   *More Than Words: Prayer and Ritual for Inclusive Communities.* Oak Park, Ill.: Meyer-Stone Books.

Schneiders, Sandra M.
  1991a   *Beyond Patching: Faith and Feminism in the Catholic Church.* New York: Paulist Press.
  1991b   *The Revelatory Text: Interpreting the New Testament as Sacred Scripture.* San Francisco: Harper and Row.
  1986   *New Wineskins: Re-Imagining Religious Life Today.* New York: Paulist Press.

Schneir, Miriam, ed.
  1972   *Feminism: The Essential Historical Writings.* New York: Vintage Books.

Scott, Anne Firor
  1992   *Natural Allies: Women's Associations in American History.* Chicago: University of Illinois Press.

Shulamit, Reinharz
  1992   *Feminist Methods in Social Research.* New York: Oxford University Press.

Simon, Rita J., and Gloria Danziger
  1991   *Women's Movements in America: Their Successes, Disappointments, and Aspirations.* New York: Praeger.

Sjoo, Monica, and Barbara Mor
  1987   *The Great Cosmic Mother: Rediscovering the Religion of the Earth.* San Francisco: Harper and Row.

Smith, Christine M.
  1992   *Preaching as Weeping, Confession, and Resistance.* Louisville: Westminster/John Knox Press.
  1989   *Weaving the Sermon: Preaching in a Feminist Perspective.* Louisville: Westminster/John Knox Press.

Soelle, Dorothee
  1990   *Thinking about God: An Introduction to Theology.* Philadelphia: Trinity Press International.
  1984   *The Strength of the Weak: Toward a Christian Feminist Identity.* Philadelphia: Westminster Press.

Southard, Naomi, and Rita Nakashima Brock
  1987   "The Other Half of the Basket: Asian American Women and the Search for a Theological Home." *Journal of Feminist Studies in Religion* 3 (Fall): 133–50.

Spretnak, Charlene, ed.
  1982   *The Politics of Women's Spirituality: Essays on the Rise of Spiritual Power within the Feminist Movement.* Garden City, N.Y.: Anchor Books.
Starhawk
  1987   *Truth or Dare: Encounters with Power, Authority, and Mystery.* San Francisco: Harper and Row.
  1982   *Dreaming the Dark. Magic, Sex and Politics.* Boston: Beacon Press.
  1979   *The Spiral Dance: A Rebirth of the Ancient Religion of the Great Goddess.* San Francisco: Harper and Row.
Steinem, Gloria
  1992   *Revolution from Within: A Book of Self-Esteem.* New York: Little.
Stokes, Allison
  1993   "Critical Mass in the Berkshires: A Research Study about Women Pastors." *Daughters of Sarah* 19 (Spring): 30–31.
Stone, Merlin
  1979   *Ancient Mirrors of Womanhood: A Treasury of Goddess and Heroine Lore from Around the World.* Boston: Beacon Press.
  1976   *When God Was a Woman.* New York: Harcourt/Brace/Jovanovich.
Storkey, Elaine
  1985   *What's Right with Feminism.* Grand Rapids, Mich.: William B. Eerdmans.
Swidler, Arlene
  1974   *Sistercelebrations: Nine Worship Experiences.* Philadelphia: Fortress.
Swidler, Arlene, and Leonard Swidler, eds.
  1977   *Women Priests: A Catholic Commentary on the Vatican Declaration.* New York: Paulist Press.
Tamez, Elsa, ed.
  1989   *Through Her Eyes: Women's Theology from Latin America.* New York: Orbis Books.
Tannen, Deborah
  1990   *You Just Don't Understand: Women and Men in Conversation.* New York: Ballantine Books.
  1986   *That's Not What I Meant! How Conversational Style Makes or Breaks Your Relations With Others.* New York: William Morrow.
Thistlethwaite, Susan
  1991   *Sex, Race, and God: Christian Feminism in Black and White.* New York: Crossroad.
Tong, Rosemarie
  1993   *Feminine and Feminist Ethics.* Belmont, Calif.: Wadsworth Publishing.
Torjesen, Karen Jo
  1993   *When Women Were Priests: Women's Leadership in the Early Church and the Scandal of Their Subordination in the Rise of Christianity.* San Francisco: HarperSanFrancisco.

Townes, Emilie M., ed.
1993   *A Troubling in My Soul: Womanist Perspectives on Evil and Suffering*. Maryknoll, N.Y.: Orbis Books.

Trebbi, Diana
1991   "Women-Church: Catholic Women Produce an Alternative Spirituality." Pp. 347–51 in Thomas Robbins and Dick Anthony, eds.
In Gods We Trust: New Patterns of Religious Pluralism in America.
2d ed. New Brunswick: Transaction Books.

Trible, Phyllis
1989   "Bringing Miriam Out of the Shadows." *Bible Review* 5 (February): 14–25, 34.
1984   *Texts of Terror: Literary-Feminist Readings of Biblical Narratives*.
Philadelphia: Fortress Press.
1978   *God and the Rhetoric of Sexuality*. Philadelphia: Fortress Press.

Ulanov, Ann Belford
1988   *The Wisdom of the Psyche*. Cambridge, Mass.: Cowley Publications.
1986   *Picturing God*. Cambridge, Mass.: Cowley Publications.

Wainwright, Elaine Mary
1991   *Towards a Feminist Critical Reading of the Gospel according to
Matthew*. New York: Walter de Gruyter.

Wallace, Ruth A.
1993   "The Social Construction of a New Leadership Role: Catholic
Women Pastors." *Sociology of Religion* 54: 31–42.
1992   *They Call Her Pastor: A New Role for Catholic Women*. Albany, N.Y.:
SUNY Press.

Wallace, Ruth A., ed.
1989   *Feminism and Sociological Theory*. Newbury Park, Calif.: Sage
Publications.

Walker, Alice
1983   *In Search of Our Mothers' Gardens: Womanist Prose*. New York:
Harbrace.

Walker, Barbara G.
1990   *Women's Rituals: A Sourcebook*. San Francisco: Harper and Row.
1988   *The Woman's Dictionary of Symbols and Sacred Objects*. San Francisco: Harper and Row.
1985   *The Crone: Woman of Age, Wisdom, and Power*. San Francisco:
Harper and Row.
1983   *The Woman' Encyclopedia of Myths and Secrets*. San Francisco:
Harper and Row.

Walters, Suzannna Danuta
1985   "Caught in the Web: A Critique of Spiritual Feminism." *Berkeley
Journal of Sociology* 30: 15–40.

von Wartenberg-Potter, Barbel
1987   *We Will Not Hang Our Harps on the Willows: Global Sisterhood and
God's Song*. Oak Park, Ill.: Meyer-Stone Books.

Weaver, Mary Jo
  1985   *New Catholic Women: A Contemporary Challenge to Traditional Religious Authority.* San Francisco: Harper and Row.
Weems, Renita J.
  1988   *Just a Sister Away: A Womanist Vision of Women's Relationships in the Bible.* San Diego: LuraMedia.
Welch, Sharon D.
  1989   *A Feminist Ethic of Risk.* Minneapolis: Augsburg/Fortress Press.
  1985   *Communities of Resistance and Solidarity: A Feminist Theology of Liberation.* Maryknoll, N.Y.: Orbis Books.
Williams, Delores S.
  1993   *Sisters in the Wilderness: The Challenge of Womanist God-Talk.* Maryknoll, N.Y.: Orbis Books.
Williams, Selma R.
  1981   *Divine Rebel: The Life of Anne Marbury Hutchinson.* New York: Holt, Rinehart and Winston.
Wilshire, Donna
  1994   *Virgin Mother Crone: Myths and Mysteries of the Triple Goddess.* Rochester, Vt.: Inner Traditions.
Winter, Miriam Therese
  1993   *The Gospel according to Mary: A New Testament for Women.* New York: Crossroad.
  1992   *WomanWitness: A Feminist Lectionary and Psalter: Women of the Hebrew Scriptures, Part Two.* New York: Crossroad.
  1991   *WomanWisdom: A Feminist Lectionary and Psalter: Women of the Hebrew Scriptures, Part One.* New York: Crossroad.
  1990   *WomanWord: A Feminist Lectionary and Psalter: Women of the New Testament.* New York: Crossroad.
  1989   "The Women-Church Movement." *The Christian Century* 106 (March 8): 258–60.
  1987   *WomanPrayer, WomanSong: Resources for Ritual.* New York: Crossroad.
Wittberg, Patricia
  1991   *Creating a Future for Religious Life: A Sociological Perspective.* New York: Paulist Press.
  1989   "Non-Ordained Workers in the Catholic Church: Power and Mobility among American Nuns." *Journal for the Scientific Study of Religion* 28 (June): 148–61.
World Council of Churches
  1988   *Ecumenical Decade, 1988–1998: Churches in Solidarity with Women: Prayers and Poems, Songs and Stories.* Geneva: WCC Publications.
Wuthnow, Robert
  1994   *Sharing the Journey: Support Groups and America's New Quest for Community.* New York: Free Press.
  1988   *The Restructuring of American Religion.* Princeton, N.J.: Princeton University Press.

Young, Pamela Dickey
    1990   *Feminist Theology/Christian Theology: In Search of Method.* Minneapolis: Fortress Press.

Zappone, Katherine
    1991   *The Hope for Wholeness: A Spirituality for Feminists.* Mystic, Conn.: Twenty-Third Publications.

Ziegenhals, Gretchen E.
    1989   "Meeting the Women of Women-Church." *The Christian Century* 106 (May 10): 492–94.

Zikmund, Barbara Brown
    1993   "Women's Organizations: Denominational Loyalty and Expressions of Christian Unity." Pp. 116–38 in Jackson Carroll and Wade Clark Roof, eds. *Beyond Establishment: Protestant Identity in a Post-Protestant Age.* Louisville: Westminster/John Knox Press.